SELECTED READINGS
FROM BEDIUZZAMAN SAID NURSİ'S
RISALE-I NUR

Published by Tughra Books

335 Clifton Ave.

Clifton, NJ, 07011, USA

www.tughrabooks.com

ISBN: 978-1-59784-928-9

Library of Congress Cataloging-in-Publication Data Available

SELECTED READINGS FROM BEDİÜZZAMAN SAİD NURSİ'S RİSALE-İ NUR

Revised Third Edition

Dr. Hakan Gök

TUGHRA
BOOKS

New Jersey

Contents

CHAPTER 5

CHAPTER 6

CHAPTER 7

CHAPTER 8

CHAPTER 9

CHAPTER 11

CHAPTER 12

Acknowledgements

My first and foremost gratitude goes to Şükran Vahide and Hüseyin Akarsu who have made the Risale-i Nur available to English language readership. Their work is invaluable.

I am grateful to Sait Aksoy for helping me to make this particular selection of topics. I would like to thank certain other colleagues, who gracefully asked me not to mention their names, for their valuable comments and contributions.

I would like to express my appreciation to the entire team of Mevlana University where I edited the great majority of this book.

Finally, my special thanks go to Dr. Dusmamat Karimov, Alixe Gök and Adem Toplu for their additional input.

Preface

Bediüzzaman Saïd Nursi (1877–1960), arguably one of the most influential scholars of the last century, wrote in *The Letters:*

> Even if those in this circle of Qur'anic teaching are leading scholars and authorities on the law (*ulama* and *mujtahidūn*), their duties in respect of the sciences of belief are only explanations, elucidations or the ordering of the *Risale-i Nur*.[1]

Since Nursi already presented everything beautifully, my position is to simplify and reorganize some of his writings in order to make it accessible for a wider English-speaking audience.

Over the years I have had numerous chances to meet many people with whom I discussed the life and works of Bediüzzaman Said Nursi. There have always been interests in reading the Risale from them. However, when they saw the size of the *Risale-i Nur* they were put off straight away. Their situation motivated me to construct a book which incorporates a careful selection of quintessential topics that Nursi wrote in various part of the *Risale-i Nur Collection.*

The topics in this book emerged as a result of a brainstorming with fellow academics in the summer of 2013. We discussed about the ways to address the needs of people, especially the youth, who

---

[1]   Said Nursi, *The Letters* (Istanbul: Nesil, 2004f) at 553.

face daily doubts thrown at their faces in modern society. Issues such as the existence of God, reality of resurrection and the need for worship as well as common social behavioral problems such as greed, backbiting and racism are explained from the perspective of Saïd Nursi.

My aim is to present a carefully chosen, digestible selections from Nursi's 14-volume, 6000-page the *Risale-i Nur Collection* to beginners. I hope this book is going to be the very first step into the fascinating writings of Bediüzzaman Saïd Nursi for many first-time readers.

Hakan Gök
Leeds, December 2018

Notes on Sources

There is only a limited variety of available printed materials of Bediüzzaman Saïd Nursi's Risale-i Nur in English. Şükran Vahide's translation sounds closer to Nursi's original writings in Ottoman Turkish. Her works are currently available from Sözler Publication. Hüseyin Akarsu's more recent translation, which is relatively easy to read and slightly reorganized from the original text, is printed by Tughra Books, New Jersey, US.

In this book, I have used both authors' translations with my personal touch, which appear only in the form of footnotes and slight reorganization of the main texts.

Page numbers given in the footnotes are taken from Nesil Publication's twin volume version of the *Risale-i Nur*. For those who are interested in accessing the original text, chapter locations are given below.

Chapter Locations

Notes on Spelling and Transliteration

Since Bediüzzaman Saïd Nursi lived in Turkey, most of his work is in Turkish. Names of people and places are used as they appear in Turkish. There are some different letters in the Turkish alphabet, and some letters are pronounced differently. The following list might guide the reader on how these letters sound in English and French.

c—j, as in *jot*.

ç—ch, as in *chop*. ş—* sh, as in *shop*.

ğ—unpronounced, lengthens preceding vowel.

ı—no equivalent, approximately as in *io* of *nation*.

ö—as in French *peu*.

ü—as in French *rue*.

Saïd (Nursi)—is pronounced *Sa'eed*.

Frequently used names and terms

Latinized term or name	Full transliteration	Meaning
Abu Bakr	Abū Bakr	The first caliph and the Prophet's closest associate
Abu Jahl	Abū Jahl	Nickname of ʿAmr ibn Hisham, means the father of ignorance
adalah	ʿadalah	justice
adhan	adhan	Call to Prayer (salah)
Ahl as-Sunnah	Ahl al-Sunnah	Sunni way of belief
Al-asma al-husna	Al-asmā al-ḥusnā	the Beautiful Names of God
Al-Farabi	Al-Fārābī	Muslim philosopher and jurist. Born in 872 in Kazakhstan, died in 950 in Syria.
Al-Ghazzali	Al-Ghazzālī	Muslim theologian, jurist, philosopher, and mystic (1058–1111, Iran)
Al-Mathnawi al-ʿArabi al-Nuri	Al-Mathnawī al-ʿArabi al-Nūriyah	One of Nursi's book, literally means 'Seedbed of the Light'
Al-ʿIsharat al-Iʿjaz	Al-Ishārāt al-Iʿjāz	One of Nursi's book, literally means 'Signs of Miraculousness'
ana	anā	Ego, self or human 'I'
ʿaqaid	ʿaqāid	the element of doctrine
Ash'ari	Ashʿarī	theological school of Islam founded by Imam Abu al-Hasan al-Ash'ari (874–936, Iraq)
ayat	ayāt	signs
balaghah	balāghah	the element of rhetoric
Dajjal	Dajjal	antichrist
Divan-ı Harb-i Örfî	Diwan-i Ḥarb-i Urfī	One of Nursi's book, literally means 'The Court Marshall'
falsafa	falsafa	philosophy
hadith	ḥadīth	Sayings and actions of the Prophet

hadith qudsi	*ḥadīth qudsī*	sayings of Allah narrated by the Prophet but not included in the Qur'an
haqiqah	*ḥaqīqah*	the element of reality
hashr	*ḥashr*	resurrection
hujjat-ul Islam	*khujjat ul Islām*	proof of Islam
Hutbe-i Şamiye	*Ḥutba-ī Shāmiya*	Damascus Sermon
Hutuvat-ı Sitte	*Ḥuṭūwāt-i Sitta*	One of Nursi's book, literally means 'Six Steps' or 'Six Tricks of Devil'
'ibadah	*'ibādah*	worship
ibda	*ibdā*	creation out of nothing
Ibn-i Sina	*Ibn Sīnā*	Muslim polymath and jurist. Born in Üzbekistan in 980 and died in Iran in 1037.
ikhlas	*ikhlās*	sincerity
iman	*imān*	belief
iman-ı tahkiki	*imān-ı taḥqīqi*	Belief through investigation
iman-ı taklidi	*imān-ı taqlīdi*	belief through emulation
insha	*inshā*	gradual building from existing material
İşarat	*Ishārāt*	One of Nursi's book, literally means 'Signs'
Islam	*Islām*	Islam
Isra'illiyat	*Isrāilliyāt*	Judaic or Judao-Christian legends in the early Islamic literature
İttihad-ı Muhammedi	*Ittiḥād-i Muḥammadī*	Muḥammadan Ünion for Muslim Unity
Jabariyya	*Jabariyya*	A school of thought which deny free will in man, means 'The Necessitarians'
jihad	*Jihād*	striving in God's cause and for humanity's good; doing one's utmost to achieve something; struggle
Jurjani	*Jurjānī*	one of the most leading scholars of the language of literature of Arabic (1010–1079, Iran)

juz'-i ikhtiyari	*juz'-i ikhtiyārī*	Free will
juz'i irada	*juz'i irādah*	Free will
kalam	kalām	Islamic Theology, literally means 'speech'
kasb	*kasb*	acquisition
kitab-ı kainat	*kitāb-ı kāināt*	book of universe
Kurush (in Turkish)	Kurush (in Turkish)	acquisition
Lemaat	Lemaāt	One of Nursi's book, literally means 'Gleams'
ma'nà-i harfi	*m'anà-i ḥarfī*	other-indicative meaning
ma'nà-i ismi	*m'anà-i ismī*	self-referential meaning
madrasa, (pl.) madaris	madrasah (pl) madāris	school of theology
Madrasat uz-Zahra'	Madrasat uz-Zahrā	Name of Nursi' project universi- ty, literally means 'The School of Brilliance'
maktab	*maktab*	school
Mu'tazilite	Mu'tazilah	School of Islamic theology based on reason and rational thought.
Muhakemat	Muḥākamāt	One of Nursi's book, means 'The Reasonings'
Münazarat	Münāẓarāt	One of Nursi's book, means 'Debates'
musabbib al-asbab	*musabbib al-asbāb*	the creator of all causes
mutakallimun	*mutakallimūn*	kalam theologians
nafs	*nafs*	self, psyche ego or soul
nazm	*naẓm*	word order
nubuvvah	*nubuwwah*	Prophethood
Nurcu (in Turkish)	Nurcu (in Turkish)	Students of *the Risale-i Nur*
Nutuk	Nuṭq	One of Nursi's book, literally means 'Speech'

qadar	qadar	Divine destiny
qibla	qiblah	The direction of the Ka'ba in Mecca in which a Muslim turns to when praying.
Qur'an	Qur'ān	Islam's Holy Book
Risale-i Nur	Risāla-i Nūr	The Epistles of Light

24 SELECTED READINGS FROM RISALE-I NUR

rububiyyah	Rubūbiyyah	God's Lordship
Rumi	Rūmī	Poet, jurist, Islamic scholar, theologian, and Sufi mystic. Born in 1207 in Tajikistan and died in 1273 in Turkey.
Said Nursi	Saīd Nursī	Said Nursi
salah	ṣalah	Prayers
Sharia	Sharīʿa	Islamic Law
Sirhindi	Sirhindī	Indian Islamic scholar of Arab origin, a Hanafi jurist, and a prominent member of the Naqshbandi Sufi order (1564– 1624, India)
Sufyan	Sufyān	Antichrist, Dajjal, who will appear in the Muslim world.
sunnah	sunnah	deeds and saying of the Prophet
surah	sūrah	verse in the Qur'an
tafsir	tafṣīr	exegesis
taqwa	taqwā	piety
tawhid	tawḥīd	the Oneness and Ünity of God
tekke	tekke	Sufi lodge; dervish lodge
ʿubudiyyah	ʿubudiyyah	worship or servanthood
uhuwwah	uḥuwwah	brotherhood
ʿulama	ʿulamā	scholars
Vahib ul Hayat	Wāhib al-ḥayāt	Bestower of Life
zakat	dhakāt	alms
Zamakshari	Zamakhsharī	Muslim scholar of theology and linguistic annalist. Born in 1075 in Üzbekistan and died in 1144 Iran.

Maps

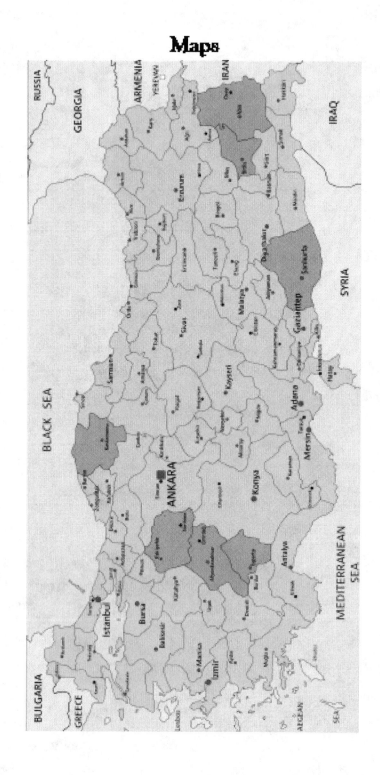

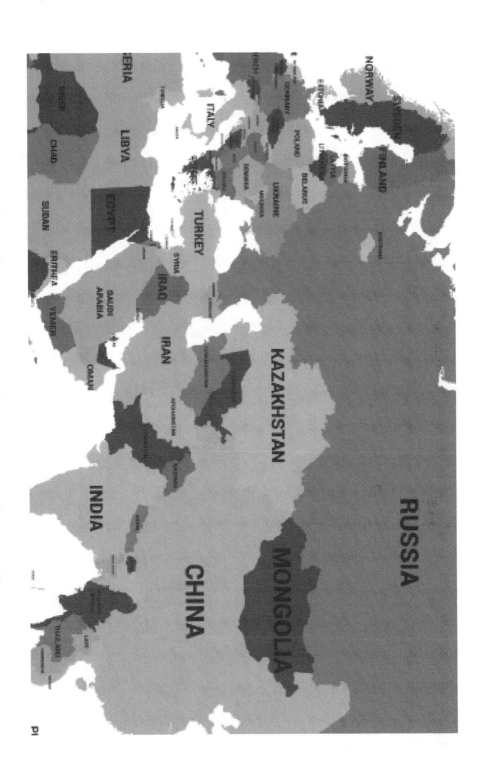

About the Author

Dr. Hakan Gök is a Research Fellow at the Center for Governance, Leadership and Global Responsibility at Leeds Beckett University. He received his PhD from Durham University.

His research interests are the problem of evil and suffering, arguments for and against the existence of God, atheist philosophy, life and discourse of Nursi, Ghazzālī, Rūmī and Sirhindī.

He is the author of 'Atheism or Theism: Perspective of Saïd Nursi', and the co-editor of 'India-Turkey: History, Culture and Politics' books.

Introduction

Human beings have always been interested in philosophical subjects such as the origins of life, the purpose of existence, the nature of death and its aftermath etc. Regardless of their philosophical or theological tendencies these key questions always occupy a place in their mind.

Throughout history, both philosophers and theologians have tried to take their best shot at answering these questions. One such attempt came from Bediüzzaman Saïd Nursi (1877–1960). Having infused positive science, philosophy and religious science, Nursi produced a set of books in which he presented his perspective on these issues.

Even though Nursi wanted his arguments to be heard and understood by the general public at the time of writing, not everyone finds Nursi's writing accessible neither in its original language, Ottoman Turkish, nor in other languages (over thirty at the time of the print of this edition) into which it has been translated. It took Nursi about twenty-four years to complete the

Risale-i Nur Collection, which comprises fourteen different books and some six thousand pages in total.

Having witnessed the collapse of both ideological and political empires during the turbulent part of the late nineteenth and early twentieth centuries, Nursi, being on the side of monotheistic theism, dedicated his life to its defense. Therefore, certain themes repeatedly appear in Nursi's writings. Some of these themes are faith, divine destiny, human free will, resurrection and the Hereafter, in addition to prophets and prophethood. Nursi describes his *Risale-i Nur* as a spiritual exegesis of the Qur'an. To any reader, the *Risale-i Nur* is very different from regular exegeses. As opposed to regular and orderly explanations of Qur'anic verses, Nursi takes a fairly different route. He picks a topic and develops semi-philosophical arguments around it, referring to relevant Qur'anic verses and *ahadith* of the Prophet. Therefore, the reader has a good understanding of the Qur'anic verses related to certain themes, giving him a totally different experience in comparison to reading a regular exegesis (*tafsir*).

My intention in this book is to give the reader a general understanding of Saïd Nursi, the context in which he lived, and the philosophy he developed. The book comprises two parts. In the first part, the reader can find a brief account of the life and the discourse of Saïd Nursi. Certain key concepts that appear in the *Risale-i Nur* are briefly explained there. The appendix contains some additional material such as photographs and diagrams to help the reader digest this part better.

The main body of the book has twelve chapters and a total of twenty selections from the *Risale-i Nur*. The first reading in Chapter One is about 'The purpose of the existence of men and the universe.' Here, Nursi explains through analogies, comparisons and metaphors that the universe and life on the planet did not come into existence by chance. It was intentional and it serves a purpose. Nursi advocates positive morality, arguing that what is permitted religiously is sufficient for men's happiness. Therefore, he puts, living in high morality is not a burden but a source of happiness both here in this life and in the Hereafter.

The second reading in Chapter One is about 'Ego, self and human I.' This is a subject which is a key to understand Nursian philosophy. There, the reader is invited to use the tool of self and ego to attain the full under- standing of God and His Attributes. In other words, ego is a measure to compare and understand the true majesty of God.

Chapter Two addresses the ever-popular Epicurean dilemma and the problem of evil. The issue always interests the public in general. If there is an all-powerful, all-knowing, all-loving god, then why would there be evil? Is God not capable of stopping evil? Is he not willing to stop evil? Or does he want evil in the world, for some reason? Nursi contends that the existence of evil is necessary in order for God to manifest his Divine Names and Attributes. He further explains that life is all about testing human beings. Evil is, therefore, a tool to differentiate between good, obedient and patient individuals from bad, rebellious and impatient ones.

Chapter Three tackles the issues surrounding divine destiny (*qadar*). There the reader can find Nursi's answers to questions such as: 'If God al- ready knows what is in one's destiny can one really talk about free will?' and 'If God creates everything including one's actions, can people be held responsible for their actions?' This chapter also gives more technical in- formation on different schools of thought such as the *Mu'tazilite,* the *Jabariyya,* and *Ahl al-Sunnah.*

In Chapter Four, the reader can find one of the most controversial topics of the twentieth and the current centuries: that is; the origin of life. Nursi gives his perspective on the question. He sets out three hypotheses about the origins of existence and life. The first theory is 'causes create this thing', the second one is 'it forms itself; it comes into existence and later ceases to exist.' The third theory is that 'it is natural; Nature necessitates and creates it.' Having refuted all three propositions with three arguments against each, Nursi concludes that life could only come into existence with the interference of an all-knowing, all-powerful all-wise Being. It is simply implausible that any of the three other agents could actually have power and intelligence to create life out of nothing.

Chapter Five consists of three separate readings. In all of them, Nursi sets off with a mini story, a comparison, in a way, and defends how reasonable it is to have a belief in God and the afterlife and live life accordingly with prayer, worship and supplication.

Nursi attempts to address another key issue in Chapter Six. That is the resurrection after death. This is indeed the very first piece he wrote in Barla, a small town near Isparta, in 1926. One might argue that the resurrection question was one of the utmost importance to Nursi since he started *The Words* with the piece called 'On Resurrection.' Most people, throughout history, have found it implausible that, once man dies and his body decomposes after burial, or is incinerated in some cases, he could possibly come back to life, i.e., be resurrected. In Chapter Six, Nursi tries to demonstrate that the existence of miniature resurrections on this planet in springtime, the lack of complete justice in this life, evil people's death before they were held accountable for their evil deeds and the very nature of the functioning of life on this planet are evidence of resurrection.

In the first of the two readings of Chapter Seven, the reader can find two possible interpretations of life. First is the view of the materialist philosophy and the second is one based on the Divine teachings of the Qur'an. Nursi meticulously contends that wisdom and virtue can be found in the divine teachings of the Qur'an. He further tries to demonstrate that competition, rivalry and hostility in order to gain worldly benefits promoted by the materialist philosophy could only be the source of conflict, clash and unhappiness.

In the second reading of Chapter Seven, Nursi tells the story of a traveler in a desert. The story was very relevant to people at the time of writing and still clear to the imagination of modern-day people. He then goes on to tell how necessary for this traveler it is to take the protection of the local ruler. From this comparison, Nursi invites his readers to take up the protection of God as He is the owner and the ruler of the universe. This simple yet powerful argument surely encourages readers to start everything with the word '*Bismillah*', in the name of God, and be selective about people they deal with, ensuring that they have the same attitude towards God. Nursi takes pains to promote fraternity and love among the people of Divine Service in Chapter Eight. It is the team that wins the game, not the individuals. Therefore, he condemns evil traits such as dispute, discord, partisanship, obstinacy, envy, leading to rancor and enmity and tries to explain how they destroy team spirit and cause disaster. Supporting his thesis with Qur'anic verses, he aims at eradicating these evil characteristics and promotes just the opposite of these, i.e., friendship, love, sympathy, collaboration and harmony.

In the second reading of Chapter Eight, Nursi explains why greed is extremely harmful for people of the Divine Service of the Qur'an. Expounding on the verse *How many a living creature there is that does not carry its own provision (in store), but God provides for them, and indeed for you. He is the All-Hearing, the All-Knowing. (Al-Ankabut 29:60)*, Nursi demonstrates that being content with what is given to you and putting your trust in God is surely better than showing greed for material benefits. He further prescribes alms-giving (*zakat*) which not only helps build a loving, sharing and caring healthy community but also helps eradicate evil, the at- tribute of greed and selfishness.

The closing reading of Chapter Eight is another social ill, that is, back- biting. Here Nursi gives the definition of backbiting and encourages his readers to avoid it, underlining the verse *Would any among you like to eat the flesh of his dead brother? (Al-Hujurat 49:12)*. He closes his piece by clarifying the four occasions, i.e., to complain, to consult for cooperation, to describe a person in a non-insulting manner and to refer to an un- ashamed sinner, when backbiting may be permissible.

Sincerity and fraternity are two inextricable qualities for Nursi. He al- ways mentions these two together in Chapter Nine, therefore, shows the piece Nursi wrote on Sincerity. In the first reading, Nursi presents his social analysis of the seven causes of the apparent dispute and lack of cooperation among Muslims.

In the second part of Chapter Nine, Nursi establishes four essential rules that he says must be observed in order to attain true sincerity. He explains that seeking Divine Pleasure as opposed to gaining public popularity must be the top priority of anyone in the Divine Service. Not criticizing his fellow brothers and sisters in a destructive way is the second rule Nursi establishes for his readers. Seeking all the strength in sincerity and truth is Nursi's third rule. In the fourth rule, Nursi advises his readers to take pride in the achievements of his brothers and sister instead of being jealous. Finally, Nursi wraps up this article stating that rivalry in order to gain material advantages, working towards earning higher worldly status, fear and greed are the main obstacles that destroy sincerity, and the people of the Divine Service must avoid falling into these traps.

Chapter Ten, which originally appears in Nursi's book called *The Flashes*, gives twenty-six spiritual cures to the sick. Since almost everyone is either sick or has someone close to them sick, this reading comes as a relief and lifts up the mood of the people who are suffering an illness and the people who have sick friends or family members. Expounding on the Prophetic *hadith*, 'Those afflicted with the severest trials are the Prophets, then the saints and those like them', Nursi regards illness as a reward rather than a punishment. He suggests that illness actually acts as an expiation of sins and helps one to gain a higher spiritual rank both in this world and in the Hereafter. He highlights the fact that people become more spiritual and do more supplication whilst ill. Illness, therefore, is something beneficial in terms of earning more spiritual rewards. Another argument Nursi puts forward is that God has many Divine Names and Attributes, each requiring certain conditions to manifest itself. In the case of an illness, the Divine Name The Healer (*Ash-Shafi*) manifests itself as people become ill, then recover. In the Appendix, the list of ninty-nine Divine Names and Attributes is given for the reader to contemplate the required conditions for these Names to manifest themselves.

Nursi gives the allegory of 'the rich man and his servant' for the second time (the first time it appears in Chapter Three on Divine Destiny) and argues that, since man has no right to claim the ownership of his body and faculties given to him, he can only thank God, not to complain.

Nursi's private letter written to one of his students Hafiz Halid Efendi on the death of his son conveniently completes Chapter Ten. This is not an ordinary letter but a letter written with the power of solace. Here Nursi presents five good news and consolation to Hafiz Halid Efendi as well as to anyone else who has lost a child. With the Qur'an's *immortal youths (al-Waqi'ah 56:17)* description of a young deceased, one finds this letter of consolation very comforting and empowering.

Chapter Eleven is the exposition of Nursi's view on fasting during the holy month of Ramadan. Nursi does not consider fasting simply as the act of refraining from eating, drinking and sexual intercourse. To him, fasting also brings social, personal and spiritual benefits. Nursi elaborates on eight wisdoms of fasting. For instance, fasting is the best way for the soul to become aware of God's bounties and makes it more thankful to Him. Fasting also makes people show more empathy towards each other as they experience hunger, thirst and all kinds of bodily weaknesses. Nursi further stresses how fasting helps people discipline their body and soul. Chapter Eleven also has another extract from *The Letters* where Nursi lectures on how thanking God is one of the most fundamental responses God expects from people and how to thank Him properly.

The final reading of this book is about the six satanic tactics and stratagems to deceive the servants of the Divine Service. Here the reader has another chance to read Nursi's interpretation of six personal weaknesses that harm the team spirit of the servants of the Qur'an. Nursi originally called this piece The Six Stratagems and it appears in several different places in the *Risale-i Nur*. The reader can instantly recognize that these six tactics were partly mentioned in Chapter Nine on Sincerity as the main obstacles that destroy sincerity. The first of the six satanic tactics is the desire for rank and position. Nursi explains how this causes rivalry and jealousy among the servants of the Qur'an and damages their harmonious cooperation. According to Nursi, the second satanic tactic is fear. Fear is given to human beings as a protective tool to help them avoid danger and stay safe. It is not given to turn them into cowards or paranoids. He suggests that reasonable caution is always essential, but running away from an arena of action due to fear is something Muslims must avoid at all times. Nursi further elaborates on greed as the third satanic tactic. The fourth tactic of Satan, to Nursi, is strong nationalist feelings which dangerously lead people to strong racism. Nursi advises his followers that the diversity of people should not cause dispute among them. The servants of the Qur'an should focus on the merits of the people, not their race or color. Egotism and laziness are the other two satanic tactics that used to draw people away from serving the Qur'an.

This book has been prepared with a genuine hope for the first-time readers to have a taste of Nursi's writings, collectively called the *Risale-i Nur*, and to develop interest in further studies and benefit from them. If the reader finds any shortcomings, they are mine.

BEDİÜZZAMAN SAİD NURSİ: HIS LIFE AND DISCOURSE

In a dusty, hot July night in 1960, a convoy of military vehicles hurried towards Halil ar-Rahman mosque in the Urfa city center, in the south-eastern Turkey. The commanding officer wiped his sweat and instructed the driver to move faster. The convoy eventually arrived at the mosque, quickly cordoned off the streets leading towards it, and secured the premises. More soldiers jumped from the back of the military trucks with axes and shovels in their hands. It was exactly half past midnight. Soldiers first removed the massive slab of marble from the top of a three-month-old grave. They quickly dug the earth and reached the green coffin. The coffin was opened, and the body swiftly transferred into a new galvanized metal coffin which had been carried on the back of one of the military trucks. Soldiers sealed the coffin and secured it on the back of a truck. They left the premises as quickly as they came.

The convoy reached the local civilian airport. It was 1 a.m. now. The galvanized coffin was transferred to a waiting C–47 military cargo plane. The plane took off shortly after 1a.m. on the 12th of July, 1960. Its destination was Afyon, a city some 900 km west of Urfa. Once the cargo plane landed on a military air strip in Afyon, the remaining 176 km were to be covered by land. The party eventually arrived at Isparta City Cemetery. It was nearly early morning. They swiftly reburied the body into a pre-dug grave. Official paperwork was signed and later locked safely in the Prime Minister's Archive in Ankara.[2] This action-packed military operation was to remove the dead body of no one other than Saïd Nursi, who had died less than four months earlier, on the 23rd of March 1960.

On the 27th of May 1960, 37 petty army officers executed a long-plotted military coup against the democratically elected Prime Minister

Adnan Menderes. PM Menderes' Democrat Party had its first election victory ten years earlier on the 22nd of May 1950[3] against the Republican People's Party (RPP) candidate and the Prime Minister Ismet Inönü. It was the beginning of Turkey's transformation from a single-party autocracy into a real democracy. With the backing of massive public support, Menderes quickly eased off the restrictions put in place by RPP more than three decades ago. Chief of these restrictions was the lifting of the ban of Islamic Prayer call (adhan) in Arabic. Menderes was to regain a majority in 1957 elections[4] for the second time only to irritate further the RPP and the Army, which were essentially the same organization. When the Army and the RPP realized that there was virtually little or no chance of gaining power through the ballot box, they intensified their focus on Plan B.

The junta arrested every single member of the parliament, 235 army generals, more than 3,500 army officers and 1,402 academics. They were quickly controlled by being sent into forced retirement or sacked. Perhaps the ultimate price of this bloody coup was paid by PM Adnan Menderes, Foreign Minister Fatin Rüştü Zorlu and the Finance Minister Hasan Polatkan. Despite President Kennedy's last minute intervention,[5] the junta executed the democratically elected Menders, Zorlu and Polatkan.

---

[2]   See Appendix 3: Official document stating the reburial of Saïd Nursi in Isparta Cemetery. (Death certificate of Nursi).

[3]   14 May 1950 Election: Democrat Party got % 52.67 of the votes gaining 415 seats of 487 seats.

[4]   27 October 1957 Election. Menderes got % 48.88 of the votes gaining 424 seats of 610

[5]   Nur Batur, "Kennedy'nin son dakika mesajı: Asmayın," 20 Haziran 2007, Sabah gazetesi, URL accessed: 15 June 2008.

This was the end of a brief episode in Turkey's struggle for democracy. It was not only the politicians and the members of the Army who suffered. Nursi's dead body was hit by the fury of the junta too.

Saïd Nursi[6] (1877–1960) is probably one of the most influential intellectuals that Turkey produced in the twentieth century. This chapter ex- amines his life via discussion of the historic and political perspectives that shaped his discourse. It presents an analysis of Nursi's intellectual shift from sociological concerns into philosophical challenges of materialism, rather than a chronological account of his life.

Nursi was born in eastern Anatolia[7] in 1877, to Kurdish parents.[8] At the time, the region where he was born was called Kurdistan and was within the borders of the Ottoman Empire. Nursi's life spread over two completely different regimes: first, the Ottoman Empire, which was a theocratic monarchy with a parliament, and then the Turkish Republic, a secular democracy built on the ashes of the Ottoman Empire in 1923. As a child of Kurdish parents, Nursi spoke the local language, Kurdish, but also Turkish, the official state language, as well as Arabic, the language of science, knowledge and religion.

In accordance with these factors, Nursi's life is conventionally divided into three periods. The first is from his birth in 1877 to 1920. Nursi himself calls this 37-year part of his life the 'Old Saïd' era. The second period is from 1920 to 1950, when Nursi produced his *magnum opus*, the *Risale-i Nur* (The Epistles of Light). Nursi called this part of his life the 'New Saïd' era. The last ten years of his life, from 1950 to 1960, are known as the 'Third Saïd' period.

---

[6] The conventional English version, 'Said Nursi', is commonly used instead of 'Saïd Nursi'

[7] In order to avoid confusion between the geographic east of the Ottoman Empire and the Republic of Turkey, I use the geographical name of Anatolia.

[8] There is a disagreement about Nursi's exact date of birth, owing to Hijri–Gregorian calendar conversion and lack of precise records. Vahide accepts 1877 as more accurate than others. See Şükran Vahide and Ibrahim M. Abu-Rabi, 'Islam in Modern Turkey an Intellectual Biography of Bediuzzaman Said Nursi.'

The Old Saïd Period (1877–1916)

Nursi spent the first thirty years of his life in eastern Anatolia studying various disciplines in different *madrasas* (religious schools). As a gifted student, Nursi needed only a short time to complete all the courses he attended. Hence, he managed to study almost all the taught sciences fairly quickly. He read and memorized most of the texts, including those that were not even part of the *madrasa's* curriculum. He was an outstandingly brilliant student. As a result, the nickname *Bediüzzaman* (nonpareil of the times) was given to him.

The end of the nineteenth century and the beginning of the twentieth century represented a challenging period for the 600-year-old Ottoman Empire. It was fighting wars on different fronts, and facing economic hardship, rising nationalism and many other political problems.

Nursi quickly awakened to the facts that the Empire was in decline and that there were a great number of problems to solve. He identified what the main flaws in the education system and formulated his own solution. At the time, the education system had two tiers; One was strictly religious education and the other was modern sciences (i.e., medicine, engineering, etc.). This caused a chasm between religious scholars who possessed little or no knowledge of modern science and scientists who had little or no religious knowledge.

Nursi came up with a project for a university called '*Madrasat uz-Zahra*' which would bring these two tiers (i.e., traditional religious teaching and modern science) together. He suggested that his university should have its central campus in Bitlis, one campus in Van and another campus in Diyarbakır. All the Arabic, Turkish and Kurdish languages would be used simultaneously. In *Münazarat,* he writes:

> ... in this university (Madrasat uz-Zahra', the sister of Al-Azhar University of Cairo) the language of Arabic is obligatory, the language of Kurdish is acceptable and the language of Turkish is to be necessary ...[9]

---

[9]   Said Nursi, *Münazarat (Istanbul: Sözler),* at 1956.

This idea would arguably have been the solution to the Kurdish Problem that remains to this day. In order to realize his ambitious project,[10] Nursi went to Istanbul, the capital city of the Empire, in 1907. He met Sultan Abdulhamid II and presented his proposal[11] to him. This was a very turbulent time in Ottoman history since the Second Constitution was about to be proclaimed. After submitting his proposal, Nursi did not receive a welcoming treatment. In fact, he was arrested and briefly detained in prison on the grounds of being mentally unfit.[12] In 1908, the Constitutional Revolution took place, led by the Young Turks. The fruit of the revolution was the re-instatement of the Parliament, which had been suspended by Sultan Abdulhamid II in 1878. The revolution saw the union of all the opposition parties against the Sultan. All nationalists, secularists, reform-minded persons and pluralists joined forces. It seemed to be a positive step towards democracy, but it led to the events that eventually completely destroyed the Ottoman Empire. Nursi, like many other Islamists, supported constitutionalism. Only through freedom and constitutional government could the empire be saved, progress achieved, and Islamic civilization established, he believed.[13]

Nursi became a well-known public figure. He gave open public speeches and wrote articles in support of constitutionalism. He be-

---

[10]   On Nursi's education reform project, Şükran Vahide writes, "It might be noted here that his ideas about educational reform were far-reaching and radical. Besides the joint teaching of the religious education and modern physical sciences, already mentioned, Nursi proposed reconciling and bringing together in the *Madrasat uz-Zahra*, the three main educational traditions of the time, the madrasas or 'religious schools', *the maktabs* or 'modern secular schools' and the Sufi *tekke*s, and the disciplines they represent. It would thus heal the rifts between them and the resultant division of society ... he was also a strong advocate of students specializing in subjects for which they had an aptitude, a radical departure from established practice."

[11]   In his proposal, Nursi writes: "The religious sciences are the light of the conscience, and the modern sciences are the light of the reason. The truth becomes manifest through the combining of the two. The students' endeavor will take flight on these two wings. When they are separated it gives rise to bigotry in the one, and wiles and skepticism in the other."

[12]   Necmeddin Şahiner, *Bilinmeyen Taraflarıyla Bediüzzaman Said Nursi: Kronolojik Hayatı* (Istanbul: Nesil, 1997) at 93.

[13]   Safa Mürsel, *Bediüzzaman Said Nursi ve Devlet Felsefesi (Istanbul: Yeni Asya Yayınları, 1976) at 223–35.*

came a founder member of İttihad-ı Muhammedi Cemiyeti (Muḥammadan Union for Muslim Unity). After the Thirty-First of March Incident in 1909,[14] he was arrested, court-martialed, and acquitted after having served 24 days in prison. In 1910, Nursi published his first book, *Nutuk* (Speech), which was a collection of his articles and speeches. In 1911, he published the defense he had presented to the Court Martial under the same title, *Divan-ı Harb-i Örfi*. This was Nursi's second published book.

Nursi left Istanbul and headed to Eastern Anatolia to live among Kurdish tribes again. He defended democracy and constitutionalism as a way forward. His ideas and exchanges were later published in two books. *Muhakemat* (The Reasonings) addressed the '*ulama* (scholars), and *Münazarat* (Discussions) addressed the general public. These two works were published in 1911 and 1913 respectively. Nursi impressed both scholars and the public with his diagnosis of the three diseases and three cures of the East. The three diseases, he said, were 'ignorance, poverty and internal conflict', and they had to be fought with the three cures of 'education, industry and unity.'[15]

He then travelled to Damascus, Syria,[16] where he gave his ground- breaking Damascus Sermon in the Umayyad Mosque to an audience of some ten thousand people, including one hundred and fifty scholars.[17]

In his speech in Arabic, Nursi identified six illnesses and offered remedies from, what he calls, 'the pharmacy of the Qur'an.' He said:

> In the conditions of the present time in these lands, I
> have learnt a lesson in the school of mankind's social

---

[14]   The Thirty-first of March Incident was a revolt against İttihad ve Terakki (the Commit-*tee of Union and Progress) who took charge of government after the Second Constitution- al Revolution. It occurred on 31 March 1325 on the Rumi calendar (13 April 1909), hence called The Thirty-first of March Incident.*

[15]   Said Nursi, *Divan-ı Harbi Örfi* (Istanbul: Nesil, 2004e) at 1921.

[16]   Syria was part of the Ottoman Empire in 1911. Following World War I Syria separated and went under the French Mandate as the Ottoman Empire lost the War.

[17]   Nursi himself reports this event in *The Rays and gives these figures. See* Said Nursi, *The Rays* (Istanbul: Nesil, 2004b) at 1148.

life and I have realized that (at the origin of) what has allowed foreigners, the West, to fly towards the future (with the wings of) progress while it arrested us and kept us, in respect of material development, in the Middle Ages, are six terrible diseases. The diseases are these:

Firstly: the rise to life of despair and hopelessness in social life. Secondly: the death of truthfulness in social and political life.

Thirdly: the love of enmity.

Fourthly: not knowing the luminous bonds that bind the believers to one another.

Fifthly: despotism, which creeps, becoming widespread as though it was various contagious diseases.

Sixthly: restricting endeavor to what is personally beneficial.

I shall explain, by means of six 'Words,' the lesson I have learnt from the pharmacy of the Qur'an, which is like a faculty of medicine. This lesson constitutes the medicine to cure our social life of those six dire sicknesses.[18]

At this stage, Nursi still mainly concentrated on the social problems of the Empire. He wanted to elucidate the ills and cures of the times' social problems. His famous Damascus Sermon was printed twice in Arabic and later reprinted in Turkish as well. Nursi left Damascus and went back to Istanbul to join the new Sultan, Mehmed Reşad, on his Balkan Journey. The mission was to gain the support of Balkan nations still living under the Ottoman flag. Although the trip was successful in the sense that it refreshed the old bonds, the upcoming events of the World War I eventually led to the separation of the Balkans from the rest of the Empire. By Nursi's own account, this Balkan trip helped him to secure the funding for *Madrasat uz-Zahra'* (the Islamic Modern University in the East), the foundations of which were eventually laid in Van in 1913. The project was abruptly

---

[18]   See Said Nursi, *Hutbe-i Şamiye* (Istanbul: Nesil, 1994) at 1961–62.

halted when the World War I broke out in 1914. Nursi had to join the militia to defend the Eastern provinces with his students. Now, his *madrasa* was both a school and a military base. Accounts by visitors to his *madrasa* describe how books and rifles were hanging on the walls side by side.[19]

Despite all the political and social turbulence, Nursi had always wanted to refresh the truths of Islam, to dispel the doubts spread by the enemies of religion, and to repulse the underground fears exploited by externalists and extremists.[20]

He explained his life mission in *The Words*:

> One time I had a dream: I was at the foot of Mount Ararat. The mountain suddenly exploded, scattering rocks the size of mountains all over the world, shaking it. Then a man appeared at my side. He told me: "Expound the aspects of the Qur'an's miraculousness you know, concisely and succinctly! I thought of the dream's meaning while still dreaming, telling myself: the explosion here symbolizes a revolution in mankind. As a result of it the guidance of the Criterion of Truth and Falsehood will be exalted everywhere and will rule. And the time will come to expound its miraculousness!"[21]

According to Nursi, Qur'anic exegesis (*tafsir*) should consist of three main parts: (1) the Element of Reality (*Haqiqah*), (2) the Element of Rhetoric (*Balaghah*), and (3) the Element of Doctrine (*'Aqaid*).

The early writings of Nursi (*Münazarat* and *Muhakemat*) places great emphasis on the element of reality in Islam. Nursi was well aware of the fact that Islam had been polluted by *Isra'illiyat* (Judaic or

---

[19]   Şahiner, *Bilinmeyen Taraflarıyla Bediüzzaman Said Nursi: Kronolojik Hayatı* at 165.

[20]   See Şükran Vahide, in Ibrahim M. Abu-Rabi, *Islam at the Crossroads: On the Life and Thought of Bediuzzaman Said Nursi* (Albany: State University of New York Press, 2003) at 8.

[21]   See 6

Judao-Christian legends in the early Islamic literature) and Ancient Greek philosophy. This caused confusion to externalists. He tried to explain that modern sciences and the Qur'an do not conflict at all.[22]

Some of the expressions in the Qur'an are representational, not factual.

Nursi started working on *Al-'Isharat al-I'jaz* (Signs of Miraculousness), which is dedicated to demonstrating the Qur'an's miraculous eloquence, in 1913. This work was never completed as he intended, owing to his capture by the Russian army in 1916. In the two hundred or so pages that Nursi managed to write, he commented on the first verses of the Qur'an with a great knowledge of the art of the Arabic language. Vahide relates contemporary scholars' admiration for Nursi's subtlety in expounding the Qur'an's word-order (*nazm*), subtlety which in places surpasses that of the great masters of the past such as Jurjani and Zamakhshari.[23]

After having spent around two years in Kostroma on the River Volga as a prisoner of war, Nursi escaped from Russia to Istanbul via Warsaw and Austria.[24]

Since Germany was the ally of the Ottoman Empire in the war, Nursi received some help from the Germans and made his way back to Istanbul. During the last few years of the Old Saïd period, Nursi produced several small books: *Lemaat*, İşarat and *Hutuvat-ı Sitte*. He was also involved in the creation of the Madrasa Teachers' Association (1919), whose aim was to maintain and raise educational standards in the *madrasas*. To fight the spread of alcoholism, Nursi took part in the foundation of the Green Crescent Society (1920). When the World War I ended in 1918, the Ottoman Empire had lost the war and was invaded by foreign troops. Nursi worked for the removal of the invaders and for independence. He eventually went back to Anatolia and withdrew into solitude. This was effectively the end of the Old Saïd era and the beginning of the New Saïd.

---

[22] See Said Nursi, *The Words* (Istanbul: Nesil, 2005) at 336., where Nursi dedicated almost this entire book for the *hakikat (reality) of Islam. For example, he explained verses like*

[23] See Şükran Vahide, *Towards the Intellectual Biography of Said Nursi, in* Said Nursi,

[24] Abu-Rabi, *Islam at the Crossroads: On the Life and Thought of Bediuzzaman Said Nursi* at 9.

The New Saïd Period (1923–1950)

During the transitional period (1916–1923), Nursi decided to take the Qur'an as his only guide and free himself from the negative influence of philosophy. He began writing his *Al-Mathnawi al-'Arabi al-Nuri*. This book was the first of the New Saïd's lifetime struggle to fight atheist and materialist philosophy championed by people like Nietzsche, Lamarck,

> *18:86: Until when he reached the place where the sun set, he found it going down into a black sea, and found by it a people. We said: O Dhu'l-Qarnayn! Either give them a chastisement or do them a benefit, and 51:48: And the earth, We have made it a wide extent; how well have We then spread (it) out.*

Darwin, Comte, Büchner, etc. Out of the 6,000 pages of Nursi's work (the *Risale-i Nur* Collection),[25] the main body was created after 1920. *The Words, The Letters, The Flashes, The Rays*, as well as *Al-Mathnawi al-'Arabi al-Nuri*, are the fruit of the New Saïd era. Describing Saïd Nursi's *Risale-i Nur*, Vahide writes:

> ... Risale-i Nur is Qur'anic interpretation ... expounding the teachings of Qur'an on the truth of belief that incorporates the traditional Islamic sciences and modern scientific knowledge, and while instilling those truths, effectively refutes the basis of materialist philosophy ... unique way in the Islamic world for the renewal of belief.[26]

In other words, the *Risale-i Nur* is a Qur'anic exegesis (*tafsir*), or a topical commentary on the Qur'an, with a unique, characteristic approach. Nursi dedicated the main body of the *Risale-i Nur* to proving the four main aims of the Qur'an: (1) the existence of the Single Maker, i.e., God, or *tawhid* (2) Prophethood or *nubuvvah* (3) the resurrection of the dead, or *hashr* and (4) justice or *adalah*.

---

[25]   ee Appendix 1: Chronology and the Diagram of Said Nursi's *Risale-i Nur Collection*.
[26]   See Şükran Vahide, *Towards the Intellectual Biography of Said Nursi* in *Said Nursi, The Flashes* (Istanbul: Nesil 2004a) at 708.

It is clear from a historical perspective why Nursi shifted his attention from social issues to philosophy, and more specifically to a refutation of materialist philosophy. With the proclamation of the Republic of Turkey in 1923 by Mustafa Kemal Atatürk, a new secular country was born out of a theocratic empire. This new regime took the Kemalist ideolgy as its official state philosophy. This ideology was characterized by six principles: republicanism, populism, nationalism, revolutionism, secularism and statism.[27]

The progress of the new nation state, according to Atatürk, had to be guided by education and science-based progress on the principles of positivism, rationalism and enlightenment. The new regime abolished the office of Caliphate in 1924 and introduced the Latin alphabet to replace the Arabic alphabet, which had been in use for several centuries.[28]

This had a devastating effect on the public at large. The positivist ideas of Auguste Comte and the materialism of Ludwig Büchner and others, which had initially become popular among secular schools in the early 1900,[29] was now the official ideology of the new republic. Islam was quickly re- moved from public life with the banning of the Arabic call to prayer and the ban on *tekkes*. Materialist philosophy entered schoolbooks together with evolutionary theories, while religion was labeled as backwardness. There was a common unpleasant reaction against these extreme actions of the new regime. After the Sheikh Saïd[30] revolt of 1925,[31] Nursi was arrested and sent into exile at Burdur, although he opposed

---

27 Abu-Rabi, *Islam at the Crossroads: On the Life and Thought of Bediuzzaman Said Nursi* at 1.
28 See Donald Everett Webster, *The Turkey of Ataturk: Social Process in the Turkish Reformation* (1939) at 245.
29 Suraiya Faroqhi, 'Approaching Ottoman History an Introduction to the Sources.'
30 Saïd Nursi and Sheikh Saïd were both popular Kurdish personalities, but they should not be mixed up. Sheik Saïd led a revolt against the newly formed Turkish Republic in order to gain Kurdish independence. The Kurdish rebels (15,000-strong) were crushed by some fifty thousand Turkish troops. Sheikh Saïd was captured and executed.
31 ee M. Şükrü Hanioğlu, *Bir Siyasi Düşünür Olarak Dr Abdullah Cevded ve Dönemi* (Istanbul) at 370–72.

the rebellion.[32] There he started writing short treaties to answer local people's questions on religion. During the first three years of his exile in Barla, he completed *The Words*. In the following years, his individual treaties were brought together to form two more books, *The Letters* and *The Flashes*. Since the main aim of these books was to revitalize for people the Islamic faith, Nursi quickly became the enemy of the regime. The state's decision to contain him in a remote village of Barla[33] did not apparently work, since he managed to gather a large audience and spread his treaties, thanks to followers copying them by hand. Nursi once again was summoned and relocated to another exile in Isparta in 1934. Although his teachings were not political, they displeased the Kemalist regime intensely because of their religious contents. The unity of the Maker (God), Prophethood, resurrection and the miraculousness of the Qur'an—these were subjects the Kemalist regime did not like at all. The Kemalist regime was to eradicate Islam and its values from public life and promote a new Western, secular and materialist lifestyle in Turkey. In 1935, Nursi and 120 of his students were arrested and charged with "opposing the reforms and belonging to a secret political organization ... exploiting religion for political ends, forming an organization that constituted a possible threat to public order and giving instruction in Sufism."[34] The court acquitted 97 of his students but sentenced Nursi to eleven months in prison on the grounds of opposition to dress

---

[32]   When Nursi was invited to the rebellion he replied: "The Turkish nation has acted as the standard-bearer of Islam for centuries. It has produced many saints and given many martyrs. The sword may not be drawn against the sons of such a nation. We are Mus- lims, we are their brothers, and we may not make brother fight brother. It is not per- missible according to the Sharia. The sword is to be drawn against external enemies; it may not be used internally. Our only salvation at this time is to offer illumination and guidance through the truths of the Qur'an and belief; it is to get rid of our greatest enemy, ignorance. Give up this attempt of yours, for it will be fruitless. Thousands of innocent men and women may perish on account of a few bandits."

[33]   Barla, at the time, was a very small isolated village on the other side of the lake Eğirdir. In his *Tarihçe-i Hayatı (Nursi's Biography)*, Nursi reports how a little boat transferred him to Barla across the lake, as there was no road access.

[34]   See Şükran Vahide, A Chronology of Said Nursi's Life, in Robert W. Olson, *The Emer- gence of Kurdish Nationalism and the Sheikh Said Rebellion, 1880–1925* (Austin: Üniver- sity of Texas Press, 1989).

code.[35] Nursi was to be exiled in Kastamonu after having served his sentence in Eskişehir. During the Kastamonu exile, he wrote *The Supreme Sign* and some parts of *The Rays*. He was once again arrested along with 126 of his students and sent to Denizli. Charges similar to those used in the Eskişehir trial were brought against him, but Nursi and his students were all acquitted and the *Risale-i Nur* was cleared. However, during the trial, which lasted some nine months, they were kept in harsh conditions in Denizli Prison. *The Fruits of Belief* was written in the prison during this difficult time. Nursi was forced to stay in Emirdağ where, by 1947, the *Risale-i Nur* was completed. Nursi was detained once again and sent to Afyon Prison where he served another twenty months, on the same charges he had previously faced. Although he and the *Risale-i Nur* were cleared once again, the process was deliberately slow in order to keep him in prison as long as possible. Now, Nursi was over seventy years of age, and owing to his periods of exile and stays in prison his health was very poor. According to the accounts of his students, the regime was deliberately trying to kill him, by means of poisoning and by exposing him to extreme cold in his prison cell.[36] The new state was run by Mustafa Kemal Atatürk and his Republican People's Party (RPP)[37] up until 1950. This 27-year period in the history of modern Turkey, known as the single-party period, is still very controversial. For some, it was a brutal dictatorship, for others, it was a necessary step towards establishing a new state. It was a period when philosophy-based ideologies were becoming increasingly influential in political systems and when Islamic societies underwent the most radical changes in the whole history of Islamic civilization.[38]

Owing to his enforced exile, Nursi rarely made contact with

---

[35] Atatürk introduced the new dress code in 1925, which made the use of the hat obliga-tory. Anyone refusing to put a hat on was punished severely.

[36] See Abu-Rabi, *Islam at the Crossroads: On the Life and Thought of Bediuzzaman Said Nursi* at xxi.

[37] The Republican People's Party was established by Atatürk on 9 September 1923. It was the only party without opposition until the General Election of 1950. The ideology of the party is Kemalism and Social Democracy.

[38] See Ahmet Davutoğlu, "Bediüzzaman and the Politics of the 20th Century" available at www.nur.org/en/nurcenter/nurlibrary/Bediuzzaman_and_the_Politics_of_the_20th_ Century_198 last accessed on 25 October 2014.

people outside his close circle of students. His main means of communication was through his letters and treaties. During the second period of his life (the New Saïd period) he hardly made any public speeches other than his court defenses. Hence, his only option was to promote the *Risale-i Nur* rather than his own leadership and charisma. On many occasions, he called himself 'a student of the *Risale-i Nur*' rather than the author of it. From 1926 on, Nursi started building up a large number of followers of his *Risale-i Nur*, corporately called the *Risale-i Nur Movement*, or *Nurcus*. Although the new regime abolished the use of the Arabic alphabet in favor of the Latin, Nursi wrote his treaties and letters using the Ottoman alphabet (Arabic), which made them readily understandable by the public at large. Here, it is important to note that the *Risale-i Nur* was printed in the modern Latin alphabet only in 1956, after all charges against it by the Afyon Court were dropped. Especially after the ban on Sufi *tekke*s and *madrasa*s, the public experienced a vacuum and a lack of guidance. The *Risale-i Nur* filled this gap and it was widely accepted and its text reproduced by people in and around Isparta.

The *Risale-i Nur* (The Epistles of Light)

According to Nursi, the *Risale-i Nur*, a collection of fourteen books and inspired directly by the Qur'an,[39] is the true commentary on the Qur'an's meanings (*tafsir ma'nawi*).[40] In *Al-Isharat al-I'jaz*, Nursi highlights four main purposes (*maqasid-i 'arba'*) that the Qur'an expounds. These are: the oneness or unity of God (*tawhid*), the nature of and the necessity for Prophethood (*nubuwwwah*), the resurrection of the dead (*ḥashr*), and justice and worship ('*adalah and 'ibadah*).[41] In order to clarify the Qur'an's exposition of these four elements, Nursi explains certain themes in his writings. Turner and Horkuç argue that six of these distinct themes appear in Nursi's writings.[42]

i. The book of universe *(kitab-ı kainat)* **and the beautiful**

---

[39]   Şahiner, *Bilinmeyen Taraflarıyla Bediüzzaman Said Nursi: Kronolojik Hayatı.*

[40]   Nursi, *The Letters* at 439.

[41]   Ibid., at 512.

[42]   Saïd Nursi, *Signs of Miraculousness* (Istanbul: Nesil, 2004d) at 1167.

Names of God (al-asma al-husna)

Throughout the *Risale-i Nur*, Nursi meticulously comments on the universe being a book written by God. He explains that, just like a mirror, the universe reflects all the different beautiful Names and Attributes of its Creator.[43] To Nursi, all beings have been created for a purpose and are the signs (*ayat*) of their Creator.[44] Therefore, the purpose of man's creation is to attain belief in God, which may be achieved by the correct interpretation of the cosmic narrative.

ii. The self, or the human 'I' (*ana*)

According to Nursi, *ana* is the trust given to man by his Creator. The first function of *ana* is to understand the Beautiful Names of God. Secondly, *ana* is a key given to man wherewith to unlock the secret of creation. *Ana,* the human 'I', is a comparison tool given to man so he can see where God stands in contrast to where he stands. In *Ana Risalesi* (The Thirtieth Word), Nursi writes:

> The All-Wise Maker gave to man as a Trust an 'I' which comprises indications and samples that show and cause to recognize the truths of the attributes and functions of His Lordship (*rububiyyah*), so that the 'I' might be a unit of measurement and the attributes of lordship and functions of Divinity might be known. However, it is not necessary for a unit of measurement to have actual existence; like hypothetical lines in geometry, a unit of measurement may be formed by hypothesis and supposition. It is not necessary for its actual existence to be established by concrete knowledge and proofs.[45]

iii. The 'self-referential' and the 'other-indicative' (*ma'nà-i ismi*, and *ma'nà-i harfi*)

To aid understanding of the meaning of life and the nature of the universe, Nursi introduced the concepts of m'anà-i ismi (the significative

---

[43]   Nursi mentions more than the classical 99 Beautiful Names of God listed in the *hadīth*.

[44]   This particular theme is also Nursi's first way of arguing for the existence of God, i.e. the teleological (design) argument, which is the focal topic of Chapter 3.

[45]   Colin Turner and Hasan Horkuc, *Said Nursi* (London, New York: I.B. Tauris 2009) at 53.

or self-referential meaning of things), and *m'anà-i harfi* (other-indicative meaning). He explains that cosmos and life can be understood correctly only through the window of *m'anà-i harfi*[46] (the meaning that signifies something other than itself). In *Al-Isharat al-I'jaz*, he explains that the Qur'an mentions beings 'not for themselves, but for another.' That is, it speaks of the universe as evidence for Almighty God's existence, unity and sublimity.[47] It is apparent from the Tenth Word on Resurrection that Nursi bases his arguments mainly on facts such as order in the universe, purpose in all creatures, and the absence of waste in the cosmos. These are two well-known theistic arguments in the philosophy of religion, the cosmological argument and the teleological argument, also known as the argument from design, which will be examined in the following chapters.

iv. Causality

Nursi tries vigorously to convince his readers that there is no necessary connection between cause and effect independent of God. Scientific materialism, which Nursi considers the greatest threat to humankind, claims that the effective cause of what is actually happening now is the combined result of the previous causes. For example, when a burning match touches dry paper, the paper burns as a result of fire caused by the match. Nursi seems to be maintaining *Ash'ari's* approach to causality, which was also endorsed by al-Ghazzali. The *Ash'ari–*al-Ghazzali line of thought dictates that the actual cause for the piece of paper burning is not the match but God's creating a new set of conditions to realize the new effect. God is the creator of all causes (*musabbib al-asbab*).

Nursi explains that people misread nature and natural events in terms of causality. He explains that God is the absolute and continuous creator. According to Nursi, there are two types of creation. These are *ibda* (creation out of nothing) and *insha* (gradual building from existing material). In *The Flashes*, Nursi writes: ac-

---

[46]   Nursi writes in the *Addendum of the 26th Word:* "According to the apparent meaning of things (*m'anà-i ismi*), which looks to each thing itself, everything is transitory, lacking,

[47]   See Nursi, *The Words* at 241.

cidental, non-existent. But according to the meaning that signifies something other than itself (*m'anà-i harfi*) and in respect of each thing being a mirror to the All-Glorious Maker's Names and charged with various duties, each is a witness, it is witnessed, and it is existent. The purification and cleansing of a person at this stage is as follows:

In his existence he is non-existent, and in his non-existence he has existence. That is to say, if he values himself and attributes existence to himself, he is in a darkness of non-existence as great as the universe. That is, if he relies on his individual existence and is unmindful of the True Giver of Existence, he has an individual light of existence like that of a fire-fly and is submerged in an endless darkness of non-existence and separation. But if he gives up egotism and sees that he is a mirror of the manifestations of the True Giver of Existence, he gains all beings and an infinite existence. For he who finds the Necessary Existent One, the manifestation of Whose Names all beings manifest, finds everything."

> Beings are created in two ways: one is creation from nothing called origination and invention; and the other is the giving of existence through bringing together existent elements and things, called composition and assembling. When in accordance with the manifestation of divine singleness and mystery of divine oneness, this occurs with an infinite ease, indeed, such ease as to be necessary. If not ascribed to divine singleness, it would be infinitely difficult and irrational, difficult to the degree of impossibility. However, the fact that beings in the universe come into existence with infinite ease and facility and no difficulty at all, and in perfect form, self-evidently shows the manifestation of divine singleness and proves that everything is directly the art of the Single One of Glory.[48]

For Nursi, in order to maintain the element of test (*sırr-ı teklif*), God uses causes to veil His actual power and majesty, but He expects people to understand that He is the

---

[48]   Nursi, *Signs of Miraculousness*.

absolute creator and controller of the events that scientific materialism explains otherwise.[49]

v. Belief and submission (*iman–islam*)

According to Nursi, the true salvation of humanity can only be achieved through a perfect balance between belief and submission. Thus, man is required to attain true belief through investigation and research. Throughout the *Risale-i Nur*, Nursi tries to make his readers move from *iman-ı taklidi* (belief through emulation) to *iman-ı tahkiki* (belief through investigation). Aware of the threat of scientific materialism, Nursi develops a reverse theme of science and nature being the evidence of their Creator.

vi. Closed doors of creation

The last theme that Nursi elaborates on is the 'closed doors of creation', which is closely connected to the second theme of *ana (the human 'I')*. In *The Words,* Nursi explains:

> The key to the world is in the hand of man and is attached to his self. For while being apparently open, the doors of the universe are in fact closed. God Almighty has given to man by way of a Trust, such a key, called the 'I', that it opens all the doors of the world; He has given him an enigmatic 'I' with which he may discover the hidden treasures of the Creator of the universe. But the 'I' is also an extremely complicated riddle and an enigma

that is difficult to solve. When its true nature and the purpose of its creation are known, as it is itself solved, so will be the universe.[50]

The Nursian view is that the purpose of human existence is to investigate and explore life and the universe so as to try to unlock the doors of creation in order to attain true belief (iman-ı tahkiki).[51]

---

[49]   In *The Words, Nursi writes:* Yes, dignity and grandeur demand that causes are a veil to the hand of power in the view of the mind, while Divine unity and glory demand that causes withdraw their hands and have no true effect. See Nursi, *The Flashes* at 808.

[50]   Nursi, *The Words* at 122.

[51]   Turner and Horkuç discuss these themes in greater detail. See ibid., at 241.

Nursi's Style

Nursi wrote the treaties in *The Words* in a very simple language. He uses allegories to make the context clear to readers who were not highly educated. Then, he reveals the truth via the allegory. By way of proof of the Maker, Nursi tells the story of two men travelling through a land. One man is empty-headed and represents the atheist philosophy, and the other is wise and represents the theist philosophy. To the empty-headed man rejecting the Deity, the wise man replies:

> Every village must have its headman; every needle must have its manufacturer and craftsman. And, as you know, every letter must be written by someone. How, then, can it be that so extremely well-ordered a kingdom should have no ruler? And how can so much wealth have no owner, when every hour a train arrives filled with precious and artful gifts, as if coming from the realm of the unseen? And all the announcements and proclamations, all the seals and stamps, found on all those goods, all the coins and the flags waving in every corner of the kingdom — can they be without an owner? It seems you have studied foreign languages a little, and are unable to read this Islamic script. In addition, you refuse to ask those who are able to read it. Come now; let me read to you the king's supreme decree.[52]

In terms of methodology, Nursi's style resembles that of Plato. In the *Laws*, Plato uses two imaginary characters, Cleinias and the Athenian Stranger, to represent opposing ideas. Similarly, Hume, in his *Dialogues Concerning Natural Religion*, speaks from the mouths of Demea, Cleanthes, and Philo to represent the cosmological theist, the experimental theist and the skeptic.

Nursi uses the word philosophy (*falsafa*) in a deprecatory sense, meaning negative philosophy (i.e. materialist, naturalist and atheist). In order to denigrate this philosophy, he makes the Qur'an speak. He never uses the expressions 'atheist philosophy' or 'theist philosophy.' He often presents a clash between *falsafa* (philosophy) and the Qur'an.

---

[52]   Turner and Horkuc, *Said Nursi* at 53–84.

The Third Saïd Period (1950–1960)

Perhaps one of the most important events in the history of modern Turkey was its first democratic, multi-party elections in 1950, after 27 years of single-party rule by the Republican People's Party (RPP). Now, the opposition Democratic Party (DP) was allowed to challenge the RPP and it won the elections by landslide.[53] One of the first actions of the DP was to lift the ban on the Arabic call to Prayer. This was clearly a massive positive step forward in terms of ending anti-religious oppression. Although the DP seriously improved democracy in Turkey, public prosecutors, brandishing the old Article 163 of the Penal Code,[54] were still free to press charges against Nursi. Indeed, the charges against the *Risale-i Nur* and the *Nurcus* kept coming until the removal of Article 163 from the Penal Code in 1991. The shift towards democracy and the rise of communist Russia after the World War II gave Nursi the opportunity to promote the *Risale-i Nur* so as to fight the imminent threat of communism. Nursi saw atheism as the common enemy of the all monotheistic religions. In 1953, he met the Greek Orthodox Patriarch and offered his views on uniting forces against aggressive atheism.[55]

Another important turning point in Nursi's life was the 1956 court acquittal of the *Risale-i Nur*, which was consequently printed and duplicated *en masse* in the Latin alphabet in both Ankara and Istanbul. Nursi called this "The *Risale-i Nur* Festival."[56] He said, 'From now on, there is no need for me to work in the service of the *Risale-i Nur*. That is to say, the *Risale-i Nur* and its students will perform my duties."[57]

---

[53]   The results of the 1950 elections were: Democrat Party: 52.68% (415 seats), Republican People's Party: 39.45% (69 seats).

[54]   Article 163 of the old Turkish Penal Code, which was removed in 1991, outlawed politically motivated religious activities and prohibited the establishment of religious organizations and political parties aimed at creating an Islamic republic.

[55]   On the issue of Nursi's Muslim–Christian dialogue, see Nursi, *The Words* at 20.

[56]   See Şükran Vahide, A Chronology of Said Nursi's Life in Z. Sarıtoprak, 'Said Nursi on Muslim-Christian Relations Leading to World Peace', *Islam and Christian Muslim Relations*, 19/1 (2008), 25–37 at 25–37.

[57]   Abu-Rabi, *Islam at the Crossroads: On the Life and Thought of Bediuzzaman Said Nursi* at xxiii.

In the last few years of his life, Nursi was a free man; his ideas and books were freely available to everyone, and he had followers in their thousands. He travelled through the places that had marked his life with important memories. In 1960, he arrived in Urfa in eastern Turkey where, at the age of 83, he died peacefully of old age in his hotel room.

Conclusion

Nursi lived through three distinctive periods of Turkish history, which affected his philosophy of life. During the last few decades of the Ottoman Empire, he was mainly concerned with saving the falling Empire. Nicknamed the 'sick man', the Ottoman Empire had been the target of other imperialist states, which saw it as a major threat to their expansion in many parts of the world. This was mainly due to the fact that the Ottoman Sultan also held the post of Caliph, the official head of the Muslims. The British Secretary for the Colonies, Gladstone, openly declared war on the Qur'an, which, he said, was the main obstacle to British imperialist ambitions.[58] Nursi's thoughts took a first turn here. He committed himself to acquiring all the knowledge available to understand the Qur'an and prove its truth. The Old Saïd period, which coincides with the last years of the Ottoman Empire, is Nursi's most politically active period. He was advocating a reform of the education system that would help stop the collapse of the Empire and in addition solve other social issues.

With the collapse of the Empire, Nursi turned to fight the materialist philosophy that have become the official ideology of the new Turkish Republic. It is clear in the *Risale-i Nur* that there is a great shift towards a *ka-lam*-style refutation of atheism in works like *The Word*, *The Letters* and *The Flashes*, which were all written during the first years of Kemalist Turkey. Nursi did not object to secularism, since he considered it to be a guarantor of freedom of faith; however, he was seriously concerned with materialism and its negative

---

[58]   The British Secretary for the Colonies, Gladstone, said: So long as the Muslims have the Qur'an, we shall be unable to dominate them. We must either take it from them, or make them lose their love of it. See Vahide, *Biography of Bediuzzaman Said Nursi: at 47.*

effects on a mainly Muslim public. He developed a unique way of *kalam*, where he merged modern science and the traditional Islamic knowledge of the *madrasa* to address the question of doubts surrounding the Qur'an. Unlike works such as *Muhakemat*, and *Al-Isharat al-I'jaz*, which were addressed to scholars, Nursi's writings in

the New Saïd period were mainly aimed at the ordinary public. Nursi explained that every reader could benefit from the *Risale-i Nur* according to his or her abilities. Although he did not make any systematic reference to the materialist philosophers by name, a large proportion of his work was dedicated to refuting their philosophy. In general, he condemned philosophy on the basis that it did not submit to revelation. He also criticized famous Muslim philosophers (*mutakallimun*) such as Ibn-i Sina and al-Farabi regarding their judgments. Nursi's *kalam* may be seen as more in line with the thought of al-Ghazzali, whom he described as *ḥujjat-ul Islam*, which literally means 'The proof of Islam.'

CHAPTER 1

THE PURPOSE OF THE EXISTENCE OF HUMANBEINGS AND THE UNIVERSE

In the Name of God, the All-Merciful, the All-Compassionate.

By the sun and its brightness; And the moon as it follows it (reflecting its light); And the day as it reveals it (the sun); And the night as it enshrouds it; And the heaven and that (All-Magnificent One) Who has built it; And the earth and that (All-Magnificent One) Who has spread it; And the human selfhood and that (All-Knowing, All-Powerful, and All-Wise One) Who has formed it to perfection, (Ash-Shams 91:1–7)

If you want to understand a little about the talisman of the wisdom of the world and the riddle of man's creation and the mystery of the reality of the prescribed prayers (*salah*), then consider this short comparison together with my own soul.

One time there was a king. As wealth he had numerous treasuries containing diamonds and emeralds and jewels of every kind. Besides these he had other, hidden, wondrous treasuries. By way of attainment he had consummate skill in strange arts, and encompassing knowledge of innumerable wondrous sciences, and great erudition in endless branches of abstruse learning. Now, like every possessor of beauty and perfection wants to see and display his own beauty and perfection, that glorious king wanted to open up an exhibition and set out displays within it in or- der to make manifest and display in the view of the people the majesty of his rule, his glittering wealth, the wonders of his art, and the marvels of his knowledge, and so that he could behold his beauty and perfection in two respects:

The First Respect: So that he himself could behold them with his own discerning eye.

The other: So that he could look through the view of others.

With this purpose in mind, the king started to construct a vast and majestic palace. He divided it into magnificent apartments and dwellings, and decorated it with every sort of jewel from his treasuries, and with his own hand so full of art adorned it with the finest and most beautiful works. He ordered it with the subtlest of the arts of his wisdom, and decked it out with the miraculous works of his knowledge. Then after completing it, he set up in the palace broad tables containing the most delicious of every kind of food and every sort of bounty. He specified an appropriate table for each group. He set out such a munificent and artful banquet that it was as though the boundless priceless bounties he spread out had come into existence through the works of a hundred subtle arts. Then he invited his people and subjects from all the regions of his lands to feast and behold the spectacle.

Later the king appointed a Supreme Commander,[59] as a teacher, to make known the purposes of the palace and the meanings of its contents; to describe its Maker and its contents to the people, make known the secrets of the palace's embellishments, teach what the arts within it were pointing to, and to explain what the well-set jewels were, and the harmonious embroideries; and to explain to those who entered the palace the way in which they indicated the perfections and arts of the palace's owner, and to inform them of

---

[59]   That is Prophet Muhammad, peace and blessings be upon him.

the correct conduct in beholding them, and to explain the official ceremonies as the king, who did not appear, wished them to be. The teacher and instructor had an assistant in each area of the palace, while he himself remained in the largest apartment among his students, making the following announcement to all the spectators. He told them:

"O people! By making this palace and displaying these things our lord, who is the king of the palace, wants to make himself known to you. You therefore should recognize Him and try to get to know Him. And with these adornments He wants to make Himself loved by you. Also, He shows His love for you through these bounties that you see, so you should love Him too by obeying Him. And through these bounties and gifts which are to be seen He shows His compassion and kindness for you, so you should show your respect for Him by offering thanks. And through these works of His perfection He wants to display His transcendent beauty to you, so you should show your eagerness to see Him and gain His regard. And through placing a particular stamp and special seal and an inimitable signet on every one of these adorned works of art that you see, He wants to show that everything is particular to Him, and is the work of His own hand, and that He is single and unique and independent and removed. You therefore should recognize that He is single and alone, and without peer or like or match, and accept that He is such." He spoke further fitting words to the spectators like these concerning the King and this station. Then the people who had entered the palace separated into two groups.

The first group: Since these people had self-knowledge, were intelligent, and their hearts were in the right place, when they looked at the wonders inside the palace, they declared: "There are great matters afoot here!" They understood that it was not in vain or some trifling plaything. They were curious, and while wondering: "I wonder what the talisman to this is and what it contains," they suddenly heard the speech the Master and Instructor was giving, and they realized that the keys to all the mysteries were with him. So they approached him and said: "Peace be upon you, O Master! By rights, a truthful and exact instructor like you is necessary for a magnificent palace such as this. Please tell us what our Lord has made known to you!" First of all the Master repeated the speech to them. They listened carefully, and accepting it, profited greatly. They acted as the King wished. And because the King was pleased at their becoming conduct and manners, he invited them to another special, elevated, ineffable palace. And he bestowed it on them in a way worthy of such a munificent king, and fitting for such obedient subjects, and suitable for such well-mannered guests, and appropriate to such an elevated palace. He made them permanently happy.

As for the second group, because their minds were corrupted and their hearts extinguished, when they entered the palace, they were defeated by their evil-commanding souls and took notice of nothing apart from the delicious foods; they closed their eyes to all the virtues and stopped up their ears to the guidance of the Master, peace and blessings be upon him, and the warnings of his students. They stuffed themselves like animals then sank into sleep. They drank elixirs which had been prepared for certain other matters and were not to have been consumed. Then they became drunk and started shouting so much they greatly upset the other spectating guests. They were ill-mannered in the face of the Glorious Maker's rules. So the soldiers of the palace's owner arrested them, and cast them into a prison appropriate to such unmannerly people.

O friend who is listening to this story with me! Of course you have understood that the Glorious Creator built this palace for the above-mentioned aims. The achievement of these aims is dependent on two things:

The First: The existence of the Master, peace and blessings be upon him, whom we saw and whose speech we heard. Because if it was not for him, all these aims would be in vain. For if an incomprehensible book has no author, it consists only of meaningless paper.

The Second is the people listening the Master's words and accepting them. That is to say, the Master's existence is the cause of the palace's existence, and the people's listening to him is the cause of the continuation of the palace's existence. In which case it can be said that if it was not for the Master, peace and blessings be upon him, the Glorious King would not have built the palace. And again it may be said that when the people do not follow the Master's (peace and blessings be upon him) instructions, the palace will of a certainty be transformed and changed.

Friend! The story ends here. If you have understood the meaning of the comparison, come and behold its reality.

The palace is this world. Its roof is the heavens illuminated with smiling stars, and its floor, the face of the earth adorned from east to west with multifarious flowers. As for the King, he is the Most Holy One, the Pre-Eternal and Post-Eternal Monarch, Whom all things in the seven heavens and the earth glorify and worship, each with its particular tongue. He is a king so powerful He created the heavens and earth in six days, then abided on the Throne. One of Power and Majesty, who, alternating night and day like two threads, one white and one black, writes His signs of the page of the universe; One to Whose command the sun, moon, and stars are subjugated. The apartments of the palace are the eighteen thousand worlds, each of which has been set in order and decorated in a fashion suitable to it. The strange arts you saw in the palace are the miracles of Divine power you see in this world, and the foods you saw there allude to the wonderful fruits of Divine mercy in this world, especially in summer, and above all in the gardens of Barla. The stove and kitchen there is the earth here, which has fire in its heart, and the face of the earth. While the jewels of the hidden treasuries you saw in the comparison are the similitudes of the manifestations of the sacred Divine Names. And the embroideries there, and the signs of the embroideries, are the well-ordered and finely worked beings and the harmonious impresses of the pen of power which adorn this world and point to the Names of the All-Powerful One of Glory.

As for the Master, he is our Master Muhammad, peace and blessings be upon him. His assistants are the other prophets, peace be upon them, and his students, the saints and purified scholars. The ruler's servants in the pal- ace indicate the angels, peace be upon them, in this world. And the guests invited to the banquet to spectate in the comparison are the jinn and man- kind in this guesthouse of the world, and the animals, who are the servants of mankind. As for the two groups, one of them here consists of the people of belief, who are the students of the All-Wise Qur'an, the interpreter of the verses and signs of the book of the universe. The other group are the people of unbelief and rebellion, who follow Satan and their evil-commanding souls; deaf and dumb, like animals, or even lower, they form the group of the misguided, who recognize the life of this world only.

First group: These are the felicitous and the good, who listened to the Master, 'the Possessor of Two Wings.' He is both the worshipping servant of God; in regard to worship he describes his Sustainer so that he is like the envoy of his community at the court of almighty God. And he is also God's messenger; with regard to messengership he conveys his Sustainer's decrees to men and the jinn by means of the Qur'an.

This happy community heeded the Messenger and listened to the Qur'an. They saw themselves invested with the prescribed prayers, which are the index of all the varieties of worship, and numerous subtle duties within elevated stations. Indeed, they saw in detail the duties and stations which the Prayers point to with their various formulas and actions. It was like this:

First: Since they observed the Divine works, and in the form of a transaction in the absence of the person concerned, saw themselves in the station of observing the wonders of the sovereignty of lordship, they performed the duty of praising and glorifying God, declaring: "*God is Most Great!*"

Second: Through being seen in the station of herald of His brilliant and wonderful works, which are the manifestations of the sacred divine names, exclaiming: "*Glory be to God! All praise be to God!*", they performed the duty of hallowing and praising God.

Third: In the station of perceiving and understanding with their inner and outer senses the bounties stored up in the treasuries of Divine mercy, they started to carry out the duty of thanks and praise.

Fourth: In the station of weighing up with the scales of their spiritual faculties the jewels in the treasuries of the Divine Names, they began the duty of praise and declaring God to be free of all faults.

Fifth: In the station of studying the Sustainer's notifications, written with the pen of power on the plan of Divine Determining, they began the duty of contemplation and appreciation.

Sixth: With beholding the subtle, delicate, fine beauties in the creation of things and in the art in beings, in the station of declaring God to be free of all defects, they took up the duty of love and yearning for their All- Glorious Creator, their All-Beauteous Maker. That is to say, after looking at the universe and works and performing the duties in the above-mentioned stations through transactions in the object of worship's absence, they rose to the degree of also beholding the transactions and acts of the All-Wise Maker, whereby, in the form of a transaction in the presence of the person concerned, they responded with knowledge and wonder in the face of the All-Glorious Creator's making Himself known to conscious beings through the miracles of His art, and declared: "Glory be unto You! How can we truly know you? What makes You known are the miracles of the works of Your art!"

Then, they responded with love and passion to that Most Merciful One's making Himself loved through the beautiful fruits of His mercy. *"You alone do we worship and from You alone do we seek help!"*, they declared.

Then they responded with thanks and praise to the True Bestower is showing His mercy and compassion through His sweet bounties, and ex- claimed: "Glory be unto You! All praise is Yours! How can we thank You as is Your due? You are utterly worthy of thanks! For all Your bounties spread through all the universe hymn Your praises and thanks through the clear tongues of their beings. All Your bounties lined up in the market of the world and scattered over the face of the earth proclaim Your praises and extol You. Through testifying to Your munificence and generosity, all the well-ordered and well-proportioned fruits of Your mercy and bounty offer You thanks before the gazes of Your creatures."

Then they responded, saying: *"God is Most Great!"* before the manifestation of Divine beauty, glory, perfection, and majesty in the mirrors of beings, ever changing on the face of the universe; they bowed reverently in their impotence, and prostrated in humility with love and wonder.

Then announcing their poverty and need, they responded with supplication and beseeching to the Possessor of Absolute Riches' displaying the abundance of His wealth and breadth of His mercy, and declared: "*From You alone do we seek help!*"

Then they responded appreciatively to the All-Glorious Maker's dis- playing the subtleties and wonders of His antique art in the exhibition of creatures, exclaiming: "What wonders God has willed!" Observing and applauding them, they declared, "How beautifully they have been made! What blessings God has bestowed!" Holding everyone witness, they said in wonder: "Come! Look at these! Hasten to the Prayers and to prosperity!"

And they responded with submission and obedience to the Monarch of Pre-Eternity and Post-Eternity's proclamation of the sovereignty of His Lordship in every corner of the universe and the manifestation of His unity. Declaring: "We hear and we obey!", they affirmed His unity.

Then, before the manifestation of the Godhead of that Sustainer of All the Worlds, they responded with worship and humble veneration, which consists of proclaiming their poverty within need, and with the Prescribed Prayers, which are the summary of worship. Thus, through performing their various duties of worship in the mighty mosque known as the abode of this world, they carried out the obligations and duties of their lives, and assumed 'the finest of forms.' They ascended to a rank above all creatures by which, through the auspiciousness of belief and assurance and 'the Trust,' they became trustworthy Vicegerents of God on the Earth. And after this field of trial and place of examination, their Munificent Sustainer invited them to eternal happiness in recompense for their belief, and to the Abode of Peace in reward for their adhering to His religion of Islam. There, He bestowed on them out of His mercy bounties so dazzling that no eye has seen them, nor ear heard them, nor have they occurred to the heart of man[2]—and so He does bestow these on them, and He gave them eternity and everlasting life. For the desirous, mirror-bearing lovers of an eternal, abiding beauty who gaze upon it will certainly not perish, but will go to eternity. The final state of the Qur'an's students is thus. May Almighty God include us among them, Amen!

As for the other group, the sinners and the wicked, when they entered the palace of this world at the age of discretion, they responded with unbelief to all the evidences of divine unity, and with ingratitude towards all the bounties, and by accusing all creatures of being valueless, insulted them in an unbelieving manner. And since they rejected and denied all the manifestations of the Divine Names, they committed a boundless crime in a short time and became deserving of endless punishment. For the capital of life and the human faculties were given to man for the duties mentioned above.

O my senseless soul and foolish friend! Do you suppose your life's duty is restricted to following the good life according to the requisites of civilization, and, if you will excuse the expression, to gratifying the physical appetites? Do you suppose the sole aim of the delicate and subtle senses, the sensitive faculties and members, the well-ordered limbs and systems, the inquisitive feelings and senses included in the machine of your life is restricted to satisfying the low desires of the base soul in this fleeting life? God forbid! There are two main aims in their creation and inclusion in your essential being:

The first consists of making known to you all the varieties of the True Bestower's bounties, and causing you to offer Him thanks. You should be aware of this, and offer Him thanks and worship.

The second is to make known to you by means of your faculties all the sorts of the manifestations of the sacred Divine Names manifested in the world and to cause you to experience them. And you, by recognizing them through experiencing them, should come to believe in them.

Thus, man develops and is perfected through the achievement of these two basic aims. Through them, man becomes a true human being.

Look through the meaning of the following comparison, and see that the human faculties were not given in order to gain worldly life like an animal.

For example, someone gave one of his servants twenty gold pieces, telling him to have a suit of clothes made out of a particular cloth. The servant went and got himself a fine suit out of the highest grade of the cloth, and put it on. Then he saw that his employer had given another of his servants a thousand gold pieces, and putting in the servant's pocket a piece of paper with some things written on it, had sent him to conclude some business. Now, anyone with any sense would know that the capital was not for getting a suit of clothes, for, since the first servant had bought a suit of the finest cloth with twenty gold pieces, the thousand gold pieces were certainly not to be spent on that. Since the second servant had not read the paper in his pocket, and looking at the first servant, had given all the money to a shopkeeper for a suit of clothes, and then received the very lowest grade of cloth and a suit fifty times worse that his friend's, his employer was bound to reprimand him severely for his utter stupidity, and punish him angrily.

O my soul and my friend! Come to your senses! Do not spend the capital and potentialities of your life on pleasures of the flesh and this fleeting life like an animal, or even lower. Otherwise, although you are fifty times superior with regard to capital than the highest animal, you will fall fifty times lower than the lowest.

O my heedless soul! If you want to understand to a degree both the aim of your life and its nature, and the form of your life, and the true meaning of your life, and its perfect happiness, then look! The summary of the aims of your life consists of nine matters:

First: To weigh up on the scales of the senses put in your being the bounties stored up in the treasuries of Divine mercy, and to offer universal thanks.

Second: To open with the keys of the faculties placed in your nature the hidden treasuries of the sacred Divine Names.

Third: To consciously display and make known through your life in the view of the creatures in this exhibition of the world the wondrous arts and subtle manifestations which the Divine Names have attached to you.

Fourth: To proclaim your worship to the Court of the Creator's lordship verbally and through the tongue of your disposition.

Fifth: Like on ceremonial occasions a soldier wears all the decorations he has received from his king, and through appearing before the him, displays the marks of his favor towards him, this is to consciously adorn yourself in the jewels of the subtle senses which the manifestations of the Divine Names have given you, and to appear in the observant view of the Pre-Eternal Witness.

Sixth: To consciously observe the salutations of living beings to their Creator, known as the manifestations of life, and their glorifications of their Maker, known as the signs of life, and their worship of the Bestower of Life (*Vahib ul Hayat*), known as the aims of life, and by reflecting on them to see them, and through testifying to them to display them.

Seventh: Through taking as units of measurement the small samples of attributes like the partial knowledge, power, and will given to your life, it is to know through those measures the absolute attributes and sacred qualities of the All-Glorious Creator. For example, since, through your partial power, knowledge, and will, you have made your house in well-ordered fashion, you should know that the Maker of the palace of the world is its Disposer, and Powerful, Knowing, and Wise to the degree it is greater than your house.

Eighth: To understand the words concerning the Creator's unity and Maker's lordship (*rububiyyah*) uttered by each of the beings in the world in its particular tongue.

Ninth: To understand through your impotence and weakness, your poverty and need, the degrees of the Divine power and dominical riches. Just as the pleasure and degrees and varieties of food are understood through the degrees of hunger and the sorts of need, so you should understand the degrees of the infinite Divine power and riches through your infinite impotence and poverty. The aims of your life, then, briefly, are matters like these. Now consider the nature of your life; its summary is this:

It is an index of wonders pertaining to the Divine Names; a scale for measuring the Divine Attributes; a balance of the worlds within the universe; a list of the mighty world; a map of the cosmos; a summary of the vast book of the universe; a bunch of keys with which to open the hidden treasuries of Divine power; and a most excellent pattern of the perfections scattered over beings and attached to time. The nature of your life consists of matters like these.

Now, the form of your life and the manner of its duty is this: your life is an inscribed word, a wisdom-displaying word written by the pen of power. Seen and heard, it points to the Divine Names. The form of your life consists of matters like these.

Now the true meaning of your life is this: its acting as a mirror to the manifestation of Divine oneness and the manifestation of the Eternally

Besought One. That is to say, through a comprehensiveness as though being the point of focus for all the Divine Names manifested in the world, it is its being a mirror to the Single and Eternally Besought One.

Now, as for the perfection of your life, it is to perceive the lights of the Pre-Eternal Sun which are depicted in the mirror of your life, and to love them. It is to display love for Him as a conscious being. It is to pass be- yond yourself with love of Him. It is to establish the reflection of His light in the center of your heart. It is due to this mystery that the Hadith Qudsi[60] was uttered, which is expressed by the following lines, and will raise you to the highest of the high:

The heavens and the earth contain me not;

Yet, how strange! I am contained in the hearts of believers.[61]

And so, my soul! Since your life is turned towards such elevated aims and gathers together such priceless treasures, is it at all worthy of reason and fairness that you should spend it on temporary gratification of the instinctual soul and fleeting worldly pleasures, and waste it? If you do not want to waste away your life, ponder over the oaths in this surah of the Qur'an, which allude to the above comparison and truths, and act accordingly:

By the sun and its brightness; And the moon as it follows it (reflecting its light); And the day as it reveals it (the sun); And the

---

[60] Hadith Qudsi (or Sacred Hadith) is a sub-category of hadith which are the sayings of Prophet Muhammad, peace and blessings be upon him. Hadith Qudsi is regarded as the words of Allah, repeated by Prophet Muhammad, peace and blessings be upon him, and recorded on the condition of an isnad (science of hadith). According to al-Jurjani, the Hadith Qudsi differs from the Qur'an in that the former are "expressed in Prophet Muhammad's words," whereas the latter are the "direct words of Allah."

[61] See, al-'Ajluni, Kashf al-Khafa, ii, 165; Ghazzali, Ihya 'Ulum ad-Din, iii, 14.

night as it enshrouds it; And the heaven and that (All-Magnificent One) Who has built it; And the earth and that (All-Magnificent One) Who has spread it; And the human selfhood and that (All-Knowing, All-Powerful, and All-Wise One) Who has formed it to perfection, And Who has inspired it with the conscience of what is wrong and bad for it, and what is right and good for it, He is indeed prosperous who has grown it in purity (away from self-aggrandizing rebellion against God); And he is indeed lost who has corrupted it (in self-aggrandizing rebellion against God). (Ash-Shams 91:1–10)

O Lord, grant blessings and peace to the Sun of the Skies of Messengership, the Moon of the Constellation of Prophethood (i.e., Prophet Muhammad), and to his Family and Companions, the stars of guidance, and grant mercy to us and to all believing men and all believing women. Amen. Amen. Amen.[62]

EGO, SELF AND HUMAN "I"

The key to the world is in the hand of man and is attached to his self. For while being apparently open, the doors of the universe are in fact closed. God Almighty has given to man by way of a Trust, such a key, called the 'I', that it opens all the doors of the world; He has given him an enigmatic 'I' with which he may discover the hidden treasures of the Creator of the universe. But the 'I' is also an extremely complicated riddle and a talisman that is difficult to solve. When its true nature and the purpose of its creation are known, as it is itself solved, so will be the universe.

The All-Wise Maker gave to man as a Trust an 'I' which comprises indications and samples that show and cause to recognize the truths of the attributes and functions of His Lordship (rububiyyah), so that the 'I' might be a unit of measurement and the Attributes of lordship and functions of Divinity might be known. However, it is not necessary for a unit of measurement to have actual existence; like hypothetical lines in geometry, a unit of measurement may be formed by hypothesis and supposition. It is not necessary for its actual existence to be established by concrete knowledge and proofs.

---

[62]   The Words, at 133–143.

Question: Why is knowledge of the Attributes and Names of God

Almighty connected to the 'I'?

The Answer: Since an absolute and all-encompassing thing has no limits or end, neither may a shape be given to it, nor may a form be conferred on it, nor may it be determined; what its quiddity is may not be comprehended. For example, an endless light without darkness may not be known or perceived. But if a line of real or imaginary darkness is drawn, then it becomes known. Thus, since God Almighty's Attributes like knowledge and power, and Names like All-Wise and All-Compassionate are all-encompassing, limitless, and without like, they may not be deter- mined, and what they are may not be known or perceived. Therefore, since they do not have limits or an actual end, it is necessary to draw a hypothetical and imaginary limit. The 'I' does this. It imagines in itself a fictitious lordship (*rububiyyah*) (greatness and supremacy), ownership, power, and knowledge: it draws a line. By doing this it places an imaginary limit on the all-encompassing attributes, saying, "Up to here, mine, after that, His;" it makes a division. With the tiny units of measurement in itself, it slowly understands the true nature of the attributes.

For example, with its imagined lordship (*rububiyyah*) over what it owns, the 'I' may understand the lordship (*rububiyyah*) of its Creator over contingent creation.

And with its apparent ownership, it may understand the true owner- ship of its Creator, saying: "Like I am the owner of this house, so too is the Creator the owner of the universe." And with its partial knowledge, it may understand His knowledge, and with its small amount of acquired art, it may understand the originative art of the Glorious Maker. For example, the 'I' says: "As I made this house and arranged it, so someone must have made the universe and arranged it," and so on. Thousands of mysterious states, attributes, and perceptions which make known and show to a degree all the Divine Attributes and functions are contained with the 'I.' That is to say, the 'I' is mirror-like, and, like a unit of measurement and tool for discovery, it has an indicative meaning; having no meaning in it- self, it shows the meaning of others. It is a conscious strand from the thick rope of the human being, a fine thread from the raiment of the essence of humanity, it is an *Alif* (the first letter of Arabic alphabet) from the book of the character of mankind, and it has two faces.

The first of these faces looks towards good and existence. With this face it is only capable of receiving favor; it accepts what is given, itself it cannot create. This face is not active; it does not have the ability to create. Its other face looks towards evil and goes to non-existence. That face is active; it has the power to act. Furthermore, the real nature of the 'I' is indicative; it shows the meaning of things other than itself. Its lordship (*rububiyyah*) is imaginary. Its existence is so weak and insubstantial that in itself it cannot bear or support anything at all. Rather, it is a sort of scale or measure, like a thermometer or barometer that indicates the degrees and amounts of things; it is a measure that makes known the absolute, all-encompassing and limitless Attributes of the Necessary Being.

Thus, he who knows his own self in this way, and realizes and acts ac- cording to it, is included in the good news of the Qur'an:

He is indeed prosperous who has grown it in purity (away from self-aggrandizing rebellion against God) (Ash-Shams 91:9)

He truly carries out the Trust, and through the telescope of his 'I', he sees what the universe is and what duties it is performing. When he obtains information about the universe, he sees that his 'I' confirms it. This knowledge will remain as light and wisdom for him, and will not be trans- formed into darkness and futility. When the 'I' fulfills its duty in this way, it abandons its imaginary lordship and supposed ownership, which are the units of measurement, and it says: "His is the sovereignty and to Him is due all praise; His is the judgment and to Him will you all be brought back." It achieves true worship. It attains the rank of 'the Most Excellent of Patterns.'

But if, forgetting the wisdom of its creation and abandoning the duty of its nature, the 'I' views itself solely in the light of its nominal and apparent meaning, if it believes that it owns itself, then it betrays the Trust, and it comes under the category of,

And he is indeed lost who has corrupted it (in self-aggrandizing rebellion against God) (Ash-Shams 91:10).

It was of this aspect of the Trust, therefore, which gives rise to all ascribing of partners to God, evil, and misguidance, that the heavens, earth, and mountains were terrified; they were frightened of associating hypothetical partners with God.

CHAPTER 2

PROBLEM OF EVIL AND SUFFER-ING

Question 1: Why are devils created? Almighty God created Satan and evils; what is the wisdom in it? Isn't it evil to create evil, and isn't it bad to cre-ate bad?

Answer: No. The creation of evil is not evil, the 'acquisition' of or desire for evil, rather, is evil. For creation and bringing into existence look to all the consequences, whereas such desire looks to a particular result, since it is a particular relation. For example, there are thousands of consequences of rain falling, and all of them are good. If through mischoice, some people receive harm from the rain, they cannot say that the creation of rain is not mercy, they cannot state that the creation of rain is evil. For it is due to their mischoice and inclination that it is evil for them. Also, there are numerous benefits in the creation of fire, and all of them are good. But if some people receive harm from fire through their misuse of it and their wrong choice, they cannot say that the creation of fire is evil; because it was not only created to burn them. Rather, they thrust their hands into the fire while cooking the food through mischoice, and made that servant inimical to themselves.

In short, the lesser evil is acceptable for the greater good. If an evil which will lead to a greater good is abandoned so that a lesser evil should not be, a greater evil will then have been perpetrated. For example, there are certainly some minor material and physical harms and evils in send- ing soldiers to fight a *jihad*, but in the *jihad* is a greater good whereby Islam is saved from being conquered by infidels. If the *jihad* is abandoned due to those lesser evils, then the greater evil will come after the greater good has gone. And that is absolute wrong. Also, for example, to amputate a finger which is infected with gangrene and has to be amputated is good and right, although it is apparently an evil. For if it is not amputated, the hand will be amputated, and that would be a greater evil.

Thus, the creation and bringing into existence of evils, harms, tribulations, satans, and harmful things, is not evil and bad, for they are created for the many important results they yield. For example, satans have not been set to pester the angels, and the angels cannot progress; their degrees are fixed and deficient. However, in the world of humanity the degrees of progress and decline are infinite. There is an extremely long distance through which to progress, from the Nimrod's and Pharaoh's as far as the veracious saints and the Prophets.

Thus, through the creation of satans and the mystery of man's accountability and the sending of Prophets, an arena of trial and examination and striving and competition has been opened so that coal-like base spirits may be differentiated and separated out from diamond-like elevated spirits. If there had been no striving and competition, the potentialities in the mine of humanity which are like diamonds and coal would have remained equal. The spirit of Abu Bakr the Truthful at the highest of the high would have remained on the same level as that of Abu Jahl at the lowest of the low. This means that since the creation of satans and evils looks to great and universal results, their being brought into existence is not evil or bad. The evils and instances of bad that arise from abuses and the particular causes known as inclination or choice pertain to man's 'acquisition' and choice, not to Divine creation.

Question 2: The great majority of humanity becomes unbelievers due to the existence of Satan. They embrace unbelief and suffer harm, despite the existence of Prophets. If, according to the rule "The majority has the word," the majority suffers evil as a result, then the creation of evil is evil and it may even be said that the sending of Prophets is not a mercy. Isn't that so?

Answer: Quantity has no importance in relation to quality. The true majority looks to quality. For example, if there are a hundred seeds of the date palm and they are not put beneath the earth and watered and so do not undergo a chemical reaction and manifest a struggle for life, they are only a hundred seeds worth virtually nothing. But if they are watered and are subject to the struggle for life, and then eighty out of the hundred rot due to their faulty make-up, but twenty become fruit-bearing trees, can you say, "watering them was evil because most of them rotted?" Of course, you cannot say that, for that twenty have become like twenty thousand. One who loses eighty and gains twenty thousand suffers no harm, and it cannot be evil.

And for example, a peahen lays one hundred eggs, and they are worth five hundred *kurush*.[63] If the hen sits on the hundred eggs and eighty are spoilt and twenty hatch into peacocks, can it be said that there was a high loss and the affair was evil; that it was bad to put the broody hen on the eggs and an evil occurred? No, it is not thus, it is rather a good. For the peacock species and egg family lost eighty eggs worth four hundred *kurush*, but gained twenty peacocks worth eighty *liras*.

Thus, through the sending of Prophets and the mystery of man's accountability, and through striving, and fighting with satans, in return for the hundreds of thousands of Prophets and millions of saints and thousands of millions of purified scholars they have gained, who are like the suns, moons, and stars of the world of humanity, mankind has lost the unbelievers and dissemblers, who are numerous in regard to quantity, in- significant in regard to quality, and like harmful beasts.

Question 3: Almighty God sends calamities and inflicts tribulations; is this not tyrannical towards the innocent in particular, and animals even?

Answer: God forbid, the sovereignty is His. He holds sway over His possessions as He wishes. Moreover, a skillful craftsman makes you a model in return for a wage and dresses you in a bejeweled garment

---

[63] Lira is Turkish unit of currency. 1 Lira equals 100 kurush as 1US Dollar equals 100 cents.

that he has most artistically fashioned. Then in order to display his art and skill, he shortens it and lengthens it, measures it and trims it, and he makes you sit down and stand up. Are you able to say to him: "You have made the garment which made me beautiful ugly. You have caused me trouble, making me sit down and stand up." Of course, you cannot say that. If you did say it, you would be crazy.

In just the same way, the All-Glorious Maker has clothed you in a most artistically wrought being bejeweled with faculties like the eye, the ear, and the tongue. In order to display the embroideries of various of His Names, He makes you ill, He afflicts you with tribulations, He makes you hungry, He fills you, He makes you thirsty; He makes you revolve in states like these. In order to strengthen the essence of life and display the manifestation of His Names, He makes you journey in numerous such conditions. If you say: "Why do you inflict these calamities on me?", as is indicated in the comparison, a hundred instances of wisdom will silence you. In any event, calm, repose, idleness, monotony, and arrest from action are forms of non-existence, and harm. Action and change are existence and good. Life finds its perfection through action, it progresses by means of tribulations. Life manifests various actions through the manifestation of the Divine Names, it is purified, finds strength, it unfolds and expands, it becomes a mobile pen to write its own appointed course; it performs its duty, and acquires the right to receive reward in the Hereafter.

Thus, the answers to the three questions in your dispute are briefly these. Explanations of them are to be found in *The Words*.

SEEKING REFUGE WITH GOD FROM SATAN

I seek refuge with God from Satan the accursed.
In the Name of God, the All-Merciful, the All-Compassionate.
And say: "My Lord! I seek refuge in You from the
promptings and provocations of the satans (of the jinn
and humankind, especially in my relations with people,
while I am performing my mission). "I seek refuge in
You, my Lord, lest they be present with me. "
(Al-Mu'minun 23:97–98)

Question 4: Although evil spirits do not interfere in the universe in any way in regard to creation, and through His mercy and favor Almighty God takes the part of the people of truth, and the attractive beauties and virtues of truth and reality strengthen and encourage the people of truth, and the repulsive ugliness of misguidance revolts the people of misguidance, what is the reason for Satan's party very often gaining the upper hand; what is the wisdom in it? And what is the reason for the people of truth always seeking refuge with God from Satan's evil?

Answer: The wisdom and purpose is this: for the most part, misguidance and evil are negative, destructive, and pertain to non-existence. While in the great majority of cases, guidance and good are positive, constructive, repairing, and pertain to existence. Everyone knows that one man can destroy in one day a building made by twenty men in twenty days. Yes, although human life continues through the existence of all the basic members and conditions of life, and is particular to the All-Glorious Creator's power, through severing a member, a tyrant may make the person manifest death, which is non-being in relation to life. The saying "Destruction is easy" has for this reason become proverbial.

It is because of this that the people of misguidance sometimes triumph over the people of truth who are most powerful with what is in reality a weak force. But the people of truth possess a stronghold so unassailable that when they take refuge in it, those fearsome enemies cannot draw close; they can do nothing. If they cause some temporary harm, according to the verse,

> Moses said to his people: "Seek help from God and be patient, persevering. The earth belongs indeed to God, and He makes it an inheritance for whom He wills of His servants. The (final, happy) outcome is in favor of the God-revering, pious." (Al-A'raf 7:128)

everlasting reward and profit make up for the damage. And that impregnable stronghold, that fortified citadel, is the Sharia of Muhammad, peace and blessings be upon him, and his Practices.

Question 5: The creation of devils, who are pure evil, and their harassing the people of belief, and many people not believing and going to Hell because of them, appears to be terrible and ugly. How does the mercy and beauty of the Absolutely Beauteous One, the Absolutely Compassionate One, the Truly Merciful One, permit this infinite ugliness and awesome calamity? Many people have asked about this question, and it occurs to many people.

Answer: In addition to the minor evils, there are numerous universal good purposes in the existence of Satan, and human attainments and perfections. Yes, however many degrees there are from a seed to a huge tree, the abilities lodged in human nature are more numerous. There are degrees from a minute particle to the sun. For these abilities and potentialities to develop, action is required, a transaction is necessary. The action of the mechanism of progress in such a transaction is brought about through striving. And striving occurs through the existence of evil spirits and harmful things. Otherwise man's station would have been constant like that of the angels. There would have been no classes in human kind, which resembles thousands of species. And it is contrary to wisdom and justice to abandon a thousand instances of good so as to avoid one minor evil.

For sure the majority of people embrace misguidance due to Satan, but importance and value look mostly to quality; they look to quantity little or not at all. If someone has a thousand and ten seeds which he buries, and under the earth the seeds undergo a chemical reaction as a result of which ten become trees and a thousand rot, the profit the man receives from the ten seeds which have become trees certainly reduces to nothing the loss he suffers from the thousand rotted ones. In exactly the same way, through the struggle against the soul and Satan, the profit, honor, enlightenment, and value for human kind gained by ten perfect men, who are like stars, certainly reduce to nothing the harm caused to mankind through the people of misguidance embracing unbelief, who are so base as to be thought of as vermin. Since this is so, divine mercy, wisdom, and justice have permitted the existence of Satan, and allowed him to molest men.

O people of belief! Your armor against this awesome enemy is the fear of God fashioned on the workbench of the Qur'an. And your shield is the Practices of the Noble Prophet (Upon whom be blessings and peace). And your weapon, seeking refuge with God from Satan, and seeking forgiveness, and taking refuge in Divine protection.[64]

---

[64] Nursi, *The Flashes* at 618.

CHAPTER 3

DIVINE DETERMINING (QADAR)

In the Name of God, the All-Merciful, the All-Compassion-ate. There is not a thing but the stores (for its life and sustenance) are with Us, and We do not send it down except in due, determined measure. (Al-Hijr 15:21)

Everything, We have written down and kept in a Manifest Record. (Ya-Sin 36:12)

Divine Determining[65] and the power of choice[66] are two important matters. We shall attempt to disclose a few of their mysteries in several 'Topics.'[67]

First topic:

Divine Determining and the power of choice are aspects of a belief pertaining to state and conscience which show the final limits of Islam and belief; they are not theoretical and do not pertain to knowledge. That is to say, a believer attributes everything to Almighty God, even his actions and self, till finally the power of choice confronts him, so he cannot evade his obligation and responsibility. It tells him: "You are responsible and under obligation." Then, so

---

65 Divine Determining (*Qadar*) is also known as fate or destiny.
66 The power of choice or faculty of will (*juz'i irada, juz'-i ikhtiyari*), also known as free will
67 I have omitted some of the topics due to their excessive complexity.

that he does not become proud at his good deeds and his achievements, Divine Determining confronts him, saying: "Know your limits; the one who does them is not you." Yes, Divine Determining and the power of choice are at the final degrees of belief and Islam; the former has been included among the matters of belief to save the soul from pride, and the latter, to make it admit to its responsibility. Obdurate evil-commanding souls clinging to Divine Determining in order to clear themselves of the responsibility of the evils they have committed, and their becoming proud and conceited on account of the virtues bestowed on them and their relying on the power of choice, are actions totally opposed to the mystery of Divine Determining and wisdom of the power of choice; they are not matters pertaining to knowledge which might give rise to such actions. For ordinary people who have not progressed spiritually there may be occasions when Divine Determining is used, and these are calamities and disasters when it is the remedy for despair and grief. But it should not be used to justify rebellion and in matters of the future so that it becomes a cause of dissipation and idleness. That is to say, Divine Determining has not been included among the matters of belief to relieve people from their obligations and responsibility, but to save them from pride and conceit. While the power of choice has been included in order to be the source of evils, not to be the source of virtues, so that people become like the Pharaoh.

Yes, as the Qur'an states, man is totally responsible for his evils, for it is he who wants the evils. Since evils are destructive, man may perpetrate much destruction with a single evil act, like burning down a house with one match, and he becomes deserving of an awesome punishment.

However, he does not have the right to take pride in good deeds; his part in them is extremely small. For what wants and requires the good deeds is Divine mercy, and what creates them is dominical power. Both request and reply, reason and cause, are from God. Man only comes to have them through supplication, belief, consciousness, and consent. As for evils, it is man's soul that wants them, either through capacity or through choice,— like in the white and beautiful light of the sun some substances become black and putrefy, and the blackness is related to their capacity—however, it is Almighty God Who creates the evils through a Divine law which comprises numerous benefits. That is to say, the cause and the request are from the soul, so that it is the soul which is responsible, while it is Almighty God Who creates the evils and brings them into existence, and since they have other results and fruits which are good, they are good.

It is for the above reason that the 'acquisition' (*kasb*) of evil, that is, the desire for evil, is evil, but the creation of evil is not evil. A lazy man who receives damage from rain, which comprises many instances of good, may not say that the rain is not mercy. Yes, together with a minor evil in its creation are numerous instances of good. To abandon that good for a minor evil becomes a greater evil. Therefore, a minor evil becomes like good. There is no evil or ugliness in Divine creation. They rather pertain to His servant's wish and to his capacity.

Furthermore, Divine Determining is both exempt from evil and ugliness with regard to results and fruits, and free from tyranny and ugliness with respect to reason and cause. Because Divine Determining looks to the true causes and acts justly. Men construct their judgments on causes which they see superficially and fall into error within the pure justice of

Divine Determining. For example, a judge finds you guilty of theft and sends you to prison. You are not a thief, but you have committed a murder which no one knows about. Thus, Divine Determining also sentenced you to imprisonment, but it sentenced you for the secret murder and acted fairly. Since the judge sentenced you for a theft of which you were in nocent, he acted unjustly. Thus, in a single thing the justice of Divine Determining and Divine creation and man's wrongful choice or acquisition were apparent in two respects; you can make analogies with this for other things. That is to say, with regard to origin and end, source and branch, cause and results, Divine Determining and creation are exempt from evil, ugliness, and tyranny.

Question: Man has no ability to create with his power of choice and has nothing apart from 'acquisition,' which is as though theoretical, so how is it that in the Qur'an he is shown to be rebellious and hostile towards the Creator of the heavens and the earth, Who complains greatly about him; the Creator mobilizes Himself and all His angels to assist His believing servants against the rebellious, affording them the greatest importance?

Answer: Because disbelief, rebellion, and evil are destruction and non-existence. However, vast destruction and innumerable instances of non-existence may result from a single theoretical matter and one instance of non-existence. Through the helmsman of a large ship abandoning his duty, the ship may sink and the labor of all those employed on it go for nothing; all those instances of destruction will result from a single instance of non-existence. Similarly, since disbelief and rebellion are non-existence and destruction, the power of choice may provoke them through a theoretical matter and cause awesome consequences. For although disbelief is only one evil, it insults the whole universe, accusing it of being worthless and futile, and denies all beings, which display proofs of Divine unity, and is contemptuous towards all the manifestations of the Divine Names. It is therefore pure wisdom that Almighty God utters severe complaints about the unbelievers, threatening them awesomely in the name of the universe and all beings and the Divine Names; it is pure justice that they should suffer eternal punishment. Since through unbelief and rebellion man takes the way of destruction, with a small act of service, he may perform a great many works. In the face of unbelief therefore, the believers are in need of Almighty God's boundless grace. For due to one troublesome child who is trying to burn down a house, ten strong men who have undertaken to protect and repair it may be obliged to beseech the child's parents, or even have recourse to the king. In the same way the believers are in need of many Divine favors in order to withstand the unmannerly people of rebellion.

In short, if the one speaking of Divine Determining and the power of choice has perfect belief and is aware of the Divine presence, he attributes the universe and himself to Almighty God, knowing them to be under His disposal. He has the right to speak of them. For since he knows himself and everything to be from Almighty God, he assumes the responsibility, basing it on his power of choice. He accepts that it is the source of evils and proclaims his Sustainer free of fault. He remains within the sphere of worship and undertakes the obligations with which he is charged by Almighty God. Moreover, he does not become proud at his good deeds and achievements; he rather looks to Divine Determining and offers thanks. He sees Divine Determining in the calamities that befall him, and endures them in patience.

However, if the one speaking of Divine Determining and the power of choice is one of the heedless and neglectful, then he has no right to speak of them. For, impelled by his misguidance, his evil-commanding soul attributes the universe to causes and divides up God's property among them. And he attributes the ownership of himself to himself. He ascribes his acts to himself and to causes. His responsibility and faults, he refers to Divine Determining. He will finally ascribe the power of choice to Almighty God, and he will consider Divine Determining last of all; thus discussion of them becomes meaningless. To discuss them is only a trick of the soul which is entirely contrary to the wisdom in them, in order to save such a person from responsibility.

...

Fourth Topic: Divine Determining is a sort of knowledge. Knowledge is dependent on the thing known. That is, it knows it as it is. The thing known is not dependent on knowledge. That is, the principles of knowledge are not fundamental so that the knowledge directs the thing known with regard to its external existence. Because the essence of the thing known and its external existence look to will and are based on power. Also, pre-eternity is not the tip of a chain reaching into the past which should be considered the end point in the existence of things and a source of compulsion. Rather, pre-eternity holds the past, the present, and the future all at once, looking at them from above like a mirror. In which case, it is not right to imagine an end to past time which stretches back within the sphere of contingency and call it pre-eternity, and to suppose that things enter that knowledge of pre-eternity in sequence, and that oneself is outside it; to reason thus is not right. Consider the following example in order to explain this mystery:

Suppose there is a mirror in your hand and the area to your right is the past and the area to your left, the future; the mirror only holds what is opposite it. Then with a movement it holds both sides, but it cannot hold all of it. However low the mirror is held, less will appear in it, and the higher it rises, the area it encompasses expands, until it can hold both sides in their entirety simultaneously. Whatever occurs in the areas reflected in the mirror in this position cannot be said to precede or follow one another, or to conform to or oppose one another. Divine Determining is part of pre-eternal knowledge, and in the words of the Hadith, pre-eternal knowledge is "at an elevated station which from its lofty view-point encompasses everything that has been and will be from pre-eternity to post-eternity." We and our reasoning cannot be outside of it so we can be like a mirror to the area of the past.

Question: Divine Determining has a connection with cause and effect. That is, this effect will occur through this cause. In which case, it may not be said that "Since so-and-so's death is determined at such-and-such a time, what fault has the man who fired the rifle through his own choice, for if he had not fired it, the other still would have died?" Why may it not be said?

Answer: Because Divine Determining specified that so-and-so's death would occur through the man's rifle. If you suppose that he did not fire the rifle, then you are supposing that Divine Determining had no connection with it, so with what would you decree his death? If you imagine cause and effect to be separate like the *Jabari-yya*,[68] or you deny Divine Determining like the *Mu'tazilites*, you leave the Sunni School and join the heretics. We people of truth say: "If he had not fired the rifle, we do not know if he would have died." The *Jabariyya* say: "If he had not fired it, he still would have died." While the *Mu'tazilites* say: "If he had not fired it, he would not have died."

...

Seventh Topic: For sure, man's faculty of will and power of choice are weak and a theoretical matter, but Almighty God, the Absolutely Wise One, made that weak and partial will a condition for the connection of His universal will. He in effect says: "My servant!

---

[68]   See Appendix 4: Schools of Thoughts (Madhhabs) in Islam.

Whichever way you wish to take with your will, I will take you there. In which case the responsibility is yours!" If the comparison is not mistaken, you take a powerless child onto your shoulders and leaving the choice to him, tell him you will take him wherever he wishes. The child wants to go to a high mountain so you take him there, but he either catches cold or falls. So of course you reprimand him, saying, "You wanted to go there," and you give him a slap. Thus, Almighty God, the Firmest of Judges, makes His servant's will, which is utterly weak, a condition, and His universal will follows it.

In short, O man! You have a will known as the power of choice which is extremely weak, but whose hand in evil acts and destruction is extremely long and in good deeds is extremely short. Give one of the hands of that will of yours to supplication, so that it may reach Paradise, a fruit of the chain of good deeds, and stretch to eternal happiness. And give its other hand to the seeking of forgiveness, so that it may be short for evil deeds and will not reach the oleander-tree of Hell, which is one fruit of that accursed tree. That is, just as supplication and reliance on God greatly strengthen the inclination to do good, so repentance and the seeking of forgiveness cut the inclination to do evil, putting an end to its transgressions.

A Question regarding Divine Determining:

In the First Topic you proved that everything about Divine Determining is good and beautiful. Even the evil that comes from it is good, and the ugliness, beautiful. But the disasters and tribulations in this world refute that statement.

Answer: O my soul and my friend who feel severe pain out of intense com- passion! The facts that all virtues and perfections return to existence and that the basis of all rebellion, calamities, and defects is non-existence are a proof that existence is pure good and non-existence, pure evil. Since non-existence is pure evil, circumstances that either result in non-existence or give an inkling of it, also comprise evil. Therefore, life, the most brilliant light of existence, proceeding through different circumstances, finds strength; it encounters varying situations and is purified; it takes on numerous qualities and produces the desired results, and enters many stages and displays comprehensively the impresses of the Bestower of Life's Names. It is due to this fact that certain things happen to living creatures in the form of grief, calamities, difficulties, and tribulations whereby the lights of existence are renewed in their lives, and the darkness of non-existence draws distant and their lives are purified. For arrest, repose, silence, idleness, rest, and monotony are all, both in quality and as conditions, non-existence. Even the greatest pleasure is reduced to nothing by monotony.

In short, since life displays the impresses of the Most Beautiful Names,

everything that happens to it is good. For example, an extremely rich and infinitely skillful person who is proficient in many crafts, for an hour and in return for a wage, clothes a miserable wretch in a bejeweled, artistically fashioned garment. This garment he made in order to make the miserable man act as a model and to display the works of his art and his extensive wealth. He works the garment on the man, gives it various forms, and alters it. In order to display every variety of his art, he cuts it, changes it, and lengthens and shortens it. Can the poor man receiving the wage be justified if he says to the person: "You are giving me trouble. You are making me bow down and stand up. By cutting and shortening this garment which makes me more beautiful, you are spoiling my beauty"? Does he have the right to tell him: "You are acting unkindly and unfairly"? Thus, like him, in order to display the impresses of His Most Beautiful Names, the All-Glorious Maker, the Peerless Creator, alters within numerous circumstances the garment of existence He clothes on living creatures, bejeweled with senses and subtle faculties like eyes, ears, the reason, and the heart. He changes it within very many situations. Among these are circumstances in the form of suffering and calamity which show the meanings of some of His Names, and the rays of mercy within flashes of wisdom, and the subtle instances of beauty within those rays of mercy.

CHAPTER 4

MATERIALISM OR GOD?

This treatise puts naturalistic atheism to death with no chance of reanimation, and totally shatters the foundation stones of unbelief.

A Reminder

This piece explains through nine impossibilities, themselves comprising at least ninety impossibilities, just how unreasonable, crude and superstitious is the way taken by those Naturalists who are atheists.[69] In order to cut short the discussion here and because these impossibilities have been explained in part in other sections of the *Risale-i Nur*, and some steps in the arguments have been skipped. It occurs to one, therefore, how is it that those famous and supposedly brilliant philosophers accepted such a blatantly obvio us superstition, and continue to pursue that way. Well, the fact is they could not see its reality. And I am ready to explain in detail and prove through clear and decisive arguments to whoever doubts it that these crude, repugnant and unreasonable impossibilities are the nec-

---

[69] Naturalism is the idea or belief that only natural laws and forces—as opposed to super- natural or spiritual—operate in the world. Naturalism is the idea or belief that nothing exists beyond the natural world. Naturalists assert that natural laws are the rules that govern the structure and behavior of the natural universe, that the changing universe at every stage is a product of these laws.

essary and unavoidable result of their way; in fact, the very gist of their creed.[70]

> *In the Name of God, the All-Merciful, the All-Compassionate. Their Messengers said: "Can there be any doubt about (the Existence, Oneness, and absolute Sovereignty of) God, the Originator of the heavens and the earth?*
> *(Ibrahim 14:10)*

By declaring through the use of a rhetorical question that there cannot and should not be any doubt about God Almighty, this verse clearly demonstrates the Divine existence and Unity.

A point to be mentioned before our discussion:

When I went to Ankara in 1922, the morale of the people of belief was extremely high as a result of the victory of the army of Islam over the Greeks. But I saw that an abominable current of atheism was treacherously trying to subvert, poison and destroy their minds. "O God!" I said, "this monster is going to harm the fundamentals of belief." At that point, since the above-mentioned verse makes self-evidently plain God's existence and unity, I sought assistance from it and wrote a treatise in Arabic consisting of a proof taken from the All-Wise Qur'an that was powerful enough to disperse and destroy that atheistic current. I had it printed in Ankara at the Yeni Gün Press. But, alas, those who knew Arabic were few and those who considered it seriously were rare. Also, its argument was in an extremely concise and abbreviated form. As a result, the treatise did not have the effect it should have done and sadly, that current of atheism both swelled and gained strength. Now, I feel compelled to explain a part of the proof in Turkish. Since certain parts of it have been fully explained in other sections of the *Risale-i Nur*, it will be written in summary form here. Those numerous proofs in part unite in this proof; so each may be seen as an element of this proof.

---

[70] What occasioned the writing of this treatise were the attacks being made on the Qur'an by those who called everything that their corrupted minds could not reach a superstition, who were using Nature to justify unbelief, and were vilifying the truths of belief in a most aggressive and ugly fashion. Those attacks stirred up in my heart an intense anger which resulted in those perverted atheists and falsifiers of the truth receiving vehement and harsh slaps. Otherwise, the way generally followed by the Risale-i Nur is a mild, polite and persuasive one.

Introduction

O people! You should be aware that there are certain phrases which are commonly used and imply unbelief. The believers also use them, but without realizing their implications. We shall explain three of the most important of them.

First phrase: Causes create this.

Second phrase: It forms itself; it comes into existence and later ceases to exist.

Third phrase: It is natural; nature necessitates and creates it.

Indeed, since beings exist and this cannot be denied, and since each being comes into existence in a wise and artistic fashion, and since each is not outside time but is being continuously renewed, then, O falsifier of the truth, you are bound to say either that the causes in the world create beings, for example, this animal; that is to say, it comes into existence through the coming together of causes, or that it forms itself, or that its coming into existence is a requirement and necessary effect of Nature, or that it is created through the power of One All-Powerful and All-Glorious. Since reason can find no way apart from these four, if the first three are definitely proved to be impossible, invalid and absurd, the way of Divine Unity, which is the fourth way, will necessarily and self-evidently and without doubt or suspicion, be proved true.

The first way: Causes create this

This imagines that the formation and existence of things and creatures occurs through the coming together of the causes in the universe. We shall mention only three of its numerous impossibilities.

First Impossibility

Imagine there is a pharmacy in which there are hundreds of jars and phials filled with quite different substances. A living potion and a living remedy are required from those medicaments. So we go to the pharmacy and see that they are to be found there in abundance, yet in great variety. We examine each of the potions and see that the ingredients have been taken in varying but precise amounts from each of the jars and phials, one ounce from this, three from that, seven from the next, and so on. If one ounce too much or too little had been taken, the potion would not have been living and would not have displayed its special quality. Next, we study the living remedy. Again, the ingredients have been taken from the jars in a particular measure so that if even the minutest amount too much or too little had been taken, the remedy would have lost its special property.

Now, although the jars number more than fifty, the ingredients have been taken from each according to measures and amounts that are all different. Is it in any way possible or probable that the phials and jars should have been knocked over by a strange coincidence or sudden gust of wind and that only the precise, though different, amounts that had been taken from each of them should have been spilt, and then arranged themselves and come together to form the remedy? Is there anything more superstitious, impossible and absurd than this? If a fool could speak, it would say: "I cannot accept this idea!" and would gallop off!

Similarly, each living being may be likened to the living potion in the comparison, and each plant to a living remedy. For they are composed of matter that has been taken in most precise measure from truly numerous and truly various substances. If these are attributed to causes and the elements and it is claimed, "Causes created these," it is unreasonable, impossible and absurd a hundred times over, just as it was to claim that the potion in the pharmacy came into existence through the phials being knocked over; by accident.

In short, the vital substances in this vast pharmacy of the universe, which are measured on the scales of Divine Determining and Decree of the All-Wise and Pre-Eternal One, can only come into existence through a boundless wisdom, infinite knowledge and all-encompassing will. The unfortunate person who declares that they are the work of blind, deaf and innumerable elements and causes and natures, which stream like floods; and the foolish, delirious person who claims that that wondrous remedy poured itself out when the phials were knocked over and formed itself, are certainly unreasonable and nonsensical. Indeed, such denial and unbelief is a senseless absurdity.

Second Impossibility

If everything is not attributed to the All-Powerful and All-Glorious God, but attributed to causes, it necessitates that many of the elements and causes present in the universe intervene in the being of every animate creature. Whereas that different and mutually opposing and conflicting causes should come together of their own accord in complete order, with the finest balance and in perfect concord in the being of a tiny creature, like a fly, is such an obvious impossibility that anyone with even an iota of consciousness would say: "This is impossible; it could not be!"

The tiny body of a fly is connected with most of the elements and causes in the universe; indeed, it is a summary of them. If it is not attributed to the Pre-Eternal and All-Powerful One, it is necessary for those material causes to be themselves present in the immediate vicinity of the fly; rather, for them all to enter into its tiny body; and even for them to enter each of the cells of its eyes, which are minute samples of its body. For if a cause is of a material nature, it is necessary for it to be present in the immediate vicinity of, and inside, its effect. And this necessitates accepting that the constituents and elements of the universe are physically present inside that minute cell, a place too small even for the tip of its antenna, and that they work there in harmony like a master.

A way such as this, then, shames even the most foolish of the Sophists.

Third Impossibility

It is an established rule that, "If a being has unity, it can only have issued from a single being, from one hand." Particularly if it displays a comprehensive life within a perfect order and sensitive balance, it demonstrates self-evidently that it did not issue from numerous hands, which are the cause of conflict and confusion, but that it issued from a single hand that is All-Powerful and All-Wise. Therefore, to attribute a well-ordered and well-balanced being which has unity such as that to the jumbled hands of innumerable, lifeless, ignorant, aggressive, unconscious, chaotic, blind and deaf natural causes, the blindness and deafness of which increase with their coming together and intermingling among the ways of numberless possibilities, is as unreasonable as accepting innumerable impossibilities all at once. If we leave this impossibility aside and assume that material causes have effects, these effects can only occur through direct contact and touch. However, the contact of natural causes is with the exteriors of living beings. And yet we see that the interiors of such beings, where the hands of material causes can neither reach nor touch, are ten times more delicate, well-ordered and perfect as regards art than their exteriors. Therefore, although tiny animate creatures, on which the hands and organs of material causes can in no way be situated, indeed they cannot touch the creatures' exteriors all at once even, are more strange and wonderful as regards their art and creation than the largest creatures, to attribute them to those lifeless, unknowing, crude, distant, vast, conflicting, deaf and blind causes can result only from a deafness and blindness compounded to the number of animate beings.

The second way: It forms itself

It too involves many impossibilities and is absurd and impossible in many aspects. We shall explain three examples of these impossibilities.

First Impossibility

O you stubborn denier! Your egotism has made you so stupid that somehow you decide to accept a hundred impossibilities all at once. For you yourself are a being and not some simple substance that is inanimate and unchanging. You are like an extremely well ordered machine that is constantly being renewed and a wonderful palace that is undergoing continuous change. Particles are working unceasingly in your body. Your body has a connection and mutual relations with the universe, in particular with regard to sustenance and the perpetuation of the species, and the particles that work within it are careful not to spoil that relationship or to break the connection. In this cautious manner they set about their work, as though taking the whole universe into account. Seeing your relationships within it, they take up their positions accordingly. And you benefit with your external and inner senses in accordance with the wonderful positions that they take.

If you do not accept that the particles in your body are tiny officials in motion in accordance with the law of the Pre-Eternal and All-Powerful One, or that they are an army, or the nibs of the pen of Divine Determining, with each particle as the nib of a pen, or that they are points inscribed by the pen of Power with each particle being a point, then in every particle working in your eye there would have to be an eye such as could see every limb and part of your body as well as the entire universe, with which you are connected. In addition to this, you would have to ascribe to each particle an intelligence equivalent to that of a hundred geniuses, sufficient to know and recognize all your past and your future, and your forbears and descendants, the origins of all the elements of your being, and the sources of all your sustenance.

To attribute the knowledge and consciousness of a thousand Plato's to a single particle of one such as you who does not possess even a particle's worth of intelligence in matters of this kind is a crazy superstition a thousand times over!

Second Impossibility

Your being resembles a thousand-domed wondrous palace in which the stones stand together in suspension and without support. Indeed, your being is a thousand times more wonderful than such a palace, for the palace of your being is being renewed continuously in perfect order.

Leaving aside your truly wonderful spirit, heart and other subtle faculties, each member of your body resembles a single-domed part of the palace. Like the stones of a dome, the particles stand together in perfect balance and order demonstrating the eye and the tongue, for example, each to be a wondrous building, extraordinary work of art, and miracle of power.

If these particles were not each officials dependent on the command of the master architect of the universe, then each particle would have to be both absolutely dominant over all the other particles in the body and absolutely subordinate to each of them; and both equal to each and, with regard to its dominant position, opposed; and both the origin and source of most of the attributes that pertain only to the Necessarily Existent One, and extremely restricted; and both in absolute form, and in the form of a perfectly ordered individual artifact that could only, through the mystery of unity, be the work of the Single One of Unity.

Anyone with even a particle of consciousness would understand what an obvious impossibility this is; to attribute such an artifact to those particles.

Third Impossibility

If your being is not 'written' by the pen of the Pre-Eternal and All-Powerful One, Who is the Single One of Unity, and is instead 'printed' by Nature and causes, there would have to be printing-blocks in Nature not only to the number of cells in your body, but to the number of their thousands of combinations, which are arranged in concentric circles. Because, for example, if this book which we hold in our hand is written, a single pen may write it relying on the knowledge of its writer. If, on the other hand, it is not written and is not attributed to its writer's pen, and if it is said that it exists of its own accord or it is ascribed to Nature, then, as a printed book, it would be necessary for there to be a different iron pen of each letter so that it could be printed. In a printing-press there have to be pieces of type to the number of letters in the alphabet so the letters in the book come into existence by means of them; pens to the number of those letters being necessary in place of a single pen.

As may be seen, sometimes a whole page is written in a single large letter from among those letters with a small pen in fine script, in which case a thousand pens would be necessary for one letter. Rather, if it took the form of your body, with all its components one within the other in concentric circles, there would have to be printing-blocks in each circle, for each component, to the number of the combinations that they form.

Now, see, if you claim this, which involves a hundred impossibilities, to be possible, then again if they are not attributed to a single pen, for those well-ordered, artistic pieces of type, faultless printing-blocks and iron pens to be made, further pens, printing-blocks and letters to the same number as themselves would be necessary. And they too would have to have been made; and they too would have to have been well-ordered and artistically fashioned. And so on. It would carry on in succession *ad infinitum*.

There, you too understand! This way of thinking is such that it involves impossibilities and superstitions to the number of particles in your body. O denier of God! See this, and quit the way of misguidance!

The third way: Nature necessitates it; nature makes it

This statement contains many impossibilities. We shall mention three of them by way of examples.

First Impossibility

If the art and creativity, which are discerning and wise, to be seen in beings and particularly in animate beings are not attributed to the pen of Divine Determining and Power of the Pre-Eternal Sun, and instead are attributed to Nature and force, which are blind, deaf and unthinking, it becomes necessary that Nature either should have present in everything machines and printing-presses for their creation, or should include in everything power and wisdom enough to create and administer the universe. The reason for this is as follows:

The sun's manifestations and reflections appear in all small fragments of glass and droplets on the face of the earth. If those miniature, reflected imaginary suns are not ascribed to the sun in the sky, it is necessary to accept the external existence of an actual sun in every tiny fragment of glass smaller than a match-head, which possesses the sun's qualities and which, though small in size, bears profound meaning; and therefore to accept actual suns to the number of pieces of glass.

In exactly the same way, if beings and animate creatures are not attributed directly to the manifestation of the Pre-Eternal Sun's Names, it becomes necessary to accept that in each being, and especially animate beings, there lies a nature, a force, or quite simply a god that will sustain an infinite power and will, and knowledge and wisdom. Such an idea is the most absurd and superstitious of all the impossibilities in the universe. It demonstrates that a man who attributes the art of the Creator of the universe to imaginary, insignificant, unconscious Nature is without a doubt less conscious of the truth than an animal.

Second Impossibility

If beings, which are most well-ordered and well-measured, wise and artistically fashioned, are not ascribed to One Who is infinitely powerful and wise and instead are attributed to Nature, it becomes necessary for there to be present in every bit of soil as many facto-ries and printing- presses as there are in Europe so that each bit of soil can be the means for the growth and formation of innumerable flowers and fruits, of which it is the place of origin and workshop. The seeds of flowers are sown in turn in a bowl of soil, which per-forms the duty of a flower-pot for them. An ability is apparent in the bowl of soil that will give shapes and forms which differ greatly from one another to all the flowers sown in it. If that ability is not attributed to the All-Glorious and All-Powerful One, such a situation could not occur without there being in the bowlful of soil immaterial, different and natural machines for each flower.

This is because the matter of which seeds, like sperm and eggs for ex- ample, consist is the same. That is, they consist of an order-less, formless, paste-like mixture of oxygen, hydrogen, carbon and nitrogen. Together with this, since air, water, heat and light also are each simple, unconscious and flow against everything in floods, the fact that the all-different forms of those flowers emerge from the soil in a most well-ordered and artistic fashion self-evidently and necessarily requires that there are present in the soil in the bowl im-material, miniature printing-presses and factories to the number of presses and factories in Europe so that they could weave this great number of living fabrics and thousands of various embroidered tex-tiles.

Thus, you can see how far the unbelieving thought of the Nat-uralists has deviated from the realm of reason. And although brain-less pretenders who imagine Nature to be creator claim to be "men of science and reason," see just how distant from reason and science is their thought, so that they have taken a superstition that is in no way possible, that is impossible, as a way for themselves. See this and laugh at them!

Question: If such extraordinary impossibilities and insurmountable difficulties occur when beings are attributed to Nature, how are those difficulties removed when they are attributed to the Single and Eternally Besought One? And how is the difficult impossibility transformed into that easy necessity?

Answer: We saw in the First Impossibility that the manifestation of the sun's reflection displays its radiance and effect through miniature imaginary suns with complete ease and lack of trouble in everything from the smallest inanimate particle to the surface of the vastest ocean. If each particle's relationship with the sun is severed, it then becomes necessary to accept that the external existence of an actual sun could subsist, with a difficulty at the level of impossibility, in each of those minute particles.

Similarly, if each being is ascribed directly to the Single and Eternally Besought One, everything necessary for each being can be conveyed to it through a connection and manifestation with an ease and facility that is at the level of necessity. If the connection is severed and each being reverts from its position as an official to being without duties, and is left to Nature and its own devices, it then becomes necessary to suppose that, with a hundred thousand difficulties and obstacles that reach the degree of impossibility, blind Nature possesses within it a power and wisdom with which to create and administer the universe so that it might bring into existence the wonderful machine of the being of an animate creature like a fly, which is a tiny index of the universe. This is impossible not just once but thousands of times over.

In short, just as it is impossible and precluded for the Necessarily Existent One to have any partner or like in respect of His Essence, so too is the interference of others in His Lordship and in His creation of beings impossible and precluded.

As for the difficulties involved in the Second Impossibility, as is proved in many parts of the *Risale-i Nur*, if all things are attributed to the Single One of Unity, all things become as easy and trouble-free as a single thing. Whereas if they are attributed to causes and Nature, a single thing becomes as difficult as all things. This has been demonstrated with numerous, decisive proofs and a summary of one of them is as follows.

If a man is connected to a king through being a soldier or an official, by reason of the strength of that connection, he may perform duties far exceeding his own individual strength. He may, on occasion, capture another king in the name of his own king. For he himself does not carry the equipment and sources of strength necessary to carry out the duties and work he performs, nor is he compelled to do so. By reason of the connection, the king's treasuries, and the army, which is behind him and is his point of support, carry his equipment and sources of strength. That is to say, the duties he performs may be as grand as the business of a king, and as tremendous as the actions of an army.

Indeed, through being an official, an ant destroyed Pharaoh's palace. Through the connection, a fly killed Nimrod off. And through the connection, the seed of a pine the size of a grain of wheat produces all the parts of a huge pine-tree.[71]

Were the connection to be severed and the man discharged from his duties as an official, he would be compelled to carry the equipment and sources of strength necessary for his work himself. He would then only be able to perform duties in accordance with the sources of strength and ammunition that he was able to carry. If he was to be required in this situation to carry out his duties with the extreme ease of the first situation, it would be necessary to load on his back the sources of an army's strength and the arsenals and

---

[71] Yes, on there being this connection, the seed receives an order from Divine Determining and displays those wonderful duties. Should the connection be severed, the creation of the seed would require more equipment, power and art than the creation of the mighty pine-tree. For it would be necessary for the pine-tree out there on the mountain, which is the work of Divine power, to be physically present together with all its limbs and parts in what is only the potential tree within the seed and is the work of Divine Determining. For the mighty tree's factory is the seed. The determined, potential tree within it becomes manifest in the external world through Divine power, and becomes a physical pine-tree.

munitions factories of a king. Even clowns who invent stories and superstitions to make people laugh would be ashamed at this fanciful idea.

In short, to attribute all beings to the Necessarily Existent One is so easy as to be necessary. While to attribute their creation to Nature is so difficult as to be impossible and outside the realm of reason.

Third Impossibility

The following two comparisons, which are included in other parts of the

Risale-i Nur, explain this impossibility.

A wild savage entered a palace which had been built in an empty desert, and completed and adorned with all the fruits of civilization. He cast an eye over its interior and saw thousands of well-ordered and artistically fashioned objects. Because of his boorishness and lack of intelligence, he said: "No one from outside had a hand in this, one of the objects from inside must have made this palace together with all of its contents," and started to investigate. However, whatever he looked at, even his untaught intelligence could not fathom out how it had made those things.

Later, he saw a notebook in which had been written the plan and program of the palace's construction, an index of its contents and the rules of its administration. For sure, the notebook too, which was without hand, eye, or implement, like the rest of the objects in the palace, was completely lacking the ability to construct and decorate the palace. But, since he saw that in comparison with all the other things, the notebook was related to the whole palace by reason of its including all its theoretical laws, he was obliged to say: "There, it is this notebook that has organized, ordered and adorned this palace, and has fashioned all these objects and set them in their places." He transformed his uncouthness into ludicrous jabber.

Thus, exactly like this comparison, a boor who subscribed to Naturalist thought, which denies God, entered the palace of the universe, which is infinitely more well-ordered, more perfect and everywhere full of miraculous instances of wisdom than the palace in the comparison. Not thinking that it was the work of art of the Necessarily Existent One, Who is outside the sphere of contingency, and shunning that idea, he saw a collection of the laws of Divine practice and an index of dominical art, which are like a slate for writing and erasing of Divine Determining in the sphere of contingency, and like a constantly changing notebook for the laws of the functioning of Divine power, and are extremely mistakenly and erroneously given the name 'Nature', and he said:

"These things require a cause and nothing else appears to have the relationship with everything like this notebook has. It is true that reason will in no way accept that this unseeing, unconscious and powerless notebook could carry out this creation, which is the work of an absolute lord- ship and requires infinite power. But since I do not recognize the Eternal Maker, the most plausible explanation is to say the notebook made it, and makes it, so I shall say that." To which we reply:

O you mistaken unfortunate! Your foolishness exceeds anything imaginable! Lift your head out of the swamp of Nature and look beyond yourself! See an All-Glorious Maker to Whom all beings from particles to planets testify with their different tongues and Whom they indicate with their fingers! Behold the manifestation of the Pre-Eternal Inscriber, Who fashions the palace and Who writes its program in the notebook! Study His decree, listen to the Qur'an! Be delivered from your delirious raving!

Second comparison: A rustic bumpkin entered the bounds of a splendid palace and saw there the uniform actions of an extremely orderly army carrying out its drill. He observed a battalion, a regiment and a division stand to attention, stand at ease and march, and open fire when commanded as though they were a single private. Since his rude, uncultured mind could not comprehend, so denied, that a commander had been given command by the country's laws and by royal decree, he imagined that the soldiers were attached to one another with strings. He thought of what wonderful string it must be, and was amazed.

Later, he continued on his way till he came upon a magnificent mosque like Hagia Sophia in Istanbul. He entered it at the time of

Friday prayer and watched the congregation of Muslims rising, bowing, prostrating and sitting at the sound of man's voice. Since he did not understand the Sharia, which consists of a collection of immaterial, revealed laws, nor the immaterial rules proceeding from the Lawgiver's command, he fancied the congregation to be bound to one another by physical string, and that this wonderful string had subjected them and was making them move like puppets. And, coming up with this idea, which is so ridiculous as to make the most ignorant roar with laughter, he went on his way.

Exactly like this comparison, an atheist who subscribed to materialist thought, which is denial and pure brutishness, entered the universe, which is a splendid barracks of the Monarch of Pre-Eternity and Post- Eternity for His innumerable forces, and a well-ordered mosque of that Pre-Eternal All-Worshipped One. He imagined the immaterial laws of the ordering of the universe, which proceed from the Pre-Eternal Monarch's wisdom, each to have material and physical existence; and supposed the theoretical laws of the sovereignty of lordship, and the rules and ordinances of the Greater *Sharia*, the *Sharia* of Creation, which are immaterial and exist only as knowledge, each to have external, material and physical existence. But to set up in place of Divine power those laws, which proceed from the Divine Attributes of knowledge and speech and only exist as knowledge, and to attribute creation to them; then to attach the name 'Nature' to them, and to deem force, which is merely a manifestation of dominical power, to be an independent almighty possessor of power, is a thousand times more low-fallen ignorance than the ignorance in the comparison.

In short, the imaginary and insubstantial thing that Naturalists call Nature, if it has an external reality, can at the very most be work of art; it cannot be the Artist. It is an embroidery, and cannot be the Embroiderer. It is a set of decrees; it cannot be the Issuer of the decrees. It is a body of the laws of creation, and cannot be the Lawgiver. It is but a created screen to the dignity of God, and cannot be the Creator. It is passive and created, and cannot be a Creative Maker. It is a law, not a power, and cannot possess power. It is the recipient, and cannot be the source.

Conclusion

Since beings exist, and as was stated at the beginning of this treatise, reason cannot think of a way to explain the existence of beings apart from the four mentioned, three of which were each decisively proved through three clear Impossibilities to be invalid and absurd, then necessarily and self-evidently the way of Divine Unity, which is the fourth way, is proved in a conclusive manner. The fourth way, in accordance with the Qur'anic verse quoted at the beginning:

Can there be any doubt about (the Existence, Oneness, and absolute Sovereignty of) God, the Originator of the heavens and the earth? (Ibrahim 14:10) demonstrates clearly so that there can be no doubt or hesitation the Divinity of the Necessarily Existent One, and that all things issue directly from the hand of His power, and that the heavens and the earth are under His sway.

O you unfortunate worshipper of causes and Nature! Since the nature of each thing, like all things, is created, for it is full of art and is being constantly renewed, and, like the effect, the apparent cause of each thing is also created; and since for each thing to exist there is need for much equipment and many tools; there must exist a Possessor of Absolute Power Who creates the nature and brings the cause into existence. And that Absolutely Powerful One is in no need of impotent intermediaries to share in His Lordship and creation. God forbid! He creates cause and effect together directly. In order to demonstrate His wisdom and the manifestation of His Names, by establishing an apparent causal relation- ship and connection through order and sequence, He makes causes and Nature a veil to the hand of His power so that the apparent faults, severities and defects in things should be ascribed to them, and in this way His dignity be preserved.

Is it easier for a watchmaker to make the cogwheels of a clock, and then arrange them and put them in order to form the clock? Or is it easier for him to make a wonderful machine in each of the cogwheels, and then leave the making of the clock to the lifeless hands of those machines? Is that not beyond the bounds of possibility? Come on, you judge with your unfair reason, and say!

And is it easier for a scribe to collect ink, pen and paper, and then using them proceed to write out a book himself? Or is it easier for him to create in the paper, pen and ink a writing-machine that requires more art and trouble than the book, and can be used only for that book, and then say to the unconscious machine: "Come on, you write it!", and himself not interfere? Is that not a hundred times more difficult than writing it himself?

Question: Yes, it is a hundred times more difficult to create a machine that writes a book rather than writing it out oneself. But is it not in a way easier, because the machine is the means for producing numerous copies of the same book?

Answer: Through His limitless power, the Pre-Eternal Inscriber continuously renews the infinite manifestations of His Names so as to display them in ever-differing ways. And through this constant renewal, He creates the identities and special features in things in such a manner that no missive of the Eternally Besought One or dominical book can be the same as any other book. In any case, each will have different features in order to express different meanings.

If you have eyes, look at the human face: you will see that from the time of Adam until today, indeed, until post-eternity, together with the conformity of their essential organs, each face has a distinguishing mark in relation to all the other faces; this is a definite fact. Therefore, each face may be thought of as a different book. Only, for the artwork to be set out, different writing-sets, arrangements, and compositions are required. And in order to both collect and situate the materials, and to include every- thing necessary for the existence of each, a completely different work- shop will be required.

Now, knowing it to be impossible, we thought of Nature as a printing press. But apart from the composition and printing, which concern the printing-press, that is, setting up the type in a specific order, the substances that form an animate being's body, the creation of which is a hundred times more difficult than that of the composition and ordering, must be created in specific proportions and particular order, brought from the furthest corners of the cosmos, and placed in the hands of the printing-press. But in order to do all these things, there is still need for the power and will of the Absolutely

Powerful One, Who creates the printing press. That is to say, this hypothesis of the printing press is a totally meaningless superstition.

Thus, like these comparisons of the clock and the book, the All-Glorious Maker, Who is powerful over all things, has created causes, and so too does He create the effects. Through His wisdom, He ties the effect to the cause. Through His will, He has determined a manifestation of the Greater *Sharia*, the *Sharia* of Creation, which consists of the Divine laws concerning the ordering of all motion in the universe, and determined the nature of beings, which is only to be a mirror to that manifestation in things, and to be a reflection of it. And through His power, He has created the face of that nature which has received external existence, and has created things on that nature, and has mixed them one with the other.

Is it easier to accept this fact, which is the conclusion of innumerable most rational proofs-in fact, is one not compelled to accept it?—or is it easier to get the physical beings that you call causes and Nature, which are lifeless, unconscious, created, fashioned and simple, to provide the numberless tools and equipment necessary for the existence of each thing and to carry out those matters, which are performed wisely and discerningly? Is that not utterly beyond the bounds of possibility? We leave it to you to decide, with your unreasonable mind!

The unbelieving Nature-worshipper replied: "Since you are asking me to be fair and reasonable, I have to confess that the mistaken way I have followed up to now is both a compounded impossibility, and extremely harmful and ugly. Anyone with even a grain of consciousness would understand from your analyses above that to attribute the act of creation to causes and Nature is precluded and impossible, and that to attribute all things directly to the Necessarily Existent One is imperative and necessary. I say: 'all praise be to god for belief,' and I believe in Him. Only, I do have one doubt:

"I believe that Almighty God is the Creator, but what harm does it do to the sovereignty of His Lordship if some minor causes have a hand in the creation of insignificant matters and thereby gain for themselves a little praise and acclaim? Does it diminish His sovereignty in some way?"

Answer: As we have conclusively proved in other parts of the *Risale-i Nur*, the mark of rulership is that it rejects interference. The most insignificant ruler or official will not tolerate the interference of his own son, even, within the sphere of his rule. The fact that, despite being Caliph, certain devout Sultans had their innocent sons murdered on the unfounded apprehension that the sons would interfere in their rule demonstrates how fundamental is this 'law of the rejection of interference' in rulership. And the 'law of prevention of participation,' which the independence intrinsic to rulership necessitates, has shown its strength in the history of mankind through extraordinary upheavals whenever there have been two governors in a town or two kings in a country.

Thus, if the sense of rulership and sovereignty, which is a mere shad-ow in human beings, who are impotent and in need of assistance, rejects interference to this degree, prevents the intervention of others, does not accept participation in its sovereignty, and seeks to preserve the independence of its position so jealously, then, if you can, compare this with an All-Glorious One Whose absolute sovereignty is at the degree of lordship, Whose absolute rulership at the degree of Divinity, absolute independence at the degree of Oneness, and absolute lack of need at the degree of absolute power, and understand what a necessary requirement and inevitable necessity of that rulership is this rejection of interference, prevention of participation, and repulsion of partners.

Concerning the second part of your doubt, you said: "If some of the worship of some insignificant beings is directed towards certain causes, what deficiency does this cause to the worship of all beings, from particles to planets, which is directed towards the Necessarily Existent One, the Absolute Object of All Worship?"

Answer: The All-Wise Creator of the universe made the universe like a tree with conscious beings as its most perfect fruit, and among conscious beings He made man its most comprehensive fruit. And man's most important fruit, indeed the result of his creation, the aim of his nature, and the fruit of his life are his thanks and worship. Would that Absolute Sovereign and Independent Ruler, that Single One of Unity, Who creates the universe in order to make

Himself known and loved, give away to others man, the fruit of the whole universe, and man's thanks and worship, his most elevated fruit? Totally contrary to His wisdom, would He make vain and futile the result of creation and fruit of the universe? God forbid! Would He be content to give away the worship of creatures to others in a way that would deny His wisdom and His Lordship? And although He demonstrates through His actions that He wishes to make Himself known and loved to an unlimited degree, would he cause His most perfect creatures to forget Him by handing over to causes their thanks and gratitude, love and worship, and cause them to deny the exalted purposes in the universe?

O friend who has given up the worship of Nature! Now it is for you to say! To which he replied:

"All praise be to God, these two doubts of mine have now been resolved. And your two proofs concerning Divine Unity which demonstrate that the only True Object of Worship is He, and that nothing other than He is worthy of worship are so brilliant and powerful that to deny them would require as much arrogance as to deny the sun and the day."

CHAPTER 5

LOGIC BEHIND WORSHIP AND SUPPLICATION

In the Name of God, the All-Merciful, the All-Compassion-
ate. God has bought from the believers their selves and
wealth because Paradise is for them. (At-Tawbah 9:111)

If you wish to understand how profitable a trade it is, and how honorable a rank, to sell one's person and property to God, to be His slave and His soldier, then listen to the following comparison.

Once a king entrusted each of two of his subjects with an estate, including all necessary workshops, machinery, horses, weapons and so forth. But since it was a tempestuous and war-ridden age, nothing enjoyed stability; it was destined either to disappear or to change. The king in his infinite mercy sent a most noble lieutenant to the two men and by means of a compassionate decree conveyed the following to them:

"Sell me the property you now hold in trust, so that I may keep it for you. Let it not be destroyed for no purpose. After the wars are over, I will return it to you in a better condition than before. I will regard the trust as your property and pay you a high price for it. As for the machinery and the tools in the workshop, they will be used in my name and at my workbench. But the price and the fee for their use shall be increased a thousand fold. You will receive all the profit that accrues. You are indigent and without resource, and unable to provide the cost of these great tasks. So let me assume the provision of all expenses and equipment, and give you all the income and the profit. You shall keep it until the time of demobilization. So see the five ways in which you shall profit! Now if you do not sell me the property, you can see that no one is able to preserve what he possesses, and you too will lose what you now hold. It will go for nothing, and you will lose the high price I offer. The delicate and precious tools and scales, the precious metals waiting to be used, will also lose all value.

You will have the trouble and concern of administering and preserving, but at the same time be punished for betraying your trust. So see the five ways in which you may lose! Moreover, if you sell the property to me, you become my soldier and act in my name. Instead of a common prisoner or irregular soldier, you will be the free lieutenant of an exalted monarch."

After they had listened to this gracious decree, the more intelligent of the two men said: "By all means, I am proud and happy to sell. I offer thanks a thousand fold." But the other was arrogant, selfish and dissipated; his soul had become as proud as the Pharaoh.[72] As if he was to stay eternally on that estate, he ignored the earthquakes and tumults of this world. He said: "No! Who is the king? I won't sell my property, nor spoil my enjoyment." After a short time, the first man reached so high a rank that everyone envied his state. He received the favor of the king, and lived happily in the king's own palace. The other by contrast fell into such a state that everyone pitied him, but also said he deserved it. For as a result of his error, his happiness and property departed, and he suffered punishment and torment. O soul full of caprices! Look at the face of truth through the telescope of this parable. As for the king, he is the Monarch of Pre-Eternity and Post-Eternity, your Sustainer and Creator. The estates, machinery, tools and scales are your possessions while in life's fold; your body, spirit and heart within those possessions, and your outward and inward senses such as the eye and the tongue, intelli-

---

[72] Pharaoh represents the cumulative evil of mankind. He is not simply the ruler of ancient Egypt.

gence and imagination. As for the most noble lieutenant, it is the Noble Messenger of God; and the most wise decree is the Wise Qur'an, which describes the trade we are discussing in this verse, *'Verily God has purchased from the believers their persons and property that Paradise might be theirs.' (At- Tawbah 9:111).* The surging field of battle is the tempestuous surface of the world, which ceaselessly changes, dissolves and reforms and causes every man to think: "Since everything will leave our hands, will perish and be lost, is there no way in which we can transform it into something eternal and preserve it?" While engaged in these thoughts, he suddenly hears the heavenly voice of the Qur'an saying: "Indeed there is, a beautiful and easy way which contains five profits within itself." What is that way? To sell the trust received back to its true owner. Such a sale yields profit fivefold.

First Profit: Transient property becomes everlasting. For this waning life, when given to the Eternal and Self-Subsistent Lord of Glory and spent for His sake, will be transmuted into eternity. It will yield eternal fruits. The moments of one's life will apparently vanish and rot like kernels and seeds. But then the flowers of blessedness and auspiciousness will open and bloom in the realm of eternity, and each will also present a luminous and reassuring aspect in the Intermediate Realm.

Second Profit: The high price of Paradise is given in exchange.

Third Profit: The value of each limb and each sense is increased a thousand fold. The intelligence is, for example, like a tool. If you do not sell it to God Almighty, but rather employ it for the sake of the soul, it will become an ill-omened, noxious and debilitating tool that will burden your weak person with all the sad sorrows of the past and the terrifying fears of the future; it will descend to the rank of an inauspicious and destructive tool. It is for this reason that a sinful man will frequently resort to drunkenness or frivolous pleasure in order to escape the vexations and injuries of his intelligence. But if you sell your intelligence to its True Owner and employ it on His behalf, then the intelligence will become like the key to a talisman, unlocking the infinite treasures of compassion and the vaults of wisdom that creation contains.

To take another example, the eye is one of the senses, a window through which the spirit looks out on this world. If you do not sell it to God Almighty, but rather employ it on behalf of the soul, by gazing upon a handful of transient, impermanent beauties and scenes, it will sink to the level of being a pander to lust and the concupiscent soul. But if you sell the eye to your All-Seeing Maker, and employ it on His behalf and within limits traced out by Him, then your eye will rise to the rank of a reader of the great book of being, a witness to the miracles of dominical art, a blessed bee sucking on the blossoms of mercy in the garden of this globe.

Yet another example is that of the tongue and the sense of taste. If you do not sell it to your Wise Creator, but employ it instead on behalf of the soul and for the sake of the stomach, it sinks and declines to the level of a gatekeeper at the stable of the stomach, a watchman at its factory. But if you sell it to the Generous Provider, the sense of taste contained in the tongue will rise to the rank of a skilled overseer of the treasuries of Divine compassion, a grateful inspector in the kitchens of God's eternal power.

So look well, O intelligence! See the difference between a tool of destruction and the key to all being! And look carefully, O eye! See the difference between an abominable pander and the learned overseer of the Divine library! And taste well, O tongue! See the difference between a stable doorkeeper or a factory watchman and the superintendent of the treasury of God's mercy!

Compare all other tools and limbs to these, and then you will understand that in truth the believer acquires a nature worthy of Paradise and the unbeliever a nature conforming to Hell. The reason for each of them attaining his respective value is that the believer, by virtue of his faith, uses the trust of his Creator on His behalf and within the limits traced out by Him, whereas the unbeliever betrays the trust and employs it for the sake of the instinctual soul.

Fourth Profit: Man is helpless and exposed to numerous misfortunes. He is indigent, and his needs are numerous. He is weak, and the burden of life is most heavy. If he does not rely on the Omnipotent One of Glory, place his trust in Him and confidently submit to Him, his conscience will always be troubled. Fruitless torments, pains and regrets will suffocate him and intoxicate him, or turn him into a beast.

Fifth Profit: Those who have experienced illumination and had unveiled to them the true nature of things, the elect who have witnessed the truth, are all agreed that the exalted reward for all the worship and glorification of God performed by your members and instruments will be given to you at the time of greatest need, in the form of the fruits of Paradise.

If you spurn this trade with its fivefold profit, in addition to being deprived of its profit, you will suffer fivefold loss.

First Loss: The property and offspring to which you are so attached, the soul and its caprice that you worship, the youth and life with which you are infatuated, all will vanish and be lost; your hands will be empty. But they will leave behind them sin and pain, fastened on your neck like a yoke.

Second Loss: You will suffer the penalty for betrayal of trust. For you will have wronged your own self by using the most precious tools on the most worthless objects.

Third Loss: By casting down all the precious faculties of man to a level much inferior to the animals, you will have insulted and transgressed against God's wisdom.

Fourth Loss: In your weakness and poverty, you will have placed the heavy burden of life on your weak shoulders, and will constantly groan and lament beneath the blows of transience and separation.

Fifth Loss: You will have clothed in an ugly form, fit to open the gates of Hell in front of you, the fair gifts of the Compassionate One such as the intelligence, the heart, the eye and the tongue, given to you to make preparation for the foundations of everlasting life and eternal happiness in the Hereafter.

Now is it so difficult to sell the trust? Is it so burdensome that many people shun the transaction? By no means! It is not in the least burdensome. For the limits of the permissible are broad, and are quite adequate for man's desire; there is no need to trespass on the forbidden. The duties imposed by God are light and few in numbers. To be the slave and soldier of God is an indescribably pleasurable honor. One's duty is simply to act and embark on all things in God's name, like a soldier; to take and to give on God's behalf; to move and be still in accordance with His permission and law. If one falls short, then one should seek His forgiveness, say:

"O Lord! Forgive our faults, and accept us as Your slaves. Make us sure holders of Your trust until the time comes when it is taken from us. Amen!" and make petition unto Him.

VIRTUES OF WORSHIP (ʿUBUDI-YYAH)

In the Name of God, the All-Merciful, the All-Compassionate.

Now O humankind! Worship your Lord. (Al-Baqarah 2:21)

If you want to understand what great profit and happiness lie in worship, and what great loss and ruin lie in vice and dissipation listen to and take heed of the following story which is in the form of a comparison:

One time, two soldiers received orders to proceed to a distant city. They set off and travelled together until the road forked. At the fork was a man who said to them, "The road on the right causes no loss at all, and nine out of ten of those who take it receive a high profit and experience great ease. While the road on the left provides no advantages, and nine out of ten of its travelers make a loss. But they are the same as regards distance. Only there is one difference: those who take the left-hand road, which has no rules and no one in authority, travel without baggage and arms. They feel an apparent lightness and deceptive ease. Whereas those travelling on the right-hand road, which is under military order, are compelled to carry a kit-bag full of nutritious rations four *okka*s or so in weight and a superb army rifle of about two *kıyyes*[73] which will overpower and rout every enemy..."

After the two soldiers had listened to what this instructive man had to say, the fortunate one took the road to the right. He loaded the weight of one *batman*[74] onto his back, but his heart and spirit were saved from thousands of *batmans* of fear and feeling obliged to others. As for the other, luckless, soldier, he left the army. He did not want to conform to the

order, and he went off to the left. He was released from bearing a load of one *batman*, but his heart was constricted by thousands of *batmans* of in- debtedness, and his spirit crushed by innumerable fears. He proceeded on his way both begging from everyone and trembling before every object and every event until he reached his destination. And there he was punished as a mutineer and a deserter.

As for the soldier who loved the order of the army, had guarded his kitbag and rifle, and taken the right-hand road, he had gone on his way being obliged to no one, fearing no one, and with an easy heart and con- science until he reached the city he was seeking. There he received a re- ward worthy of an honorable soldier who had carried out his duty faithfully.

O rebellious soul, know that one of those two travelers represents those who submit to the Divine Law, while the other represents the rebellious and those who follow their own desires. The road is the road of life, which comes from the Spirit World, passes through the grave, and carries on to the Hereafter. As for the kit bag and rifle, they are worship and fear of God. There is an apparent burden in worship, but there is an ease and lightness in its meaning that defies description. For in the Prescribed Prayers the worshipper declares, "I bear witness that there is no god but God." That is to say, he finds the door of a treasury of mercy in everything because he believes and says, "There is no Creator and Provider other than Him. Harm and benefit are in His hand. He is both All-Wise; He does

---

[73] 1 *okka approximately equals 2.8 lbs. or 1,300 grams. Kıyye, another name for okka. 1 batman equals to 8 okkas or 5-30 lbs.* Egypt.

[74] *Batman is an old unit of measurement. 1 batman equal 7.6 kilos.*

nothing in vain, and He is All-Compassionate; His bounty and mercy are abundant." And he knocks on the door with his supplication. Moreover, he sees that everything is subjugated to the command of his own Sustainer, so he takes refuge in Him. He places his trust in Him and relies on Him, and is fortified against every disaster; his belief gives him complete confidence.

Indeed, like with every true virtue, the source of courage is belief in God, and worship. And as with every iniquity, the source of cowardice is misguidance.

In fact, for a worshipper with a truly illuminated heart, it is possible that even if the globe of the earth became a bomb and exploded, it would not frighten him. He would watch it with pleasurable wonder as a marvel of the Eternally Besought One's power. But when a famous degenerate philosopher with a so-called enlightened mind but no heart saw a comet

VIRTUES OF WORSHIP (☐UBUDI-YYAH) 121

in the sky, he trembled on the ground, and exclaimed anxiously: "Isn't that comet going to hit the earth?" (On one occasion, America was quaking with fear at such a comet, and many people left their homes in the middle of the night.)

Yes, although man is in need of numberless things, his capital is as nothing, and although he is subject to endless calamities, his power too is as nothing. Simply, his capital and power extend only as far as his hand can reach. However, his hopes, desires, pains, and tribulations reach as far as the eye and the imagination can stretch. Anyone who is not totally blind can see and understand then what a great profit, happiness, and bounty for the human spirit, which is thus impotent and weak, and needy and wanting, are worship, affirmation of God's unity, and reliance on God and submission to Him.

It is obvious that a safe way is preferable to a harmful way, even if the possibility of its safety is only one in ten. But on the way of worship, which our matter here, there is a nine out of ten possibility of it leading to the treasury of eternal happiness, as well as its being safe. While it is established by the testimony—which is at the degree of consensus—of innumerable experts and witnesses that besides being without benefit, and the dissolute even confess to this, the way of vice and dissipation ends in eternal misery. According to the reports of those who have uncovered the mysteries of creation this is absolutely certain.

In short, like that of the Hereafter, happiness in this world too lies in worship and being a soldier for Almighty God. In which case, we should constantly say: "Praise be to God for obedience to him and success," and we should thank Him that we are Muslims...

VIRTUES OF PERFORMING FIVE DAILY PRAYERS (SALAH)

In the Name of God, the All-Merciful, the All-Compassionate.
The Prescribed Prayers are the pillars of religion.[75]

If you want to understand with the certainty that two plus two equals four just how valuable and important are the Prescribed Prayers, and with what little expense they are gained, and how crazy and harmful is the person who neglects them, pay attention to the following story which is in the form of a comparison:

One time, a mighty ruler gave each of two of his servants twenty-four gold pieces and sent them to settle on one of his rich, royal farms two months' distance away. "Use this money for your tickets," he commanded them, "and buy whatever is necessary for your house there with it. There is a station one day's distance from the farm. And there is both road-transport, and a railway, and boats, and airplanes. They can be benefited from according to your capital."

The two servants set off after receiving these instructions. One of them was fortunate so that he spent a small amount of money on the way to the station. And included in that expense was some

---

[75] The hadith reported in *Tirmidhi, Iman, 8; Ibn Majah, Fitan, 12; Musnad, v, 231; al-Hakim, Al-Mustadrak, ii, 76.*

business so profitable and pleasing to his master that his capital increased a thousand fold. As for the other servant, since he was luckless and a lay about, he spent twenty-three pieces of gold on the way to the station, wasting it on gam- bling and amusements. A single gold piece remained. His friend said to him: "Spend this last gold piece on a ticket so that you will not have to walk the long journey and starve. Moreover, our master is generous; perhaps he will take pity on you and forgive you your faults, and put you on an airplane as well. Then we shall reach where we are going to live in one day. Otherwise you will be compelled to walk alone and hungry across a desert which takes two months to cross." The most unintelligent person can understand how foolish, harmful, and senseless he would be if out of obstinacy he did not spend that single remaining gold piece on a ticket, which is like the key to a treasury, and instead spent it on vice for passing pleasure. Is that not so?

O you who do not perform the Prescribed Prayers! And O my own soul, which does not like to pray! The ruler in the comparison is our Sustainer, our Creator. Of the two travelling servants, one represents the devout who perform their Prayers with fervor, and the other, the heedless who neglect their Prayers. The twenty-four pieces of gold are life in every twenty-four-hour day. And the royal domain is Paradise. As for the station, that is the grave. The journey is man's passage to the grave, and on to the resurrection, and the Hereafter. Men cover that long journey to different degrees according to their actions and the strength of their fear of God. Some of the truly devout have crossed a thousand-year distance in a day like lightning. And some have traversed a fifty-thousand-year distance in a day with the speed of imagination. The Qur'an of Mighty Stature alludes to this truth with two of its verses. In Surat Al-Haj (22:47) the Qur'an says: 'And they urge you to hasten the punishment. But Allah will never fail in His promise. And indeed, a day with your Lord is like a thousand years of those which you count. And Surat Al-Ma'arij (70:4) reads, 'The angels and the Spirit will ascend to Him during a Day the extent of which is fifty thousand years.'

The ticket in the comparison represents the Prescribed Prayers. A single hour a day is sufficient for the five Prayers together with taking the ablutions. So what a loss a person makes who spends twenty-three hours on this fleeting worldly life, and fails to spend one hour on the long life of the Hereafter; how he wrongs his own self; how unreasonably he be- haves. For would not anyone who considers himself to be reasonable understand how contrary to reason and wisdom such a person's conduct is, and how far from reason he has become, if, thinking it reasonable, he gives half of his property to a lottery in which one thousand people are participating and the possibility of winning is one in a thousand, and does not give one twenty-fourth of it to an eternal treasury where the possibility of winning has been verified at ninety-nine out of a hundred?

Moreover, the spirit, the heart, and the mind find great ease in prayer. And it is not tiring for the body. Furthermore, with the right intention, all the other acts of someone who performs the Prescribed Prayers become like worship. He can make over the whole capital of his life to the Hereafter in this way. He can make his transient life permanent in one respect.

CHAPTER 6

RESURRECTION AND THE HERE-AFTER

The reasons for my writing these treatises in the form of metaphors, comparisons and stories are to facilitate comprehension and to show how rational, appropriate, well founded and coherent are the truths of Islam. The meaning of the stories is contained in the truths that conclude them; each story is like an allusion pointing to its concluding truth. Therefore, they are not mere fictitious tales, but veritable truths.

In the Name of God, the Compassionate, the Merciful.

Look, then, at the imprints of God's Mercy how He revives the dead earth after its death: certainly then it is He Who will revive the dead (in a similar way). He has full power over everything. (Ar- Rum 30:50)

Brother, if you wish for a discussion of resurrection and the Hereafter in simple and common language, in a straightforward style, then listen to the following comparison, together with my own soul.

Once two men were travelling through a land as beautiful as Paradise (by that land, we intend the world). Looking around them, they saw that everyone had left open the door of his home and his shop and was not paying attention to guarding it. Money and property were readily accessible, without anyone to claim them. One of the two travelers grasped hold of all that he fancied, stealing it and usurping it. Following his inclinations, he committed every kind of injustice and abomination. None of the people of that land moved to stop him. But his friend said to him:

"What are you doing? You will be punished, and I will be dragged into misfortune along with you. All this property belongs to the state. The people of this land, including even the children, are all soldiers or government servants. It is because they are at present civilians that they are not interfering with you. But the laws here are strict. The king has installed telephones everywhere and his agents are everywhere. Go quickly, and try to settle the matter."

But the empty-headed man said in his obstinacy: "No, it is not state property; it belongs instead to some endowment, and has no clear or obvious owner. Everyone can make use of it as he sees fit. I see no reason to deny myself the use of these fine things. I will not believe they belong to anyone unless I see him with my own eyes." He continued to speak in this way, with much philosophical sophistry, and an earnest discussion took place between them.

First the empty-headed man said: "Who is the king here? I can't see him," and then his friend replied:

"Every village must have its headman; every needle must have its manufacturer and craftsman. And, as you know, every letter must be written by someone. How, then, can it be that so extremely well ordered a kingdom should have no ruler? And how can so much wealth have no owner, when every hour a train[76] arrives filled with precious and artful gifts, as if coming from the realm of the unseen? And all the announcements and proclamations, all the seals and stamps, found on all those goods, all the coins and the flags waving in every corner of the kingdom— can they be without an owner? It seems you have studied foreign languages a little, and are unable

---

[76]   Indicates the cycle of a year. Indeed, every spring is a carload of provisions coming from the realm of the unseen.

to read this Islamic script. In addition, you refuse to ask those who are able to read it. Come now, let me read to you the king's supreme decree."

The empty-headed man then retorted: "Well, let us suppose there is a king; what harm can he suffer from the minute use I am making of all his wealth? Will his treasury decrease on account of it? In any event, I can see nothing here resembling prison or punishment."

His friend replied: "This land that you see is a maneuvering ground. It is, in addition, an exhibition of his wonderful royal arts. Then again it may be regarded as a temporary hospice, one devoid of foundations. Do you not see that every day one caravan arrives as another departs and vanishes? It is being constantly emptied and filled. Soon the whole land will be changed; its inhabitants will depart for another and more lasting realm. There everyone will be either rewarded or punished in accordance with his services."

That treacherous empty-headed one retorted rebelliously: "I don't believe it. Is it at all possible that a whole land should perish, and be transferred to another realm?"

His faithful friend then replied: "Since you are so obstinate and rebellious, come, let me demonstrate to you, with twelve out of the innumerable proofs available, that there is a Supreme Tribunal, a realm of reward and generosity and a realm of punishment and incarceration, and that just as this world is partially emptied every day, so too a day shall come when it will be totally emptied and destroyed.[77]

---

[77] Rumi tells the story of an Embryo in the Womb in his *Mathnawi*. What if someone said to an embryo in the womb, "Outside of your world of black nothing is a miraculously ordered universe; a vast Earth covered with tasty food; mountains, oceans and plains, fragrant orchards and fields full of crops; a luminous sky beyond your reach, with a sun, moonbeams, and uncountable stars; and there are winds from south, north and west, and gardens replete with sweet flowers like a banquet at a wedding feast.

The wonders of this world are beyond description. What are you doing living in a dark prison, Drinking blood through that narrow tube?" But the womb-world is all an embryo knows. And it would not be particularly impressed. By such amazing tales, saying dismissively: "You're crazy. That is all a deluded fantasy."

First Aspect: Is it at all possible that in any kingdom, and particularly so splendid a kingdom as this, there should be no reward for those who serve obediently and no punishment for those who rebel? Reward and punishment are virtually non-existent here; there must therefore be a Supreme Tribunal somewhere else.

Second Aspect: Look at the organization and administration of this kingdom! See how everyone, including the poorest and the weakest, is provided with perfect and ornate sustenance. The best care is taken of the sick. Royal and delicious foods, dishes, jewel encrusted decorations, embroidered garments, splendid feasts—all are to be found here. See how every- one pays due attention to his duties, with the exception of empty-headed people such as yourself. No one transgresses his bounds by as much as an inch. The greatest of all men is engaged in modest and obedient service, with an attitude of fear and awe. The ruler of this kingdom must possess, then, great generosity and all-embracing compassion, as well as, at the same time, great dignity, exalted awesomeness and honor. Now generosity requires liberality; compassion cannot dispense with beneficence; and awesomeness and honor make it imperative that the discourteous be chastised. But not even a thousandth part of what that generosity and awesomeness require is to be seen in this realm. The oppressor retains his power, and the oppressed, his humiliation, as they both depart and migrate from this realm. Their affairs are, then, left to the same Supreme Tribunal of which we speak.

Third Aspect: See with what lofty wisdom and ordering affairs are managed, and with what true justice and balance transactions are effected! Now a wise polity requires that those who seek refuge under the protecting wing of the state should receive favor, and justice demands that the rights of subjects be preserved, so that the splendor of the state should not suffer. But here in this land, not a thousandth part of the requirements of such wisdom and justice is fulfilled; for example, empty-headed people such as yourself usual-

---

One day you will look back and laugh at yourself. You'll say, "I can't believe I was so asleep! How did I ever forget the truth? How ridiculous to believe that sadness and sick- ness. Are anything other than bad dreams."

ly leave this realm unpunished. So again we say, matters are postponed for the consideration of a Supreme Tribunal.

Fourth Aspect: Look at these innumerable and peerless jewels that are displayed here, these unparalleled dishes laid out like a banquet! They demonstrate that the ruler of these lands is possessed of infinite generosity and an inexhaustible treasury. Now such generosity and such a treasury deserve and require a bounteous display that should be eternal and include all possible objects of desire. They further require that all who come as guests to partake of that display should be there eternally and not suffer the pain of death and separation. For just as the cessation of pain is pleasurable, so too is the cessation of pleasure painful! Look at these displays and the announcements concerning them! And listen to these heralds proclaiming the fine and delicate arts of a miracle-working monarch, and demonstrating his perfections! They are declaring his peerless and invisible beauty, and speaking of the subtle manifestations of his hidden beauteousness; he must be possessed, then, of a great and astounding invisible beauty and perfection. This flawless hidden perfection requires one who will appreciate and admire it, who will gaze on it ex- claiming, *Ma'sha Allah!*, thus displaying it and making it known.

As for concealed and peerless beauty, it too requires to see and be seen, or rather to behold itself in two ways. The first consists of contemplating itself in different mirrors, and the second of contemplating itself by means of the contemplation of enraptured spectators and astounded admirers. Hidden beauty wishes, then, to see and be seen, to contemplate itself eternally and be contemplated without cease. It desires also permanent existence for those who gaze upon it in awe and rapture. For eternal beauty can never be content with a transient admirer; moreover, an admirer destined to perish without hope of return will find his love turning to enmity whenever he imagines his death, and his admiration and respect will yield to contempt. It is in man's nature to hate the unknown and the unaccustomed. Now everyone leaves the hospice of this realm very quickly and vanishes, having seen only a light or a shadow of the perfection and beauty for no more than a moment, without in any way being satiated. Hence, it is necessary that he should go towards an eternal realm where he will contemplate the Divine beauty and perfection.

Fifth Aspect: See, it is evident from all these matters that that peerless Being is possessed of most great mercy. For he causes aid to be swiftly ex- tended to every victim of misfortune, answers every question and petition; and mercifully fulfills even the lowliest need of his lowliest subject. If, for example, the foot of some herdsman's sheep should hurt, he either provides some medicine or sends a veterinarian.

Come now, let us go; there is a great meeting on that island. All the nobles of the land are assembled there. See, a most noble commander, bearing exalted decorations, is pronouncing a discourse, and requesting certain things from that compassionate monarch. All those present say: "Yes, we too desire the same," and affirm and assent to his words. Now listen to the words of that commander favored by his monarch:

"O monarch that nurtures us with his bounty! Show us the source and origin of these examples and shadows you have shown us! Draw us nigh to your seat of rule; do not let us perish in these deserts! Take us into your presence and have mercy on us! Feed us there on the delicious bounty you have caused us to taste here! Do not torment us with desperation and banishment! Do not leave your yearning, thankful and obedient subjects to their own devices; do not cause them to be annihilated!" Do you not hear him thus supplicating? Is it at all possible that so merciful and powerful a monarch should not totally fulfill the finest and highest aim of his most beloved and noble commander?

Moreover, the purpose of that commander is the purpose of all men, and its fulfillment is required by the pleasure, the compassion and the justice of the king, and it is a matter of ease for him, not difficulty, causing him less difficulty than the transient places of enjoyment contained in the hospice of the world. Having spent so much effort on these places of witnessing that will last only five or six days, and on the foundation of this kingdom, in order to demonstrate instances of his power, he will, without doubt, display at his seat of rule true treasures, perfections and skills in such a manner, and open before us such spectacles, that our intellects will be astonished.

Those sent to this field of trial will not, then, be left to their own devices; palaces of bliss or dungeons await them.

Sixth Aspect: Come now, look! All these imposing trains, planes, machines, warehouses, and exhibitions show that a majestic king exists and governs behind a veil.[78] Such a sovereign requires subjects worthy of himself. But his subjects are gathered in a guesthouse that is filled and emptied daily. Moreover, his subjects now are gathered on a testing ground for maneuvers, a ground that is changed hourly. Again, his subjects stay in an exhibition hall for a few minutes to behold examples of his beneficence, priceless products of his miraculous art. But the exhibition alters each moment. Whatever leaves does not return, and whatever comes is destined to go. All of this proves that there are permanent palaces and lasting abodes, as well as gardens and treasuries full of the pure and exalt-

---

[78] When an army is told to "take up your weapons and fix your bayonets," according to the rules of war while on maneuver, it resembles a forest of oaks. When a garrison's soldiers are commanded on a festive day to wear their parade uniforms and medals, the army resembles an ornate garden full of flowers of every color. This is how it is with all of Earth's species of unfeeling plants and trees that, like jinn, humanity, and animals, are only one of the infinitely various armies of the Eternal King, when they receive the order Be! And it is in the struggle for life's maintenance, and the command "Take up your weapons and equipment to defend yourselves and maintain your lives!" At that time, all those plants and trees fix their bayonets, in the form of trees and plants with thorns, and resemble a splendid army standing on the parade or battleground.

Each spring day and week is like a festive day for each vegetable species. Each species presents itself to the Eternal King's watching and witnessing gaze, with the jeweled decorations He has bestowed on them, as if on parade to display the precious gifts He has given them. It is as if they were obeying His command to "wear the garments produced by Divine artistry and put on the decorations (flowers and fruit) made by His Creativity." At such a time, the face of Earth represents a garrison on a magnificent parade on a splendid festive day that is brilliant with the soldiers' uniforms and jeweled decorations. Such a purposeful and well-arranged equipment and decoration demonstrates, to all who are not blind, that they occur only due to the command of a king with infinite power and unlimited wisdom.

ed originals of the samples, beyond what we see here. This is why we exert ourselves here. We work here, and he rewards us there with a form and degree of happiness suited to our capacity.

Seventh Aspect: Come, let us walk a little, and see what is to be found among these civilized people. See, in every place, at every corner, photographers are sitting and taking pictures. Look, everywhere there are scribes sitting and writing things down. Everything is being recorded. They are registering the least significant of deeds, the most commonplace of events. Now look up at the tall mountain; there you see a supreme photographer installed, devoted to the service of the king;[79] he is taking pictures of all that happens in the area. The king must, then, have issued this order; "Record all the transactions made and deeds performed in the kingdom." In other words, that exalted personage is having all events registered and photographically recorded. The precise record he is keeping must without doubt be for the sake of one day calling his subjects to ac- count.

Now is it at all possible that an All-Wise and All-Preserving Being, who does not neglect the most banal doings of the lowest of his subjects, should not record the most significant deeds of the greatest among his subjects, should not call them to account, should not reward and punish them? After all, it is those foremost among his subjects that perform deeds offensive to his glory, contrary to his pride and unacceptable to his compassion, and those deeds remain unpunished in this world. It must be, therefore, that their judgment is postponed to a Supreme Court.

---

[79] Let us point out here that the figure of the "supreme photographer devoted to the service of the king" is an indication of the Preserved Tablet. The reality and existence of the Preserved Tablet has been proved in the Twenty-Sixth Word as follows: a little portfolio suggests the existence of a great ledger; a little document points to the existence of a great register; and little drops point to the existence of a great water tank. So too the retentive faculties of men, the fruits of trees, the seeds and kernels of fruit, being each like a little portfolio, a Preserved Tablet in miniature or a drop proceeding from the pen that inscribes the great Preserved Tablet—they point to, indicate and prove the existence of a Supreme Retentive Faculty, a great register, an exalted Preserved Tablet. Indeed, they demonstrate this visibly to the perceptive intellect.

Eighth Aspect: Come, let me read to you the decrees issued by that mon- arch. See, he repeatedly makes the following promises and dire threats: "I will take you from your present abode and bring you to the seat of my rule. There I shall bestow happiness on the obedient and imprison the disobedient. Destroying that temporary abode, I shall found a different realm containing eternal palaces and dungeons."

He can easily fulfill the promises that he makes, of such importance for his subjects. It is, moreover, incompatible with his pride and his power that he should break his promise. So look, o confused one! You assent to the claims of your mendacious imagination, your distraught intellect, your deceptive soul, but deny the words of a being who cannot be compelled in any fashion to break his promise, whose high stature does not admit any such faithlessness, and to whose truthfulness all visible deeds bear witness. Certainly you deserve a great punishment. You resemble a traveler who closes his eyes to the light of the sun and looks instead upon his own imagination. His fancy wishes to illuminate his awesomely dark path with the light of his brain, although it is no more than a glowworm. Once that monarch makes a promise, he will by all means fulfill it. Its fulfillment is most easy for him, and moreover most necessary for us and all things, as well as for him too and his kingdom.

There is therefore, a Supreme Court, and a lofty happiness.

Ninth Aspect: Come now! Look at the heads of these offices and groups.[80] Each has a private telephone to speak personally with the king. Sometimes too they go directly to his presence. See what they say and unanimously report, that the monarch has prepared a most magnificent and awesome place for reward and punishment. His promises are emphatic and his threats are most stern. His pride and dignity are such that he would in no way stoop to the abjectness inherent in the breaking of a promise. The bearers of this

---

[80] For example, by heads of offices we mean the Prophets and the Saints. As for the tele- phone, it is a link and relation with God that goes forth from the heart and is the mirror of revelation and the receptacle of inspiration. The heart is like the earpiece of that telephone.

report, who are so numerous as to be universally accepted, further report with the strong unanimity of consensus that "the seat and headquarters of the lofty monarchy, some of whose traces are visible here, is in another realm far distant from here. The buildings existing in this testing-ground are but temporary, and will later be exchanged for eternal palaces. These places will change. For this magnificent and unfading monarchy, the splendor of which is apparent from its works, can in no way be founded or based on so transient, impermanent, unstable, insignificant, changing, defective and imperfect matters. It is based rather on matters worthy of it, eternal, stable, permanent and glorious." There is, then, another realm, and of a certainty we shall go toward it.

Tenth Aspect: Come, today is the vernal equinox.[81] Certain changes will take place, and wondrous things will occur. On this fine spring day, let us go for a walk on the green plain adorned with beautiful flowers. See, other people are also coming toward it. There must be some magic at work, for buildings that were mere ruins have suddenly sprung up again here, and this once empty plain has become like a populous city. See, every hour it shows a different scene, just like a cinema screen, and takes on a different shape. But notice, too, that among these complex, swiftly changing and multifarious scenes perfect order exists, so that all things are put in their proper places. The imaginary scenes presented to us on the cinema screen cannot be as well-ordered as this, and millions of skilled magicians would be incapable of this artistry. This monarch whom we cannot see must, then, have performed even greater miracles.

O foolish one! You ask: "How can this vast kingdom be destroyed and reestablished somewhere else?"

---

[81]   The vernal equinox is equivalent to the beginning of spring. As for the green plain covered with flowers, this is the face of the earth in springtime. The changing scenes and spectacles are an allusion to the different groups of vernal beings, the classes of summer creation, and the sustenance for men and animals, that the All-Powerful and Glorious Maker, the All-Wise and Beauteous Creator, from the beginning of spring to the end of summer, brings forth in orderly succession, renews with the utmost compassion, and dispatches uninterruptedly.

You see that every hour numerous changes and revolutions occur, just like that transfer from one realm to another that your mind will not accept. From this gathering in and scattering forth it can be deduced that a certain purpose is concealed within these visible and swift joining and separations, these compounding and dissolving. Ten years of effort would not be devoted to a joining together destined to last no longer than an hour. So these circumstances we witness cannot be ends in themselves; they are a kind of parable of something beyond themselves, an imitation of it. That exalted being brings them about in miraculous fashion, so that they take shape and then merge, and the result is preserved and recorded, in just the same way that every aspect of a maneuver on the battleground is written down and recorded. This implies that proceedings at some great concourse and meeting will be based on what happens here. Further, the results of all that occurs here will be permanently displayed at some supreme exposition. All the transient and fluctuating phenomena we see here will yield the fruit of eternal and immutable form.

All the variations we observe in this world are then, for the sake of a supreme happiness, a lofty tribunal, for the sake of exalted aims as yet un known to us.

Eleventh Aspect: Come, o obstinate friend! Let us embark on a plane or a train travelling east or west, that is, to the past or the future. Let us see what miraculous works that being has accomplished in other places. Look, there are marvels on every hand like the dwellings, open spaces and exhibitions we see. But they all differ with respect to art and to form. Note well, however, what order betokening manifest wisdom, what indications if evident compassion, what signs of lofty justice, and what fruits of comprehensive mercy, are to be seen in these transient dwellings, these impermanent open spaces, these fleeting exhibitions. Anyone not totally devoid of insight will understand a certainty that no wisdom can be imagined more perfect than his, no providence more beauteous than his, no compassion more comprehensive than his, and no justice more glorious than his.

If, for the sake of argument, as you imagine, no permanent abodes, lofty places, fixed stations, lasting residences, or resident and contented population existed in the sphere of his kingdom; and if the truths of his wisdom, compassion, mercy and justice had no realm in which to manifest themselves fully (for this impermanent kingdom is no place for their full manifestation)—then we would be obliged to deny the wisdom we see, to deny the compassion we observe, to deny the mercy that is in front of our eyes, and to deny the justice the signs of which are evident. This would be as idiotic as denying the sun, the light of which we clearly see at midday. We would also have to regard the one from whom proceed all these wise measures we see, all these generous acts, all these merciful gifts, as a vile gambler or treacherous tyrant (God forbid!). This would be to turn truth on its head. And turning a truth into its opposite is impossible, according to the unanimous testimony of all rational beings, excepting only the idiot sophists who deny everything.

There is, then, a realm apart from the present one. In it, there is a supreme tribunal, a lofty place of justice, an exalted place of reward, where all this compassion, wisdom, mercy and justice will be made fully manifest.

Twelfth Aspect: Come, let us return now. We will speak with the chiefs and officers of these various groups, and looking at their equipment will inquire whether that equipment has been given them only for the sake of subsisting for a brief period in that realm, or whether it has been given for the sake of obtaining a long life of bliss in another realm. Let us see. We cannot look at everyone and his equipment. But by way of example, let us look at the identity card and register of this officer. On his card, his rank, salary, duty, supplies and instructions are recorded. See, this rank has not been awarded him for just a few days; it may be given for a pro- longed period. It says on his card: "You will receive so much salary on such-and-such a day from the treasury." But the date in question will not arrive for a long time to come, after this realm has been vacated. Similarly, the duty mentioned on his card has not been given for this temporary realm, but rather for the sake of earning a permanent felicity in the proximity of the king. Then, too, the supplies awarded him cannot be merely for the sake of subsisting in this hospice of a few days' duration; they can only be for the sake of a long and happy life. The instructions make it quite clear that he is destined for a different place, that he is working for another realm.

Now look at these registers. They contain instructions for the use and disposition of weapons and equipment. If there were no realm other than this, one exalted and eternal, that register with its categorical instructions and that identity card with its clear information, would both be quite meaningless. Further, that respected officer, that noble commander, that honored chief, would fall to a degree lower than that of all men; he would be more wretched, luckless, abased, afflicted, indigent and weak than everyone. Apply the same principle to everything. Whatever you look upon bears witness that after this transient world another and eternal world exists.

O friend! This temporary world is like a field. It is a place of instruction, a market. Without doubt a supreme tribunal and ultimate happiness will succeed it. If you deny this, you will be obliged also to deny the identity cards of all the officers, their equipment and their orders; in fact, you will have to deny too all the order existing in the country, the existence of a government in it and all the measures that the government takes. Then you will no longer deserve the name of man or the appellation of conscious. You will be more of a fool than the sophists.

Beware, do not imagine that the proofs of the transfer of creation from one realm to another are restricted to these twelve. There are indications and proofs beyond counting and enumeration, all showing that this impermanent, changing kingdom will be transformed into a permanent and immutable realm. There are also innumerable signs and evidences that men will be taken from this temporary hospice and sent to the eternal seat of rule of all creation.

I will show one proof in particular that is stronger than all the twelve aspects taken together.

Come now, look, in the midst of the great assembly visible in the distance the same noble commander whom we previously saw on the island, adorned with numerous decorations, is making an announcement. Let us go and listen. See, that luminous and most noble commander is conveying a supreme edict, beautifully inscribed. He says:

"Prepare yourselves; you will go to another and permanent realm, a realm such that this one will appear as a dungeon by comparison. You will go to the seat of rule of our king, and there receive his compassion and his bounty, if you heed this edict well and obey it. But if you rebel and disobey it, you will be cast into awesome dungeons." Such is the message that he conveys. If you look at the decree, you will see that it bears such a miraculous seal that it cannot in any way be imitated. Everyone apart from idiots such as yourself knows of a certainty that the decree is from the king. Moreover, the noble commander bears such bright decorations that everyone except those blind like yourself understands full well that he is the veracious conveyer of the king's orders.

Is it at all possible that the teaching of transfer from one realm to an- other, challengingly conveyed by that noble commander in the supreme edict he has received, should at all be open to objection? No, it is not possible, unless we deny all that we have seen.

Now, o friend, it is your turn to speak. Say what you have to say.

"What should I say? What can be said to contradict all of this? Who can speak against the sun at midday? I say only: Praise be to God. A hundred thousand thanks that I have been saved from the dominance of fancy and vain imagination, and delivered from an eternal dungeon and prison. I have come to believe that there is an abode of felicity in the proximity of the monarch, separate from this confused and impermanent hospice."

Our comparison indicating the truth of resurrection and the Hereafter is now complete. Now with God's grace, we will pass on to the most exalted truth. We shall set forth twelve interrelated Truths, corresponding to the twelve Aspects discussed above, as well as an Introduction.

IS GOD REALLY CAPABLE OF RESURRECTING THE DEAD?

Third Fundamental Point

The Agent possesses the power. Without doubt, the matters necessitating the resurrection of the dead exist. Also, the One Who will bring it about is powerful to the utmost degree. There is no deficiency in His power. The greatest things and the smallest are the same in relation to His power. It is as easy for Him to create the spring as to create a flower. Yes, One so powerful that this world together with all its suns, stars, worlds, particles, and substance bear witness to His sublimity and power with endless tongues. Does any doubt or misgiving have the right to consider bodily resurrection remote from such a power?

It is plain to see that every age within this world an All-Powerful One of Glory creates a new, travelling, orderly universe. Indeed, He makes a new, well-ordered world each day. He perpetually creates and changes with perfect wisdom transient worlds and universes one after the other on the face of the heavens and the earth. He hangs on the string of time regular worlds to the number of the centuries, years, indeed, days, and through them demonstrates the tremendousness of His power. He attaches to the head of the globe the huge flower of spring which he adorns with a hundred thousand embroideries of resurrection as though it was a single flower, and through it displays the perfection of His wisdom and the beauty of His art. Can it be said of such a One, "How can He bring about the resurrection of the dead, and how can He transform this world into the Hereafter?" The verse,

> Your creation and your resurrection are but as (the creation and resurrection) of a single soul. Surely God is All-Hearing, All-Seeing. (Luqman 31:28)

proclaims the All-Powerful One's perfect power, that nothing at all is difficult for Him, that like the smallest thing, the greatest presents no difficulties for His power, and that it is as easy for His power to create innumerable individuals as to create as a single one.

We have explained the verse's essential meaning briefly in the Conclusion to the Tenth Word, and in detail in the treatise entitled *Nokta* (The Point), and in the Twentieth Letter. In connection with the discussion here, we shall elucidate a part of it in the form of three 'Matters', as follows:

Divine Power is essential, in which case, impotence cannot intervene in it. Also, it is connected to the inner dimensions of things, so obstacles cannot become interpenetrated with it. Also, its relation is according to laws, so particulars are equal to universals, minor things are like comprehensive ones. We shall prove these three matters.

First Matter: Pre-Eternal Power is the necessary inherent quality of the Most Pure and Holy Divine Essence. That is to say, it is of necessity intrinsic to the Essence, it can in no way be separated from It. Since this is so, the Essence which necessitates that power clearly cannot be affected by impotence, the opposite to power. For if that were the case, it would entail the combining of opposites. Since the Essence cannot be affected by impotence, self-evidently it cannot intervene in the power which is the inherent quality of that Essence. Since impotence cannot intervene in that essential power, clearly there can be no degrees in it. For the degrees of existence of a thing are though the intervention of its opposites.

For example, the degrees of heat are through the intervention of cold, and the degrees of beauty through the intervention of ugliness; further examples can be made in the same way. Since in contingent beings these qualities are not true, natural, and inherent, necessary qualities, their opposites may enter them. With the existence of degrees, diversity, variance, and change arose in the world. Since there can be no degrees in Pre- Eternal power, of necessity, those things decreed by it will be the same in relation to it. The greatest will be equal to the smallest, and particles the same as the stars. The resurrection of all mankind will be as easy for that power as the raising to life of a single individual; the creation of spring as easy as the giving of form to a single flower. Whereas if attributed to causes, the creation of a single flower would be as difficult as the spring.

It has been proved in the footnote to the last section of the Fourth Degree of 'God is Most Great' in the Second Station of this Word, and in the Twenty-Second Word, and in the Twentieth Letter and in its Addendum, that when the creation of beings is attributed to the Single One of Unity, all things become as easy as one thing. If they are attributed to causes, the creation of a single thing becomes as difficult and problematical as that of all things.

Second Matter: Divine power is related to the inner face of things. Yes, the universe has two faces like a mirror. One is its external face, which resembles the colored face of the mirror, the other is its face which looks to its Creator. This resembles the mirror's shining face. Its external face is the arena of opposites. It is where matters like beautiful and ugly, good and evil, big and small, difficult and easy appear. It is because of this that the All-Glorious Maker has made apparent causes a veil to the disposal of His power, so that the hand of power should not appear to the mind to be directly concerned with matters that on the face of it are insignificant or unworthy. For majesty and dignity require it to be thus. But He did not give a true effect to causes and intermediaries, because the unity of one- ness requires that they have none.

As for the face of beings, which looks to its Creator, in everything it is shining, it is clean. The colors and distortions of individuality do not intervene in it. This aspect faces its Creator without intermediary. There are no chains and disposition of causes in it. Cause and effect cannot intrude on it. It contains nothing contorted or askew. Obstacles cannot interfere in it. A particle becomes brother to the sun.

In short, Divine power is both simple, and infinite, and essential. The place connected to Divine power has neither intermediary, nor stain, nor is it the scene of rebellion. Therefore, within the sphere of Divine power great does not take pride of place over small. The community does not take preference over the individual. Universals cannot expect more from Divine power than particulars.

Third Matter: Divine power's relation is according to laws. That is to say, it regards many and few, great and small as the same. We shall make this abstruse matter easier to understand with a number of comparisons.

In the universe, transparency, reciprocity, balance, order, disengagedness, and obedience are all matters which render many equal to few, and great equal to small.

First Comparison: This explains the Mystery of Transparency.

For example, the sun's image and reflection, which are its radiance and manifestation, display the same identity on the sea's surface and in every drop of the sea. If the globe of the earth was composed of varying fragments of glass and exposed to the sun without veil, the sun's reflection would be the same in every fragment and on the whole face of the earth, without obstruction or being divided into pieces or being diminished. If, let us suppose, the sun acted with will and through its will conferred the radiance of its light and image of its reflection, it would not be more difficult for it to confer its radiance on the whole surface of the earth than to confer it on a single particle.

Second Comparison: This concerns the Mystery of Reciprocity.

For example, let us suppose there is a vast ring composed of living beings, that is, of human beings, each holding a mirror. At its center is an individual holding a candle. The radiance and manifestation reflected in all the mirrors surrounding the central point will be the same, and its relation will be without obstacle, fragmentation or being diminished.

Third Comparison: This concerns the Mystery of Balance.

For example, there are an enormous set of scales which are extremely ac- curate and sensitive. Whichever of two suns or two stars or two mountains or two eggs or two particles are placed in its two pans, it will require the same force to raise one pan of those huge sensitive scales to the sky and lower the other to the ground.

Fourth Comparison: This concerns the Mystery of Order.

For example, a huge ship can be turned as easily as a tiny toy boat.

Fifth Comparison: This concerns the Mystery of Disengagedness.

For example, a nature disengaged from individuality regards all particulars from the smallest to the greatest as the same and enters them without being diminished or fragmented. The qualities present in the aspect of external individuality do not interfere and cause confusion; they do not alter the view of a disengaged nature such as that. For example, a fish like a needle possesses such a disengaged nature the same as a whale. Or a microbe bears an animal nature the same as a rhinoceros.

Sixth Comparison: This demonstrates the Mystery of Obedience.

For example, a commander causes a single private to advance with the command "Forward march!" the same as he causes an army to advance. The truth of the mystery of this comparison about obedience is as follows:

As is proved by experience, everything in the universe has a point of perfection, and everything has an inclination towards that point. Increased inclination becomes need. Increased need becomes desire. Increased de- sire becomes attraction, and attraction, desire, need, and inclination are each seeds and kernels which together with the essences of things con- form to the creative commands of Almighty God. The absolute perfection of the true nature of contingent beings is absolute existence. Their particular perfections are an existence peculiar to each which makes each being's abilities emerge from the potential to the actual. Thus, the obedience of the whole universe to the Divine command "Be!" is the same as that of a particle, which is like a single soldier. Contained all together in the obedience and conformity of contingent beings to the pre-eternal command of "Be!" proceeding from the Pre-Eternal will are inclination, need, desire, and attraction, which are also manifestations of Divine will. The fact that when subtle water receives the command to freeze, with a refined inclination it may split a piece of iron demonstrates the strength of the mystery of obedience.

If these six comparisons are observed in the potentialities and actions of contingent beings, which are both defective, and finite, and weak, and have no actual effect, without doubt it will be seen that everything is equal in relation to Pre-Eternal power, which is both pre-eternal, and post-eternal, and creates the whole universe out of pure non-existence, and being manifested through the works of its tremendousness leaves all minds in wonderment. Nothing at all can be difficult for it. Such a power cannot be weighed on the small scales of these mysteries, neither are they proportionate. They have been mentioned to bring the subject closer to the understanding and to dispel any doubts.

Summary and the Result

Since pre-eternal power is infinite, and it is the inherent, necessary quality of the Most Pure and Holy Essence; and since the stainless, veilless inner aspect of everything is turned to it and faces it, and is in balance with respect to contingency, which consists of the equal possibility of being and non-being; and since this inner face is obedient to the order of creation and the Divine laws of the universe which form the Greater Sharia, the Sharia of Creation, and it is disengaged from and free of obstacles and different characteristics; certainly, like the smallest thing, the greatest cannot resist that power, nor expect more from it than the smallest. In which case, the raising to life of all beings with spirits at the resurrection is not more difficult for Divine power than raising a fly to life in the spring. Thus, the decree of:

> Your creation and your resurrection are but as (the creation and resurrection) of a single soul. Surely God is All-Hearing, All-Seeing. (Luqman 31:28)

is no exaggeration; it is true and correct. And our claim that "the Agent possesses the power" has been proved true in decisive fashion; there is nothing to hinder it in this respect.

FOURTH FUNDAMENTAL POINT

Just as there are things necessitating the resurrection of the dead and Great Gathering, and the One Who will bring it about possesses the power to do so, so the world possesses the potential for the resurrection of the dead and Great Gathering. There are four 'Matters' in this assertion of mine that 'this place is possible.'

The First is the possibility of this world's death.

The Second **is its actual death.**

The Third is the possibility of the destroyed, dead world being reconstructed and resurrected in the form of the Hereafter.

The Fourth is its actual reconstruction and resurrection, which are possible.

First Matter: The death of creation is possible. That which is subject to the law of development must evolve to a final end. That which develops to a final end must have a limited lifetime and, therefore, a fixed natural end. That which has a fixed end inevitably dies. Humanity is a microcosm subject to death; the universe can be regarded as a macro-human being and therefore also subject to death. Accordingly, it will perish and be resurrected on the morning of the Last Day. Just as a living tree (a miniature universe) cannot save itself from annihilation, the "branches of creatures" growing from "the Tree of Creation" will pass away.

If the universe is not destroyed by an external destructive event, with the Eternal Will's permission, it eventually will begin to die. Even scientists say this. According to the Qur'an, it will give a sharp cry, and then the following things will happen: *When the sun shall be darkened; when the stars shall be thrown down; when the mountains shall be set moving (At- Takwir 81:1–3)* and *When heaven is split open; when the stars are scattered; when the seas swarm over (Al-Infitaar 82:1–3).*

A Subtle, Allusive Matter

Just as water freezes to its own detriment, and ice melts to its own detriment, and a kernel gains strength to the detriment of the shell, and a word becomes coarse to the detriment of the meaning, and the spirit weakens on account of the body, and the body becomes finer on account of the spirit, so too this world, the dense world, becomes transparent and refined with the functioning of the machine of life on account of the Hereafter, which is the subtle world. Creative power sprinkling the light of life on dense, lifeless, extinguished, dead objects with an astonishing activity is a sign that it dissolves, burns, and illuminates this dense world with the light of life on account of the subtle world.

No matter how weak reality is, it does not die; it is not annihilated like a form. Rather, it travels in individuals and forms. Reality grows, develops, and gradually expands, while the shell and the form wear out, become finer, and break up. They are renewed in a better form so as to become suit- able to the stature of the stable and expanded reality. In regard to increase and decrease, reality and form are in inverse proportion. That is to say, the more substantial form grows, the weaker reality becomes. The less substantial form becomes, to that degree the reality grows stronger.

Thus, this law encompasses all things included in the law of the process of perfection. This means that a time is certain to come when the Manifest World, which is the shell and form of the mighty reality of the universe, will break up, with the permission of the All-Glorious Creator. Then it will be renewed in a better form. The meaning of the verse *On the Day when the earth is changed into another earth (Ibrahim 14:48)* will be realized.

In short, the death of the world is possible. Moreover, there can be no doubt that it is possible.

Second Matter: This is the actual death of the world. The proof of this matter is the consensus of all the revealed religions; the testimony of all sound natures; the indication of all the changes, transformations, and alterations in the universe; the testimony to the number of centuries and years through their deaths in this guesthouse of the world, of all living worlds and mobile worlds to the death of the world itself.

If you want to imagine the death agonies of the world as the Qur'an points them out, think of how the parts of the universe are bound to one another with an exact, exalted order. They are held with such a hidden, delicate, subtle bond and are so bound within an order that on a single one of the lofty heavenly bodies receiving the command: "Be!" or, "Leave your orbit!", the world will go into its death agonies. The stars will collide, the heavenly bodies reel, a great din will strike up in infinite space like the devastating sound of millions of cannon-balls and great guns the size of globes. Clashing and colliding with one another, sending out showers of sparks, the mountains taking flight, the seas burning, the face of the earth will be flattened.

Thus, through this death and those agonies the Pre-Eternal One of Power will shake up the universe. He will purify the universe, and Hell and the matters of Hell will draw to one side, and Paradise and the matters appropriate for Paradise draw to the other, and the world of the Hereafter will become manifest.

Third Matter: The return to life of the world, which will die, is possible. For, as is proved in the Second Fundamental Point, there is no deficiency in Divine power, and the things necessitating it are extremely powerful. The matter is within the realm of the possible. And if a possible matter has something extremely powerful necessitating it, and there is no deficiency in the power of the agent, it may be regarded not as possible, but as actual.

An Allusive Point

If the universe is studied carefully, it will be seen that within it are two elements that have spread everywhere and become rooted; with their traces and fruits like good and evil, beauty and ugliness, benefit and harm, perfection and defect, light and darkness, guidance and misguidance, light and fire, belief and unbelief, obedience and rebellion, and fear and love, opposites clash with one another in the universe. They are constantly manifested through change and transformation. Their wheels turn like the workshop of the crops of some other world.

Of a certainty, the branches and results, which are opposites, of those two elements will continue into eternity; they will become concentrated and separate from one another. Then they will be manifested in the form of Paradise and Hell. Since it is out of this transient world that the permanent world will be made, its fundamental elements will certainly go to eternity and permanence.

Indeed, Paradise and Hell are the two fruits of the branch of the tree of creation, which stretches, inclines, and goes towards eternity; they are the two results of the chain of the universe; the two storehouses of this flood of Divine activity; the two pools of beings, which flow in waves to- wards eternity; and the place of manifestation, the one of Divine favor, the other of Divine wrath. When the hand of power shakes up the universe with a violent motion, those two pools will fill up with the appropriate matters.

The secret of this Allusive Point is as follows:

As eternal benevolence and pre-eternal wisdom necessitated, the Pre- Eternally All-Wise One created this world to be a place of trial, an arena of examination, a mirror to His Most Beautiful Names, and a page for the pen of Divine Determining and power. Now, trial and examination are the cause of growth and development. And growth causes the disposition to unfold. And this unfolding causes the abilities to become apparent. And this emergence of the abilities causes the relative truths to become evident. And the relative truths' becoming evident causes the embroideries of the manifestations of the All-Glorious Maker's Most Beautiful Names to be displayed, and the universe to be transformed into a missive of the Eternally Besought One. It is through this mystery of examination and the mystery of man's accountability that the diamond-like essences of elevated spirits are purified of the coal-like matter of base spirits, and the two separated out from one another.

Thus, since it was for mysteries such as these, and for other most subtle and elevated instances of wisdom which we do not yet know of that the Pre-Eternally All-Wise One willed the world in this form, He also willed the change and transformation of this world for those instances of wisdom. He mixed together opposites for its change and transformation, and brought them face to face. Combining harm with benefit, including evil with good, and mingling ugliness with beauty, He kneaded them together like dough, and made the universe subject to the law of change and mutation, and the principle of transformation and perfection.

A day will come when this assembly of examination is closed, and the period of trial is finished, and the Divine Names have carried out their de- cree, and the pen of Divine Determining has completed writing its missives, and Divine power completed the embroideries of its art, and beings have fulfilled their duties, and creatures accomplished their acts of service, and everything has stated its meaning, and this world produced the seedlings of the Hereafter, and the earth has displayed and exhibited all the miracles of power of the All-Powerful Maker, and all the wonders of His art, and this transient world has attached to the string of time the tableaux forming the panoramas of eternity.

For the eternal wisdom and pre-eternal beneficence of the All-Glorious Maker necessitate truths like the results of the examination and trial, the truths of those Divine Names' manifestations, the truths of the missives of the pen of Divine Determining, the originals of those sample-like embroideries of art, the aims and benefits of the duties of beings, the wages of the acts of service of creatures, the truths of the meanings the book of the universe stated, the sprouting of the seeds of innate dis- position, the opening of a Supreme Court of Judgment, the displaying of the sample-like panoramas taken from this world, the rending of the veil of apparent causes, and the surrendering of everything directly to the All- Glorious Creator. Since the All-Glorious Maker's pre-eternal wisdom and beneficence necessitate these truths, they require the purification of those opposites in order to deliver the world from change and transience, transformation and extinction, and to separate out the causes of change and the matters of conflict. And most certainly they will bring about the resurrection and purify those opposites in order to obtain these results.

Thus, as a result of this purification Hell will take on its eternal and dreadful form, and its inmates will manifest the threat *And you, O disbelieving criminals! Get you apart this Day! (Ya-Sin 36:59);* while Paradise will assume its everlasting and majestic form, and its people and companions will manifest the address of:

Peace be upon you! Well you have faired and are purified (from the foul residues of sin, and delivered from all suffering), so enter it (Paradise) to abide! (Az-Zumar 39:73)

As is proved in the Second Question of the First Station of the Twenty- Eighth Word, through His perfect power, the Pre-Eternally All-Wise One will give the inhabitants of these two houses eternal and permanent bodies which will not be subject to dissolution, change, old age, or decline. For there will be no causes of change, which are the cause of decline.

Fourth Matter: This is possible, it will occur. Indeed, after dying, the world will be resurrected as the Hereafter. After being destroyed, the One Who made the world will repair and reconstruct it in an even better form, and will convert it into one of the mansions of the Hereafter. Just as the proof of this is, foremost, the agreement of the Holy Qur'an together with all its verses comprising thousands of rational proofs and all the revealed scriptures, so do the Attributes of the All-Glorious One pertaining to His might and those pertaining to His beauty, and all His Beautiful Names, clearly indicate its occurrence. So too did He promise He would create the resurrection and Great Gathering through all His heavenly decrees which He sent to His Prophets. And since He has promised, most certainly shall

He bring it about. You may refer to the Eighth Truth of the Tenth Word concerning this matter.

Also, just as foremost Muhammad the Arabian, peace and blessings be upon him, with the strength of his thousand miracles, and all the Prophets and Messengers, saints and the righteous agreed on its occurrence and gave news of it, so does the universe together with all its creational signs tell of its occurrence.

In short, The Tenth Word with all its truths, and the Twenty-Eighth Word with all its proofs in the 'Especially' in its Second Station, have demonstrated with the certainty of the sun's rising in the morning after setting the previous evening that after the setting of the life of this world, the sun of truth will appear once more in the form of the life of the Hereafter.

Thus, seeking assistance from the Divine Name of All-Wise and benefiting from the effulgence of the Qur'an, from the beginning up to here our explanations have taken the form of four 'Fundamental Points' in order to prepare the heart for acceptance, the soul for surrender, and to convince the reason. But who are we that we should speak of this matter? What does this world's true Owner, the universe's Creator, these beings' Master, say? We should listen to Him. Can others dare to interfere officiously while the Owner of this domain speaks?

We must listen to the Pre-Eternal Discourse of the All-Wise Maker which He delivers addressing all the ranks of those of each successive century in the mosque of the world and place of instruction which is the earth, with thousands of decrees like,

When the earth quakes with a violent quaking destined for it;

And the earth yields up its burdens;

And human cries out, "What is the matter with it?" On that day, she will recount all its tidings,

As your Lord has inspired her to do so.

On that day, all humans will come forth in different companies, to be shown their deeds (that they did in the world).

And so, whoever does an atom's weight of good will see it;

And whoever does an atom's weight of evil will see it. (Az-Zalzalah 99:1–8) which causes the earth to tremble, and,

Give glad tidings to those who believe and do good, righteous deeds: for them are Gardens through which rivers flow. Every time they are provided with fruits (of different color, shape, taste, and fragrance, and that are constantly renewed) therefrom, they say, "This is what we were provided with before. " For they are given to them in resemblance (to what was given to them both in the world, and just before in the Gardens, familiar in shape and color so that they may not be unattractive due to being unknown). Furthermore, for them are spouses eternally purified (of all kinds of worldly uncleanliness). They will abide there (forever). (Al-Baqarah 2:25) which fills all creatures with joy and eagerness. We must give heed to these decrees of the Possessor of All Dominion, the Owner of This World and the

Next, and we must say, "We believe in it and we affirm it."

> (In acknowledgement of their imperfection, and their perception of the truth of the matter,) the angels said: "All-Glorified You are (in that You are absolutely above having any defect and doing anything meaningless, and Yours are all the attributes of perfection). We have no knowledge save what You have taught us. Surely You are the All-Knowing, the All-Wise." (Al-Baqarah 2:32)
>
> O our Sustainer, do not punish us if we forget or do wrong. (Al-Baqarah 2:286)
>
> O God, grant blessings to our master Muhammad, and to the Family of our master Muhammad, as You granted blessings to our master Abraham and to the Family of our master Abraham; indeed, all praise is Yours, all splendor.

CHAPTER 7

READING THE UNIVERSE THROUGH THE LENSES OF THE QUR'AN

In the Name of God, the All-Merciful, the All-Compassionate. And he who has been given wisdom has been given great good. (Al-Baqarah 2:269)

This piece consists of a brief comparison between the sacred wisdom of the All-Wise Qur'an and the wisdom of philosophy and science, and a concise summary of the instruction and training which Qur'anic wisdom gives to man in his personal life and social life, and an indication of the Qur'an's superiority to other Divine words, and to all speech. There are Four Principles in this Word.

First Principle

Look through the telescope of the following story which is in the form of a comparison, and see the differences between Qur'anic wisdom and that of philosophy and science:

One time, a renowned Ruler who was both religious and a fine craftsman wanted to write the All-Wise Qur'an in a script worthy of the sacredness in its meaning and the miraculousness in its words, so that its marvel-displaying stature would be arrayed in wondrous apparel. The artist-King therefore wrote the Qur'an in a truly wonderful fashion. He used all his precious jewels in its writing. In order to indicate the great variety of its truths, he wrote some of its embodied letters in diamonds and emeralds, and some in rubies and agate, and other sorts in brilliants and coral, while others he inscribed with silver and gold. He adorned and decorated it in such a way that everyone, those who knew how to read and those who did not, were full of admiration and astonishment when they beheld it. Especially in the view of the people of truth, since the outer beauty was an indication of the brilliant beauty and striking adornment in its meaning, it became a truly precious antique. Then the Ruler showed the artistically wrought and bejeweled Qur'an to a European philosopher and to a Muslim scholar. In order to test them and for reward, he commanded them: "Each of you write a work about the wisdom and purposes of this!" First the philosopher, then the scholar composed a book about it. However, the philosopher's book discussed only the decorations of the letters and their relationships and conditions, and the properties of the jewels, and described them. It did not touch on their meaning at all, for the European had no knowledge of the Arabic script. He did not even know that the embellished Qur'an was a book, a written piece, expressing a meaning. He rather looked on it as an ornamented antique. He did not know any Arabic, but he was a very good engineer, and he described things very aptly, and he was a skillful chemist, and an ingenious jeweler. So this man wrote his work according to those crafts.

As for the Muslim scholar, when he looked at the Qur'an, he understood that it was the Perspicuous Book, the All-Wise Qur'an. This truth-loving person neither attached importance to the external adornments, nor busied himself with the ornamented letters. He became preoccupied with something that was a million times higher, more elevated, more subtle, more noble, more beneficial, and more comprehensive than the matters with which the other man had busied himself. For discussing the sacred truths and lights of the mysteries beneath the veil of the decorations, he wrote a truly fine commentary. Then the two of them took their works and presented them to the Illustrious Ruler. The Ruler first took the philosopher's work. He looked at it and saw that the self-centered and nature-worshipping man had worked very hard, but had written nothing of true wisdom. He had understood nothing of its meaning. Indeed, he had confused it and been disrespectful towards it, and ill-mannered even. For supposing that source of truths, the Qur'an, to be meaningless decoration, he had insulted it as being valueless in regard to meaning. So the Wise Ruler hit him over the head with his work and expelled him from his presence.

Then he looked at the work of the other, the truth-loving, scrupulous scholar, and saw that it was an extremely fine and beneficial commentary, a most wise composition full of guidance. "Congratulations! May God bless you!", he said. Thus, wisdom is this and they call those who possess it knowledgeable and wise. As for the other man, he was a craftsman who had exceeded his mark. Then in reward for the scholar's work, he commanded that in return for each letter ten gold pieces should be given him from his inexhaustible treasury.

If you have understood the comparison, now look and see the reality: The ornamented Qur'an is this artistically fashioned universe, and the Ruler is the Pre-Eternal All-Wise One. As for the two men, one—the European—represents philosophy and its philosophers, and the other, the Qur'an and its students. Yes, the All-Wise Qur'an is a most elevated expounder, a most eloquent translator of the Mighty Qur'an of the Universe. Yes, it is the Criterion which instructs man and the jinn concerning the signs of creation inscribed by the pen of power on the pages of the universe and on the leaves of time. It regards beings, each of which is a meaningful letter, as bearing the meaning of another, that is, it looks at them on account of their Maker. It says, "How beautifully they have been made! How exquisitely they point to their Maker's beauty!", thus showing the universe's true beauty. But the philosophy they call natural philosophy or science has plunged into the decorations of the letters of beings and into their relationships, and has become bewildered; it has confused the way of reality. While the letters of this mighty book should be looked at as bearing the meaning of another, that is, on account of God, they have not done this; they have looked at beings as signifying themselves. That is, they have looked at beings on account of beings, and have discussed them in that way. Instead of saying, "How beautifully they have been made," they say "How beautiful they are," and have made them ugly. In doing this they have insulted the universe, and made it complain about them. Indeed, *philosophy without religion is a sophistry divorced from reality and an insult to the universe.*

Second Principle

A comparison between the moral training the wisdom of the All-Wise Qur'an gives to personal life and what philosophy and science teach:

> The sincere student of philosophy is a pharaoh, but he is a contemptible pharaoh who worships the basest thing for the sake of benefit; he recognizes everything from which he can profit as his 'Lord.' And that irreligious student is obstinate and refractory, but he is wretched together with his obstinacy and accepts endless abasement for the sake of one pleasure. And he is abject together with his recalcitrance and shows his abasement by kissing the feet of satanic individuals for the sake of some base benefit. And that irreligious student is conceited and domineering, but since he can find no point of support in his heart, he is an utterly impotent blustering tyrant. And that student is a self-centered seeker of benefit whose aim and endeavor is to gratify his animal appetites; a crafty egotist who seeks his personal interests within certain nationalist interests.

However, the sincere student of Qur'anic wisdom is a servant, but he does not stoop to worship even the greatest of creatures; he is an esteemed slave who does not take a supreme benefit like Paradise as the aim of his worship. And its student is humble; he is righteous and mild, yet outside the limits of his Maker's leave, he would not voluntarily lower and abase himself before anything other than his Maker. And he is weak and in want, and he knows his weakness and poverty, but he is self-sufficient due to the wealth which his All-Generous Lord has stored up for him in the Hereafter, and he is strong since he relies on his Master's infinite power. And he acts and strives only for God's sake, for God's pleasure, and for virtue.

Thus, the training the two give may be understood from the comparison of the two students.

Third Principle

The training philosophy and science and Qur'anic wisdom give to human social life is this:

Philosophy accepts 'force' as its point of support in the life of society. It considers its aim to be 'benefits.' The principle of its life it recognizes to be 'conflict.' It holds the bond between communities to be 'racialism and negative nationalism.' Its fruits are 'gratifying the appetites of the soul and increasing human needs.' However, the mark of force is 'aggression.' The mark of benefit—since they are insufficient for every desire—is 'jostling and tussling.' While the mark of conflict is 'strife.' And the mark of racialism—since it is nourished by devouring others—is 'aggression.' It is for these reasons that it has negated the happiness of mankind.

Fourth Principle

If you want to understand the Qur'an's superiority among all the Divine scriptures and its supremacy over all speech and writings, then consider the following two comparisons:

The First: A king has two forms of speech, two forms of address. One is to speak on his private telephone with a common subject concerning some minor matter, some private need. The other, under the title of sublime sovereignty, supreme vicegerent, and universal rulership, is to speak with an envoy or high official for the purpose of making known and promulgating his commands, to make an utterance through an elevated decree proclaiming his majesty.

The Second: One man holds the mirror he is holding up to the sun. He receives light containing the seven colors according to the capacity of the mirror. He becomes connected to the sun through that relation and converses with it, and if he directs the light-filled mirror towards his dark house or his garden covered by a roof, he will benefit, not in relation to the sun's value, but in accordance with the capacity of the mirror. Another man, however, opens up broad windows out of his house or out of the roof over his garden. He opens up ways to the sun in the sky. He converses with the perpetual light of the actual sun and speaks with it, and says in gratitude through the tongue of his disposition: "O you beauty of the world who gilds the face of the earth with your light and makes the faces of the flowers smile! O beauty of the skies, fine sun! You have furnished my little house and garden with light and heat the same as you have them." Whereas the man with the mirror cannot say that. The reflection and works of the sun under that restriction are limited; they are in accordance with the restriction. Look at the Qur'an through the telescope of these two comparisons and see its miraculousness and understand its sacredness.

The Qur'an says:

> If all the trees on the earth were pens, and all the sea were ink, with seven more seas added thereto, the words of God (Hic decrees, the acts of all His Names and Attributes manifested as His commandments, and the events and creatures He creates) would not be exhausted in the writing. Surely God is the All-Glorious with irresistible might (Whom none can frustrate, and Whom nothing can tire), the All-Wise. (Luqman 31:27)

Now, the reason the Qur'an has been given the highest rank among the infinite words of God is this: the Qur'an has come from the Greatest Divine Name and from the greatest level of every Name. It is God's Word in respect of His being Sustainer of All the Worlds; it is His decree through His title of God of All Beings; an address in regard to His being Creator of the Heavens and the Earth; a speech in regard to absolute lordship; a pre-eternal address on account of universal Divine sovereignty; a notebook of the favors of the Most Merciful One from the point of view of His all-embracing, comprehensive mercy; a collection of communications at the beginnings of which are sometimes ciphers related to the sublime majesty of the Godhead; a wisdom-scattering holy scripture which, descending from the reaches of the Greatest Name, looks to and inspects the all-comprehensive domain of the Supreme Throne. It is for these reasons that the title of Word of God has been given with complete worthiness to the Qur'an.

In respect to the other Divine Words, they are speech which has become evident through a particular regard, a minor title, through the partial manifestation of a particular Name; through a particular lordship, special sovereignty, a private mercy. Their degrees vary in regard to particularity and universality. Most inspiration is of this sort, but its degrees vary greatly. For example, the most particular and simple is the inspiration of the animals. Then there is the inspiration of the ordinary people; then the inspiration of ordinary angels; then the inspiration of the saints, then the inspiration of the higher angels. Thus, it is for this reason that a saint who offers supplications directly without means by the telephone of the heart says: "My heart tells me news of my Sustainer." He does not say, "It tells me of the Sustainer of All the Worlds." And he says: "My heart is the mirror, the throne, of my Sustainer." He does not say, "It is the throne of the Sustainer of All the Worlds." For he can manifest the address to the extent of its capacity and to the degree nearly seventy thousand veils have been raised. Thus, however much higher and more elevated is the decree of a king promulgated in respect of his supreme sovereignty than the insignificant speech of a common man, and however much more abundantly the effulgence of the sun in the sky may be benefited from than the manifestation of its reflection in the mirror, and however greater is its superiority, to that degree the Qur'an of Mighty Stature is superior to all other speech and all other books.

After the Qur'an, at the second level, the Holy Books and Revealed Scriptures have superiority according to their degree. They have their share from the mystery of that superiority. If all the fine words of all men and jinn which do not issue from the Qur'an were to be gathered together, they still could not attain to the sacred rank of the Qur'an and imitate it. If you want to understand a little of how the Qur'an comes from the Greatest Name and from the greatest level of every Name, consider the universal, elevated statements of *Ayat al-Kursi* and the following verses:

And with Him are the keys of the Unseen. (Al-An'am 6:59)

O God! Lord of All Dominion. (Al-'Imran 3:26)

He draws the night as a veil over day, each seeking the other in rapid succession; He created the sun, the moon, and the stars, [all] subject to His command. (Al-A'raf 7:54)

O Earth, swallow up your water! And O Sky, withhold your rain! (Hud 11:44)

The heavens and the earth and all within them extol and glorify Him. (Al-Isra' 17:44)

Your creation and your resurrection are but as (the creation and resurrection) of a single soul. Surely God is All-Hearing, All-Seeing. (Luqman 31:28)

We did indeed offer the Trust to the heavens, and the earth, and the mountains. (Al-Ahzab 33:72)

The Day that We roll up the heavens like a scroll rolled up for books [completed]. (Al-Anbiya 21:104)

No just estimate have they made of God, such as is due to Him: on the Day of Judgment the whole of the earth will be but His handful. (Az-Zumar 39:67)

If We had sent down this Qur'an on a mountain, you would cer- tainly see it humble itself, splitting asunder for awe of God. Such parables We strike for humankind so that they may reflect (on why the Qur'an is being revealed to humankind, and how great and important their responsibility is). (Al-Hashr 59:21)

And study the Surahs which begin *al-Hamdulillah*, or *Tusabbi-hu*, and see the rays of this mighty mystery. Look too at the openings of the *Alif. Lam. Mim.*'s, the *Alif. Lam. Ra.*'s, and the *Ha. Mim.*'s, and understand the Qur'an's importance in the sight of God.

If you have understood the valuable mystery of this Fourth Principle, you have understood that revelation mostly comes to the

Prophets by means of an angel, and inspiration is mostly without means. You will have also understood the reason why the greatest saint cannot attain to the level of a Prophet. And you will have understood too the Qur'an's sublimity and its sacred grandeur and the mystery of its elevated miraculousness. So too you will have understood the mystery of the necessity of the Prophet Muhammad's Ascension, that is, that he went to the heavens, to *the furthest Lote-tree*, to *the distance of two bow-lengths*, offered supplications to the All-Glorious One, Who is *closer to him than his jugular vein*, and in the twinkling of an eye returned whence he came. Indeed, just as the Splitting of the Moon was a miracle of his Messengership whereby he demonstrated his Prophethood to the jinn and mankind, so the Ascension was a miracle of his worship and servitude to God whereby he demonstrated to the spirits and angels that he was God's Beloved.

O God, grant blessings and peace to him and to his Family as befits Your mercy, and in veneration of him. Amen.

THE VIRTUE OF BISMILLAH

In the name of God, the merciful, the compassionate
And from Him do we seek help.

All praise be to God, the Sustainer of All the Worlds,
and blessings and peace be upon our master Muham-
mad, and on all his Family and Companions.

Bismillah, "In the Name of God," is the start of all things good. We too shall start with it. Know, O my soul! Just as this blessed phrase is a mark of Islam, so too it is constantly recited by all beings through their tongues of disposition. If you want to know what an inexhaustible strength, what an unending source of bounty is *Bismillah*, listen to the following story which is in the form of a comparison. It goes like this:

Someone who makes a journey through the deserts of Arabia has to travel in the name of a tribal chief and enter under his protection, for in this way he may be saved from the assaults of bandits and

secure his needs. On his own he will perish in the face of innumerable enemies and needs. And so, two men went on such a journey and
entered the desert. One of them was modest and humble, the other
proud and conceited. The humble man assumed the name of a tribal
chief, while the proud man did not. The first travelled safely wherever he went. If he encountered bandits, he said: "I am travelling in the
name of such-and-such tribal leader," and they did not molest him. If
he came to some tents, he was treated respectfully due to the name.
But the proud man suffered indescribable calamities throughout
his journey. He both trembled before everything and begged from
everything. He was abased and became an object of scorn.

My proud soul! You are the traveler, and this world is a desert.
Your impotence and poverty have no limit, and your enemies and
needs are endless. Since it is thus, take the name of the Pre-Eternal
Ruler and Post- Eternal Lord of the desert and be saved from begging before the whole universe and trembling before every event.

Yes, this phrase is a treasury so blessed that your infinite impotence and poverty bind you to an infinite power and mercy; it makes
your impotence and poverty a most acceptable intercessor at the
Court of One All-Powerful and Compassionate. The person who acts
saying, "In the Name of God," resembles someone who enrolls in the
army. He acts in the name of the government; he has fear of no
one; he speaks, performs every matter, and withstands everything
in the name of the law and the name of the government.

At the beginning we said that all beings say "In the Name of
God" through the tongue of disposition. Is that so?

Indeed, it is so. If you were to see that a single person had come
and had driven all the inhabitants of a town to a place by force and
compelled them to work, you would be certain that he had not acted in his own name and through his own power, but was a soldier,
acting in the name of the government and relying on the power of
the king.

In the same way, all things act in the name of Almighty God, for
minute things like seeds and grains bear huge trees on their heads;
they raise loads like mountains. That means all trees say: "In the
Name of God" fill their hands from the treasury of mercy, and of-

fer them to us. All gardens say: "In the Name of God," and become cauldrons from the kitchens of Divine power in which are cooked numerous varieties of different foods. All blessed animals like cows, camels, sheep, and goats, say: "In the Name of God," and produce springs of milk from the abundance of mercy, offering us a most delicate and pure food like the water of life in the name of the Provider. The roots and rootlets, soft as silk, of plants, trees, and grasses say: "In the Name of God," and pierce and pass through hard rock and earth.

Mentioning the name of God, the name of the Most Merciful, everything becomes subjected to them. The roots spreading through hard rock and earth and producing fruits as easily as the branches spread through the air and produce fruits, and the delicate green leaves retaining their moisture for months in the face of extreme heat, deal a slap in the mouths of Naturalists and jab a finger in their blind eyes, saying: "Even heat and hardness, in which you most trust, are under a command. For like the Staff of Moses, each of those silken rootlets conform to the command of, *And We said, O Moses, strike the rock with your staff (Al-Baqarah 2:60)* and split the rock. And the delicate leaves fine as cigarette paper recite the verse *"O fire," We ordered, "Be cool and peaceful for Abraham!" (Al-Anbiya 21:69)* against the heat of the fire, each like the members of Abraham, peace and blessings be upon him.

Since all things say: "In the Name of God," and bearing God's bounties in God's name, give them to us, we too should say: "In the Name of God." We should give in the name of God, and take in the name of God. And we should not take from heedless people who neglect to give in God's name.

Question: We give a price to people, who are like tray-bearers. So what price does God want, Who is the true owner?

The Answer: Yes, the price the True Bestower of Bounties wants in return for those valuable bounties and goods is three things: one is remembrance, another is thanks, and the other is reflection. Saying, "In the Name of God" at the start is remembrance, and, *"All praise be to God"* at the end is thanks. And perceiving and thinking of those bounties, which are priceless wonders of art, being miracles of power of the Unique and Eternally Besought One and gifts of His mercy, is reflection. However foolish it is to kiss the foot of a lowly man who conveys to you the precious gift of a king and not to recognize the gift's owner, it is a thousand times more foolish to praise and love the apparent source of bounties and forget the True Bestower of Bounties.

O my soul! If you do not wish to be foolish in that way, give in God's name, take in God's name, begin in God's name, and act in God's name. And that's the matter in a nutshell!

CHAPTER 8

FRATERNITY, GREED, ENMITY AND BACKBITING

In the Name of God, the All-Merciful, the All-Compassionate.

The believers are but brothers, so make peace between your brothers; and keep from disobedience to God in reverence for Him and piety (particularly in your duties toward one another as brothers), so that you may be shown mercy (granted a good, virtuous life in the world as individuals and as a community, and eternal happiness in the Hereafter). (Al-Hujurat 49:10)

Goodness and evil can never be equal. Repel evil with what is better (or best). Then see: the one between whom and you there was enmity has become a bosom friend. (Fussilat 41:34)

They spend (out of what God has provided for them,) both in ease and hardship, ever-restraining their rage (even when provoked and able to retaliate), and pardoning people (their offenses). God loves (such) people who are devoted to doing good, aware that God is seeing them. (Al-'Imran 3:134)

FRATERNITY

Dispute and discord among the believers, and partisanship, obstinacy and envy, leading to rancor and enmity among them, are repugnant and vile, are harmful and sinful, by the combined testimony of wisdom and the supreme humanity that is Islam, for personal, social, and spiritual life. They are in short, poison for the life of man. We will set forth six of the extremely numerous aspects of this truth.

First aspect

They are sinful in the view of truth.

O unjust man nurturing rancor and enmity against a believer! Let us suppose that you were on a ship, or in a house, with nine innocent people and one criminal. If someone were to try to make the ship sink, or to set the house on fire, because of that criminal, you know how great a sinner he would be. You would cry out to the heavens against his sinfulness. Even if there were one innocent man and nine criminals aboard the ship, it would be against all rules of justice to sink it.

So too, if there are in the person of a believer, who may be compared to a dominical dwelling, a Divine ship, not nine, but as many as twenty innocent attributes such as belief, Islam, and neighborliness; and if you then nurture rancor and enmity against him on account of one criminal attribute that harms and displeases you, attempting or desiring the sinking of his being, the burning of his house, then you too will be a criminal guilty of a great atrocity.

Second aspect

They are also sinful in the view of wisdom, for it is obvious that enmity and love are opposites, just like light and darkness; while maintaining their respective essences, they cannot be combined.

If love is truly found in a heart, by virtue of the predomination of the causes that produce it, then enmity in that heart can only be metaphorical, and takes on the form of compassion. The believer loves and should love his brother, and is pained by any evil he sees in him. He attempts to reform him not with harshness but gently. It is for this reason that the Hadith of the Prophet says, "No believer should be angered with another and cease speaking to him for more than three days."[82]

If the causes that produce enmity predominate, and true enmity takes up its seat in a heart, then the love in that heart will become metaphorical, and take on the form of artifice and flattery.

O unfair man! See now what a great sin is rancor and enmity toward a brother believer! If you were to say that ordinary small stones are more valuable than the Ka'ba in Mecca and greater than Mount Uhud in al-Madinah, it would be an ugly absurdity. So too, belief which has the value of the Ka'ba, and Islam which has the splendor of Mount Uhud, as well as other Islamic attributes, demand love and concord; but if you prefer to belief and Islam certain shortcomings which arouse hostility, but in reality are like the small stones you too will be engaging in great injustice, foolishness, and sin!

The unity of belief necessitates also the unity of hearts, and the oneness of our creed demands the oneness of our society. You cannot deny that if you find yourself in the same regiment as someone, you will form a friendly attachment to him; a brotherly relation will come into being as a result of your both being submitted to the orders of a single commander. You will similarly experience a fraternal relation through living in the same town with someone. Now there are ties of unity, bonds of union, and relations of fraternity as numerous as the Divine Names that are shown and demonstrated to you by the light and consciousness of belief. Your Creator, Owner, Object of Worship, and Provider is one and the same for both of you; thousands of things are and the same for you. Your Prophet, your religion, your *qibla* are one and the same; hundreds of things are one and the same for you. Then too your village is one, your state is one, your country is one; tens of things are one and the same for you. All of these things held in common dictate oneness and unity, union and concord, love and brotherhood, and indeed the cosmos and the planets are similarly

---

[82] *Bukhari, Adab, 57, 62; Isti'dhan, 9; Muslim, Birr, 23, 25, 26; Abu Dawud, Adab, 47; Tir- midhi, Birr, 21, 24; Ibn Majah, Muqaddima, 7; Musnad, i, 176, 183; iii, 110, 165, 199, 209, 225; iv, 20, 327, 328; v, 416, 421, 422.*

interlinked by unseen chains. If, despite all this, you prefer things worthless and transient as a spider's web that give rise to dispute and discord, to rancor and enmity, and engage in true enmity towards a believer, then you will understand—unless your heart is dead and your intelligence extinguished—how great is your disrespect for that bond of unity, your slight to that relation of love, your transgression against that tie of brotherhood!

Third aspect

In accordance with the meaning of the verse, *No bearer of burdens can bear the burden of another, (Al-An'am 6:164)* which expresses pure justice, to nurture rancor and enmity towards a believer is like condemning all the innocent attributes found in him on account of one criminal attri- bute, and is hence an act of great injustice. If you go further and include in your enmity all the relatives of a believer on account of a single evil attribute of his, then, in accordance with the following verse in which the active participle is in the intensive form, *Verily man is much given to wrongdoing (Ibrahim 14:34)* you will have committed a still greater sin and transgression, against which truth, the Sharia and the wisdom of Islam combine to warn you. How then can you imagine yourself to be right, and say: "I am in the right"?

In the view of truth, the cause for enmity and all forms of evil is in itself evil and is dense like clay: it cannot infect or pass on to others. If someone learns from it and commits evil, that is another question. Good qualities that arouse love are luminous like love; it is part of their function to be transmitted and produce effects. It is for this reason that the proverb has come into being, "The friend of a friend is a friend," and also that it is said, "Many eyes are beloved on account of one eye."

So, O unjust man! If such be the view of truth, you will understand now, if you have the capacity for seeing the truth, how great an offence it is to cherish enmity for the likeable and innocent brothers and relatives of a man you dislike.

Fourth aspect

It is a sin from the point of view of personal life. Listen to the following four principles which are the base of this Fourth Aspect.

First Principle: When you know your way and opinions to be true, you have the right to say, "My way is right and the best." But you do not have the right to say, "Only my way is right." According to the sense of "The eye of contentment is too dim to perceive faults; it is the eye of anger that exhibits all vice;"[83] your unjust view and distorted opinion cannot be the all-decisive judge and cannot condemn the belief of another as invalid.

Second Principle: It is your right that all that you say should be true, but not that you should say all that is true. For one of insincere intention may sometimes take unkindly to advice, and react against it unfavorably.

Third Principle: If you wish to nourish enmity, then direct it against the enmity in your heart, and attempt to rid yourself of it. Be an enemy to your evil-commanding soul and its caprice and attempt to reform it, for it inflicts more harm on you than all else. Do not engage in enmity against other believers on account of that injurious soul. Again, if you wish to cherish enmity, there are unbelievers and atheists in great abundance; be hostile to them. In the same way that the attribute of love is fit to receive love as its response, so too enmity will receive enmity as its own fitting response. If you wish to defeat your enemy, then respond to his evil with good. For if you respond with evil, enmity will increase, and even though he will be outwardly defeated, he will nurture hatred in his heart, and hostility will persist. But if you respond to him with good, he will repent and become your friend. The meaning of the lines: *If you treat the noble nobly, he will be yours, and if you treat the vile nobly, he will revolt,*[84] is that it is the mark of the believer to be noble, and he will become submitted to you by noble treatment. And even if someone is apparently ignoble, he is noble with respect to his belief. It often happens that if you tell an evil man, "You are good, you are good," he will be-

83   'Ali Mawardi, *Adab al-Dunya wa ad-Din, 10; Diwan al-Shafi'i, 91.*

84   Mutanabi, See *Al-'Urf al-Tayyib fi Sharh Diwan at-Tayyib, 387.*

come good; and if you tell a good man, "You are bad, you are bad," he will become bad. Hearken, therefore, to these sacred principles of the Qur'an, for happiness and safety are to be found in them:

> If they pass by futility, they pass by it in honorable disdain. (Al-Furqan 25:72)
> If you forgive, pardon, and relent, verily God is All-Relenting, Merciful. (At-Taghabun 64:14)

Fourth Principle: Those who cherish rancor and enmity transgress against their own souls, their brother believer, and Divine mercy. For such a person condemns his soul to painful torment with his rancor and enmity. He imposes torment on his soul whenever his enemy receives some bounty, and pain from fear of him. If his enmity arises from envy, then it is the most severe form of torment. For envy in the first place consumes and destroys the envier, and its harm for the one envied is either slight or non-existent.

The cure for envy: Let the envious reflect on the ultimate fate of those things that arouse his enmity. Then he will understand that the beauty, strength, rank, and wealth possessed by his rival are transient and tem- porary. Their benefit is slight, and the anxiety they cause is great. If it is a question of personal qualities that will gain him reward in the Hereafter, they cannot be an object of envy. But if one does envy another on account of them, then he is either himself a hypocrite, wishing to destroy the goods of the Hereafter while yet in this world, or he imagines the one whom he envies to be a hypocrite, thus being unjust towards him.

If he rejoices at the misfortunes he suffers and is grieved by the bounties he receives, it is as if he is offended by the kindness shown towards him by Divine Determining and Divine Mercy, as if he were criticizing and objecting to them. Whoever criticizes Divine Determining is striking his head against an anvil on which it will break, and whoever objects to Divine Mercy will himself be deprived of it.

How might justice and sound conscience accept that the response to something worth not even a day's hostility should be a year's rancor and hostility? You cannot condemn a brother believer for some evil you experience at his hand for the following reasons:

Firstly, Divine Determining has a certain share of responsibility. It is necessary to deduct that share from the total and respond to it with contentment and satisfaction.

Secondly, the share of the soul and Satan should also be deducted, and one should pity the man for having been overcome by his soul and await his repentance instead of becoming his enemy.

Thirdly, look at the defect in your own soul that you do not see or do not wish to see; deduct a share for that too. As for the small share which then remains, if you respond with forgiveness, pardon, and magnanimity, in such a way as to conquer your enemy swiftly and safely, then you will have escaped all sin and harm. But if, like some drunken and crazed person who buys up fragments of glass and ice as if they were diamonds, you respond to worthless, transient, temporary, and insignificant happenings of this world with violent enmity, permanent rancor, and perpetual hostility, as if you were going to remain in the world with your enemy for all eternity, it would be extreme transgression, sinfulness, drunkenness, and lunacy.

If then you love yourself, do not permit this harmful hostility and desire for revenge to enter your heart. If it has entered your heart, do not listen to what it says. Hear what truth-seeing *Hafiz* of Shiraz says: "The world is not a commodity worth arguing over." It is worthless since it is transient and passing. If this is true of the world, then it is clear how worthless and insignificant are the petty affairs of the world! *Hafiz* also said: "The tranquility of both worlds lies in the understanding of these two words: generosity towards friends, forbearance towards enemies."

Question: "I have no choice, there is enmity within my disposition. I cannot overlook those who antagonize me."

Answer: If evil character and bad disposition do not exhibit any trace, and you do not act with ill intention, there is no harm. If you have no choice in the matter, then you are unable to abandon your enmity. If you recognize your defect and understand that you are wrong to have that attribute, it will be a form of repentance and seeking of forgiveness for you, thus delivering you from its evil effects. In fact, we have written this Topic of the Letter in order to make possible such a seeking of forgiveness, to distinguish right from wrong, and to prevent enmity from being displayed as rightful.

A case worthy of notice: I once saw, as a result of biased partisanship, a pious scholar of religion going so far in his condemnation of another scholar with whose political opinions he disagreed as to imply that he was an unbeliever. He also praised with respect a dissembler who shared his own opinions. I was appalled at these evil results of political involvement. I said: "I take refuge with God from Satan and politics," and from that time on withdrew from politics.

Fifth aspect

Obstinacy and partisanship are extremely harmful in social life.

Question: There is a Hadith which says: 'Difference among my people is an instance of Divine Mercy,'[85] and difference requires partisanship.

The sickness of partisanship also delivers the oppressed common people from the oppressor elite, for if the elite of a town or village join together, they will destroy the oppressed common people. If there is partisanship, the oppressed may seek refuge with one of the parties and thus save himself.

It is also from the confrontation of opinions and the contradiction of views that truth becomes apparent in its full measure."

Answer to the first part of the question: The difference intended in the Hadith is a positive difference. That is, each party strives to promote and diffuse its own belief; it does not seek to tear down and destroy that of the other, but rather to improve and reform it. Negative difference is rejected by the Hadith, for it aims in partisan and hostile fashion at mutual destruction, and those who are at each other's throats cannot act positively.

To the second part of the question, we say: If partisanship is in the name of truth, it can become a refuge for those seeking their rights. But as for the partisanship obtaining now, biased and self-centered, it can only be a refuge for the unjust and a point of support for them. For if a devil comes to a man engaged in biased partisanship, encourages him in his ideas and takes his side, that

---

[85]   Al-'Ajluni, *Kashf al-Khafa, 64; Al-Manawi, Fayd al-Qadir, i, 210–12.*

man will call down God's blessings on the Devil. But if the opposing side is joined by a man of angelic nature, then he will—may God protect us!—go so far as to invoke curses upon him.

To the third part of the question, we say: If the confrontation of views takes place in the name of justice and for the sake of truth, then the difference concerns only means; there is unity with respect to aim and basic purpose. Such a difference makes manifest every aspect of the truth and serves justice and truth. But what emerges from a confrontation of views that is partisan and biased, and takes place for the sake of a tyrannical, evil-commanding soul, that is based on egotism and fame-seeking—what emerges from this is not the 'flash of truth,' but the fire of dissension. Unity of aim is necessary, but opposing views of this kind can never find a point of convergence anywhere on earth. Since they do not differ for the sake of the truth, they multiply *ad infinitum*, and give rise to divergences that can never be reconciled.

In short, if one does not make of the exalted rules, "Love for the sake of God, dislike for the sake of God, judgment for the sake of God"[86] the guiding principles of one's conduct, dispute and discord will result. If one does not say, "dislike for the sake of God, judgment for the sake of God" and take due account of those principles, one's attempts to do justice will result in injustice.

An event with an important lesson: Imam 'Ali, may God be pleased with him, once threw an unbeliever to the ground. As he drew his sword to kill him, the unbeliever spat in his face. He released him without killing him. The unbeliever said: "Why did you not kill me?" He replied: "I was going to kill you for the sake of God. But when you spat at me, I became angered and the purity of my intention was clouded by the inclinations of my soul. It is for this reason that I did not kill you." The unbeliever replied: "If your religion is so pure and disinterested, it must be the truth."

An occurrence worthy of note: When once a judge showed signs of anger while cutting off the hand of a thief, the just ruler who chanced to observe him dismissed him from his post. For if he had cut the hand in the name of the Sharia, his soul would have felt pity for the

---

[86]   *Bukhari, Iman, 1; Abu Dawud, Sunna, 2; Musnad, v, 146.*

victim; he would have cut it off in a manner devoid of both anger and mercy. Since the inclinations of his soul had had some share in his deed, he did not perform the act with justice.

A regrettable social condition and an awesome disease affecting the life of society, fit to be wept over by the heart of Islam is to forget and abandon internal enmities when foreign enemies appear and attack is a demand of social welfare recognized and enacted even by the most primitive peoples. What then ails those who claim to be serving the Islamic community that at a time when numberless enemies are taking up positions to attack, one after the other, they fail to forget their petty enmities, and instead prepare the ground for the enemies' attacks? It is disgraceful savagery, and treason committed against the social life of Islam.

A story to be pondered over: There were two groups of the Hasanan, a tribe of nomads, hostile to each other. Although more than maybe fifty people had been killed on each side, when another tribe such as the Sibgan or Haydaran came out against them, those two hostile groups would forget their enmity and fight together, shoulder to shoulder, until the opposing tribe had been repelled, without ever once recalling their internal dissensions.

O Believers! Do you know how many tribes of enemies have taken up position to attack the tribe of the people of belief? There are more than a hundred of them, like a series of concentric circles. The believers are obliged to take up defensive positions, each supporting the other and giving him a helping hand. Is it then at all fitting for the people of belief that with their biased partisanship and hostile rancor they should facilitate the attack of the enemy and fling open the doors for him to penetrate the fold of Islam? There are maybe seventy circles of enemies, including the misguided, the atheist, and the unbeliever, each of them as harmful to you as all the terrors and afflictions of this world, and each of them regarding you with greed, anger and hatred. Your firm weapon, shield and citadel against all of them is none other than the brotherhood of Islam. So realize just how contrary to conscience and to the interests of Islam it is to shake the citadel of Islam on account of petty hostilities and other pretexts! Know this, and come to your senses!

According to a noble Hadith of the Prophet, peace be upon him, noxious and awesome persons like the Dajjal[87] and Sufyan[88] will come to rule over the godless at the end of time, and exploiting the greed, discord and hatred amongst the Muslims and mankind, they will need only a small force to reduce humanity to anarchy and the vast world of Islam to slavery.

O people of faith! If you do not wish to enter a humiliating condition of slavery, come to your senses and enter and take refuge in the citadel of *Indeed the believers are brothers (Al-Hujurat 49:10)* to defend yourselves against those oppressors who would exploit your differences! Otherwise you will be able neither to protect your lives nor to defend your rights. It is evident that if two champions are wrestling with each other, even a child can beat them. If two mountains are balanced in the scales, even a small stone can disturb their equilibrium and cause one to rise and the other to fall. So O people of belief! Your strength is reduced to nothing as a result of your passions and biased partisanships, and you can be defeated by the slightest forces. If you have any interest in your social solidarity, then make of the exalted principle of "The believers are together like a well-founded building, one part of which supports the other"[89] your guiding principle in life! Then you will be delivered from humiliation in this world and wretchedness in the Hereafter.

Sixth aspect

Spiritual life and correctness of worship will suffer as a result of enmity and rancor, since the purity of intention that is the means of

---

[87]   Al-Dajjal, the Antichrist, is a fierce opponent of Jesus. He is a person rebelling against Divine revelation and the Prophet. See Zeki Sarıtoprak, 'Islam's Jesus', (2014) at 94.

[88]   'Sufyan is an irreligious person who is believed to emerge among Muslims to try to destroy Islam.

[89]   *Bukhari, Salah, 88; Adab, 36; Mazalim, 5; Muslim, Birr, 65; Tirmidhi, Birr, 18; Nasa'i, Zakat, 67; Musnad, vi, 104, 405, 409.*

salvation will be damaged. For a biased person will desire superiority over his enemy in the good deeds that he performs and will be unable to act purely for the sake of God. He will also prefer, in his judgment and dealings, the one who takes his side; he will be unable to be just. Thus the purity of intention and the justice that are the bases of all good acts and deeds will be lost on account of enmity and hostility.

The Sixth Aspect is extremely complex, but we will cut it short here since this is not the place to enlarge on it.

GREED

In the Name of God, the All-Merciful, the All-Compassionate.

Surely God it is He Who is the All-Providing, Lord of all might, and the All-Forceful. (Adh-Dhariyat 51:58)

How many a living creature there is that does not carry its own

provision (in store), but God provides for them, and indeed for you.

He is the All-Hearing, the All-Knowing. (Al-Ankabut 29:60)

O people of belief! You will have understood by now how harmful is enmity. Understand too that greed is another terrible disease, as harmful for the life of Islam as enmity. Greed brings about disappointment, deficiency, and humiliation; it is the cause of deprivation and abjection. The humiliation and abjection of the Jews, who more than any other people have leaped greedily upon the world, is a decisive proof of this truth. Greed demonstrates its evil effects throughout the animate world, from the most universal of species to the most particular of individuals. To seek out one's sustenance while placing one's trust in God will, by contrast, bring about tranquility and demonstrate everywhere its beneficent effects.

Thus, fruit trees and plants, which are a species of animate be-ing insofar as they require sustenance, remain contentedly rooted where they are, placing their trust in God and not evincing any greed; it is for this reason that their sustenance hastens toward them. They breed too far more offspring than do the animals. The animals, by contrast, pursue their sustenance greedily, and for this reason are able to attain it only imperfectly and at the cost of great effort. With-in the animal kingdom it is only the young who, as it were, evince their trust in God by proclaiming their weakness and impotence; hence it is that they receive in full measure their rightful and del-icate sustenance from the treasury of Divine mercy. But savage beasts that pounce greedily on their sustenance can hope only for an illicit and coarse sustenance, attained through the expenditure of great effort. These two examples show that greed is the cause of deprivation, while trust in God and contentment are the means to God's mercy.

In the human kingdom, the Jews have clung to the world more greedily and have loved its life with more passion than any other people, but the usurious wealth they have gained with great efforts is merely illicit property over which they exercise temporary stewardship, and it benefits them little. It earns them, on the contrary, the blows of abjection and humiliation, of death and insult, that are rained down on them by all peoples. This shows that greed is a source of humiliation and loss. There are in addition so many instances of a greedy person being exposed to loss that "the greedy is subject to disappointment and loss" has become a universally accepted truth. This being the case, if you love wealth, seek it not with greed but with contentment, so that you may have it in abundance. The content and the greedy are like two men who enter the audience-hall of a great personage. One of them says to himself: "It is enough that he should admit me so that I can escape from the cold outside. Even if he motions me to sit in the lowest position, I will count it as a kindness." The second man says arrogantly, as if he had some right in the matter and everyone were obliged to respect him: "I should be assigned the highest position." He enters with greed and fixes his gaze on the highest positions, wishing to advance toward them. But the master of the audience-hall turns him back and seats him in a lower position. Instead of thanking him as he should, he is angered against him in his heart and criticizes him. The lord of the palace will be offended by him.

The first man enters most humbly and wishes to sit in the lowest position. His modesty pleases the lord of the audience-hall, and he invites him to sit in a higher position. His gratitude increases, and his thankfulness is augmented.

Now this world is like an audience-hall of the Most Merciful One. The surface of the globe is like a banqueting spread laid out by His mercy. The differing degrees of sustenance and grades of bounty correspond to the seating positions in the audience-hall.

Furthermore, even in the most minute of affairs everyone can experience the evil effects of greed. For example, everyone knows in his heart that when two beggars request something, he will be offended by the one who greedily importunes him, and refuse his request; whereas he will take pity on the peaceable one and give him what he asks.

Or to give another example, if you are unable to fall asleep at night and

wish to do so, you may succeed if you remain detached. But if you desire sleep greedily, and say: "Let me sleep, let me sleep," then sleep will quit you entirely.

Yet another example is this, that if you greedily await the arrival of someone for some important purpose and continually say: "He still hasn't come," ultimately you will lose patience and get up and leave. But one minute later the person will come, and your purpose will be frustrated.

The reason for all this is as follows. The production of a loaf of bread requires a field to be cultivated and harvested, the grain to be taken to a mill, and the loaf to be baked in an oven. So too in the arrangement of all things there is a certain slow deliberation decreed by God's wisdom. If on account of greed one fails to act with slow deliberation, one will fail to no- tice the steps one must mount in the arrangement of all things; he will either fall or be unable to traverse the steps, and in either event will not reach his goal.

O brothers giddied by preoccupation with your livelihood, and drunk on your greed for this world! Greed is harmful and pernicious; how is it then that you commit all kinds of abject deed for the sake of your greed; accept all kinds of wealth, without concern for licit or illicit; and sacrifice much of the Hereafter? On account of your greed you even abandon one of the most important pillars of Islam, the payment of *zakat*, although *zakat* is for everyone a means of attracting plenty and repelling misfortune. The one who does not pay *zakat* is bound to lose the amount of money he would otherwise have paid: either he will spend it on some useless object, or it will be taken from him by some misfortune.

In a veracious dream that came to me during the fifth year of the First

World War, the following question was put to me:

"What is the reason for this hunger, financial loss, and physical trial that now afflicts the Muslims?"

I replied in the dream:

"From the wealth He bestows upon us, God Almighty required from us either a tenth or a fortieth[90] so that we may benefit from the grateful prayers of the poor, and rancor and envy may be prevented. But in our greed and covetousness we refused to give *zakat*, and God Almighty has taken from us a thirtieth where a fortieth was owed, and an eighth where a tenth was owed.

"He required of us to undergo, for no more than one month each year, a hunger with seventy beneficial purposes. But we took pity on our instinctual souls, and did not undergo that temporary pleasurable hunger God Almighty then punished us by compelling us to fast for five years, with a hunger replete with seventy kinds of misfortune.

"He also required of us, out of each period of twenty-four hours, one hour to be spent in a form of Divine drill, pleasing and sublime, luminous and beneficial. But in our laziness we neglected the duty of prayer. That single hour was joined to the other hours and wast-

---

[90]   A tenth, that is, or wealth like corn that every year yields a new crop; and a fortieth of whatever yielded a commercial profit in the course of the year.

ed. As penance, God Almighty then caused us to undergo a form of drill and physical exertion that took the place of prayer."

I then awoke, and upon reflection realized that an extremely important truth was contained in that dream. As proven and explained in the Twenty-Fifth Word, when comparing modern civilization with the principles of the Qur'an, all immorality and instability in the social life of man proceeds from two sources:

The First: "Once my stomach is full, what do I care if others die of hunger?"

The Second: "You work, and I will eat."

That which perpetuates these two is the prevalence of usury and interest on the one hand, and the abandonment of zakat on the other. The only remedy able to cure these two awesome social diseases lies in implementing zakat as a universal principle and in forbidding usury. Zakat is a most essential support of happiness not merely for individuals and particular societies, but for all of humanity. There are two classes of men: the upper classes and the common people. It is only zakat that will induce compassion and generosity in the upper classes toward the common people, and respect and obedience in the common people toward the upper classes. In the absence of zakat, the upper classes will descend on the common people with cruelty and oppression, and the common people will rise up against the upper classes in rancor and rebellion. There will be a constant struggle, a persistent opposition between the two classes of men. It will finally result in the confrontation of capital and labor, as happened in Russia.

O people of nobility and good conscience! O people of generosity and liberality! If acts of generosity are not performed in the name of zakat, there are three harmful results. The act may have no effect, for if you do not give in the name of God, you are in effect imposing an obligation, and imprisoning some wretched pauper with a sense of obligation. Then you will be deprived of his prayer, a prayer which would be most acceptable in the sight of God. In reality you are nothing but an official entrusted with the distribution of God Almighty's bounties among His servants; but if you imagine yourself to be the owner of wealth, this is an act of ingratitude for the bounties you have received. If, on the contrary, you give in the name of *zakat*, you will be rewarded for having given in the name of God Almighty; you will have offered thanks for bounties received. The needy person too will not be compelled to fawn and cringe in front of you; his self-respect will not be injured, and his prayer on your behalf will be accepted. See how great is the difference between, on the one hand, giving as much as one would in *zakat*, but earning nothing but the harm of hypocrisy, fame, and the imposition of obligation; and, on the other hand, performing the same good deeds in the name of *zakat*, and thereby fulfilling a duty, and gaining a reward, the virtue of sincerity, and the prayers of those whom you have benefited?

> Glory be unto You; we have no knowledge save that which you have taught us; indeed, you are All-Knowing, All-Wise. (Al-Baqarah 2:32)

O God, grant blessings and peace to our master Muhammad, who said: "The believer is with respect to the believer like a firm building, of which one part supports the other," and who said too that "Contentment is a treasure that never perishes,"[91] and to his Family and his Companions. And praise be to God, the Sustainer of All the Worlds.

BACKBITING

In his Name, be He glorified!

And there is nothing but it glorifies Him with praise.

In *The Words*,[92] a single Qur'anic verse having the effect of discouraging and restraining was shown to induce repugnance at backbiting in six miraculous ways. It was shown too how abominable a thing is backbiting in the view of the Qur'an, and that there is therefore no need for any further explanation of the subject. Indeed, after the Qur'an has made its declaration, there is neither the possibility nor the need for anything further.

---

[91]   'Suyuti, *Al-Fath al-Kabir, ii, 309; Ahmad al-Hashimi, Mukhtar al-Ahadith an-Nabawiya, Istanbul, 1967, 99.*

[92]   Nursi, *The Words* at 169.

The Qur'an reproaches the backbiter with six reproaches in the verse, *Would any among you like to eat the flesh of his dead brother?* *(Al-Hujurat 49:12)* and forbids him to commit this sin with six degrees of severity. When the verse is directed to those persons actually engaged in backbiting, its meaning is the following.

As is well-known, the *hamza* at the beginning of the verse has an interrogative sense. This interrogative sense penetrates all the words of the verse like water, so that each word acquires an additional meaning. Thus the first word asks, with its *hamza*: "Is it that you have no intelligence capable of discrimination, so that you fail to perceive the ugliness of this thing?"

The second word *like* asks: "Is your heart, the seat of love and hatred,

so corrupted that it loves the most repugnant of things?"

The third word *any among you* asks: "What befell your sense of social and civilized responsibility that you are able to accept something poisonous to social life?"

The fourth word *to eat the flesh* asks: "What has befallen your sense of humanity that you are tearing your friend apart with your fangs like a wild animal?"

The fifth word *of his brother* asks: "Do you have no fellow-feeling, no sense of kinship, that you are able to sink your teeth into some wretch who is tied to you by numerous links of brotherhood? Do you have no intelligence that you are able to bite into your own limbs with your own teeth, in such lunatic fashion?"

The sixth word *dead* asks: "Where is your conscience? Is your nature so corrupt that you abandon all respect and act so repugnantly as to consume your brother's flesh?"

According then to the total sense of the verse, as well as the indications of each of its words, slander and backbiting are repugnant to the intelligence and the heart, to humanity and conscience, to nature and social consciousness.

You see then that the verse condemns backbiting in six miraculous degrees and restrains men from it in six miraculous ways. Backbiting is the vile weapon most commonly used by the people of enmity, envy, and obstinacy, and the self-respecting people will never stoop to employing so unclean a weapon. Some celebrated person once said: "I never stoop to vexing my enemy with backbiting, for backbiting is the weapon of the weak, the low, and the vile."

Backbiting consists of saying that which would be a cause of dislike and displeasure to the person in question if he were to be present and hear it. Even if what is said is true, it is still backbiting. If it is a lie, then it is both backbiting and slander and a doubly loathsome sin.

Backbiting can be permissible in a few special instances:

First: If a complaint be presented to some official, so that with his help evil be removed and justice restored.

Second: If a person contemplating co-operation with another comes to seek your advice, and you say to him, purely for the sake of his benefit and to advise him correctly, without any self-interest: "Do not co-operate with him; it will be to your disadvantage."

Third: If the purpose is not to expose someone to disgrace and notoriety, but simply to make people aware, and one says: "That foolish, confused man went to such-and-such a place."

Fourth: If the subject of backbiting is an open and unashamed sinner; is not troubled by evil, but on the contrary takes pride in the sins he commits; finds pleasure in his wrongdoing; and unhesitatingly sins in the most evident fashion.

In these particular cases, backbiting may be permissible, if it be done without self-interest and purely for the sake of truth and communal welfare. But apart from them, it is like a fire that consumes good deeds like a flame eating up wood.

If one has engaged in backbiting, or willingly listened to it, one should say: "O God, forgive me and him concerning whom I spoke ill," and say to the subject of backbiting, whenever one meets him: "Forgive me."

The Enduring One, He is the Enduring One

Saïd Nursi

CHAPTER 9

SINCERITY

In the Name of God, the All-Merciful, the All-Compassionate.

Verily We sent the Book down to you in truth, so worship God in

sincerity, for God's is sincerely practiced religion. (Az-Zumar 39:2)

All men will perish, except the scholars, and all scholars will perish except those who act in accordance with their knowledge, and all of them will perish except the sincere, and even the sincere are in great danger.[93]

The above verse and the noble saying of the Prophet (*hadith*) demonstrate together how important a principle of Islam is sincerity. From among the innumerable points concerning sincerity, we will briefly expound only five.

> **Note:** An auspicious sign of blessed Isparta which causes one to offer thanks is that compared with other places, there is no visible rivalry and dispute

---

[93]   Al-Ajluni, *Kashf al-Khafa, 2:415; Al-Ghazzali, Ihya 'Ulum ad-Din, 3:414.*

between the pious, those who follow the Sufi path, and the religious scholars. Even if the required true love and union is not present, comparatively speaking, there is no harmful rivalry and conflict.

First Point

Question: Why is it that while the worldly and the neglectful, and even the misguided and hypocrites, co-operate without rivalry, the people of religion, the religious scholars, and those who follow the Sufi path, oppose each other in rivalry, although they are the people of truth and concord? Agreement belongs in reality to the people of concord and dispute to the hypocrites; how is it that these two have changed places?

Answer: We will set forth seven of the extremely numerous causes of this painful, disgraceful and awesome situation, one that causes the zealous to weep.

First Cause

Just as dispute among the people of the truth does not arise from lack of the truth, so too the agreement prevailing among the people of neglect does not arise from any possession of truth. Rather it is that a specific duty and particular function has been assigned to the classes in society, like 'the worldly', those engaged in politics, and those who have received a secular education, and thus the functions of the various groups, societies, and communities have been defined and become distinguished from one another. Similarly, the material reward they are to receive for their functions in order to maintain a livelihood, as well as the moral reward that consists in the attention they receive from men for the sake of their ambition and pride-this too is established and specified.[94] There is therefore nothing held in

---

[94] Be aware that the attention of men cannot be demanded, but only given. If it is given, one should not delight in it. If one delights in it, sincerity is lost and hypocrisy takes its place. The attention of men, if accompanied by the desire for honor and fame, is not a reward and a prize, but a reproach and chastisement for lack of sincerity. Such attention of men, such honor and fame, harm sincerity, the source of vitality for all good deeds, and even though they yield a slight

common to the degree that it might produce conflict, dissension and rivalry. However evil be the path that they tread, they will be able to preserve unity and agreement.

But as for the people of religion, the scholars, and those who follow the path, the duty of each is concerned with all men; their material reward is not set and specified; and their share in social esteem and acceptance and public attention is not predetermined. Many may be candidates for the same position; many hands may stretch out for each moral and material reward that is offered. Hence it is that conflict and rivalry arise; concord is changed into discord, and agreement into dispute.

Now the cure and remedy for this appalling disease is sincerity. Sincerity may be attained by preferring the worship of God to the worship of one's own soul, by causing God's pleasure to vanquish the pleasure of the soul and the ego, and thus manifesting the meaning of the verse, *Verily my reward is from God alone (Hud 11:29)* by renouncing the material and moral reward to be had from men[95] and thus manifesting the meaning of the verse:

Nothing rests with the Messenger but to convey the Message fully. (It is your responsibility to act in accordance therewith and) God knows whatever you reveal and do openly, and whatever you conceal (in your bosoms) and do secretly. (Al-Maedah 5:99) and by

---

pleasure as far as the gate of the tomb, on the other side of that gate they take on the form of torment. One should not therefore desire the attention of men, but flee and shy away from it. Be warned, all you who worship fame and run after honor and rank!

[95] One should also take as one's guide the quality of preferring others to oneself, the same quality of the Companions that is praised in the Qur'an. For example, when giving a present or performing an act of charity, one should always prefer the recipient to oneself, and without demanding or inwardly desiring any material reward for religious service, know one's act to be purely God's grace and not impose a sense of obligation on men. Nothing worldly should be sought in return for religious service, for otherwise sincerity will be lost. Men have many rights and claims, and may even deserve zakat. But it cannot be demanded. When one receives something, it cannot be said that "This is the reward for my service." Rather in perfect contentment one should always prefer to oneself others who are more deserving. Thus manifesting the meaning of They prefer others to themselves, though poverty be their lot (al-Hashr, 59:9), one may be saved from this terrible danger and gain sincerity.

knowing that such matters as goodly acceptance, and making a fa-vorable impression, and gaining the attention of men are God's con-cern and a favor from Him, and that they play no part in conveying the message, which is one's own duty, nor are they necessary for it, nor is one charged with gaining them-by knowing this a person will be successful in gaining sincerity, otherwise it will vanish.

Second Cause

The agreement among the people of misguidance is on account of their abasement, and the dispute among the people of guidance is on account of their dignity. That is to say that the people of ne-glect-those misguided ones sunk in worldly concerns-are weak and abased because they do not rely on truth and reality. On account of their abasement, they need to augment their strength, and because of this need they wholeheartedly embrace the aid and co-operation of others. Even though the path they follow is misguidance, they preserve their agreement. It is as if they were making their godless-ness into a form of worship of the truth, their mis- guidance into a form of sincerity, their irreligion into a form of solidarity, and their hypocrisy into concord, and thus attaining success. For genuine sin-cerity, even for the sake of evil, cannot fail to yield results, and what-ever man seeks with sincerity, God will grant him it.[96]

But as for the people of guidance and religion, the religious schol-ars and those who follow the Sufi path, since they rely upon truth and reality, and each of them on the road of truth thinks only of his Sustainer and trusts in His help, they derive dignity from their belief. When they feel weakness, they turn not toward men, but toward God and seek help from Him. On account of difference in outlook, they feel no real need for the aid of the one whose outlook apparently opposes their own, and see no need for agreement and unity. Indeed, if obsti-nacy and egoism are present, one will imagine himself to be right and the other to be wrong; discord and rivalry take the place of concord and love. Thus sincerity is chased away and its function disrupted.

---

[96]   Yes, "Whoever seeks earnestly shall find" is a rule of truth. Its scope is compre-hensive and includes the matter under discussion.

Now the only remedy for the critical consequences of this terrible state consists of Nine Commands:

1. To act positively, that is, out of love for one's own outlook, avoiding enmity for other outlooks, not criticizing them, interfering in their beliefs and sciences, or in any way concerning oneself with them.

2. To unite within the fold of Islam, irrespective of particular outlook, remembering those numerous ties of unity that evoke love, brotherhood and concord.

3. To adopt the just rule of conduct that the follower of any right outlook has the right to say, "My outlook is true, or the best," but not that "My outlook alone is true," or that "My outlook alone is good," thus implying the falsity or repugnance of all other outlooks.

4. To consider that union with the people of truth is a cause of Divine help and the high dignity of religion.

5. To realize that the individual resistance of the most powerful person against the attacks through its genius of the mighty collective force of the people of misguidance and falsehood, which arises from their solidarity, will inevitably be defeated, and through the union of the people of truth, to create a joint and collective force also, in order to preserve justice and right in the face of that fearsome collective force of misguidance.

6. In order to preserve truth from the assaults of falsehood,

7. To abandon the self and its egoism,

8. And give up the mistaken concept of self-pride,

9. And cease from all insignificant feelings aroused by rivalry.

If this nine-fold rule is adhered to, sincerity will be preserved and its function perfectly performed.[97]

---

[97] It is even recorded in authentic *hadith of the Prophet that at the end of time the truly pious among the Christians will unite with the People of the Qur'an and fight their common enemy, irreligion. And at this time, too, the people of religion and truth need to unite sincerely not only with their own brothers and fellow believers, but also with the truly pious and spiritual ones the Christians, temporarily*

Third Cause

Disagreement among the people of truth does not arise from lack of zeal and aspiration, nor does union among the people of misguidance arise from loftiness of aspiration. That which impels the people of guidance to the misuse of their high aspiration and hence to disagreement and rivalry is the desire for heavenly reward that is counted as a praiseworthy quality in respect of the Hereafter, and extreme eagerness with respect to duties pertaining to the Hereafter. Thinking to oneself, "Let me gain this reward, let me guide these people, let them listen to me," he takes up a position of rivalry towards the true brother who faces him and who stands in real need of his love, assistance, brotherhood and aid. Saying to oneself, "Why are my pupils going to him? Why don't I have as many pu- pils as him?" he falls prey to egoism, inclines to the chronic disease of ambition, loses all sincerity, and opens the door to hypocrisy.

The cure for this error, this wound, this awesome sickness of the spirit, is the principle that "God's pleasure is won by sincerity alone," and not by a large following or great success. For these latter are functions of God's will; they cannot be demanded, although they are sometimes given. Sometimes a single word will result in someone's salvation and hence the pleasure of God. Quantity should not receive too much attention, for sometimes to guide one man to the truth may be as pleasing to God as guiding a thousand. Moreover sincerity and adherence to the truth require that one should desire the Muslims to benefit from anyone and at any place they can. To think "Let them take lessons from me so that I gain the reward" is a trick of the soul and the ego.

O man greedy for reward in the Hereafter and the performance of deeds entitling you to that reward! There have been certain Prophets who had only a limited following but received the infinite reward of the sacred duty of Prophethood. The true achievement lies, then, not in gaining a vast following, but in gaining God's pleasure. What do you imagine yourself to be, that saying, "Let everyone listen to me," you forget your function, and interfere in what

---

from the discussion and debate of points of difference in order to combat their joint enemy-aggressive atheism.

is strictly God's concern? To gain acceptance for you and to have people gather round you is God's concern. So look to your own duty and concern, and do not meddle with God's concerns.

Moreover, it is not only men who earn reward for those who hear and speak the truth. The sentient and spiritual beings of God and His angels have filled the universe and adorned its every part. If you want plentiful reward, take sincerity as your foundation and think only of God's pleasure. Then every syllable of the blessed words that issue forth from your mouth will be brought to life by your sincerity and truthful intention, and going to the ears of innumerable sentient beings, they will illumine them and earn you reward. For when, for example, you say, "Praise and thanks be to God," millions of these words, great and small, are written on the page of the air by God's leave. Since the All-Wise Inscriber did nothing prodigally or in vain, He created innumerable ears, as many as were needed to hear those multiple blessed words. If those words are brought to life in the air by sincerity and truthful intent, they will enter the ears of the spirit beings like some tasty fruit in the mouth. But if God's pleasure and sincerity do not bring those words to life, they will not be heard, and reward will be had only for the single utterance made by the mouth. Pay good attention to this, you Qur'an reciters who are sad that your voices are not more beautiful and that more people do not listen to you!

Fourth Cause

In just the same way that rivalry and disagreement among the people of guidance do not arise from failure to foresee consequences or from shortsightedness, so too wholehearted agreement among the people of misguidance does not result from farsightedness or loftiness of vision. Rather the people of guidance, through the influence of truth and reality, do not succumb to the blind emotions of the soul, and follow instead the farsighted inclinations of the heart and the intellect. Since, however, they fail to preserve their sense of direction and their sincerity, they are unable to maintain their high station and fall into dispute.

As for the people of misguidance, under the influence of the soul and caprice, and the dominance of sense-perception, which is blind to all consequences and always prefers an ounce of immediate pleasure to a ton of future pleasure, they come together in eager concord for the sake of instant benefit and immediate pleasure. Indeed, lowly and heartless worshippers of the ego are bound to congregate around worldly and immediate pleasures and benefits. It is true that the people of guidance have set their faces to the rewards of the Hereafter and its perfections, in accordance with the lofty instructions of the heart and the intellect, but even though a proper sense of direction, a complete sincerity and self-sacrificing union and concord are possible, because they have failed to rid themselves of egoism, and on account of deficiency and excess, they lose their union, that lofty source of power, and permit their sincerity to be shattered. Their duty in regard to the Hereafter is also harmed. God's pleasure is not had easily.

The cure and remedy for this serious disease is to be proud of the company of all those travelling the path of truth, in accordance with the principle of love for God's sake; to follow them and defer leadership to them; and to consider whoever is walking on God's path to be probably better than oneself, thereby breaking the ego and regaining sincerity. Salvation is also to be had from that disease by knowing that an ounce of deeds performed in sincerity is preferable to a ton performed without sincerity, and by preferring the status of a follower to that of a leader, with all the danger and responsibility that it involves. Thus sincerity is to be had, and one's duties of preparation for the Hereafter may be correctly performed.

Fifth Cause

Dispute and disagreement among the people of guidance are not the result of weakness, and the powerful union of the people of misguidance is not the result of strength. Rather the lack of union of the people of guidance comes from the power that results from the support provided by perfect belief, and the union of the people of neglect and misguidance comes from the weakness and impotence they experience as a result of their lack of any inward support. The weak form powerful unions precisely because of their need for union.[98] Since the strong do not feel a similar need, their unions are weak. Lions do not need union like foxes and therefore live as individuals, whereas wild goats form a herd to protect themselves against wolves. The community and collective personality of the weak is strong, and the community and collective personality of the strong is weak. There is a subtle allusion to this in the Qur'an in the *words, And women in the city said (Yusuf 12:30)* the verb *"said"* being in the masculine form, although it should be feminine for two reasons [women is a feminine noun, and also a plural-so-called 'broken' plurals in Arabic are always regarded as feminine]. But by contrast see the words, *the desert Arabs said (Al-Hujurat 49:14)* the verb said in this case being in the feminine, even though its subject designates a community of men. Herein lies an indication, that an association of weak, meek and soft women gains strength, toughness and force, and even acquires a certain kind of virility. The use of the masculine form of the verb is therefore most appropriate. Strong men, by contrast, and in particular Bedouin Arabs, trust in their own strength; therefore their associations are weak, for they assume a stance of softness and caution and take on a kind of femininity, for which the use of the feminine form of the verb is most suitable. Similarly the people of truth submit to and place their reliance in the firm source of support that is belief in God; hence they do not present their needs to others or request aid and assistance from them. If they do sometimes make the request, they will not adhere to the persons concerned at all cost. But the worldly ignore in their worldly affairs the true source of support; they fall into weakness and impotence, and experiencing an acute need of assistance, come together sacrificing themselves wholeheartedly.

The people of truth do not recognize and seek the true strength that is to be found in union; hence they fall into dispute, as an evil

---

[98] Among the most powerful and effective organizations in the West is the American Organization for Women's Rights and Liberty, even though women are called the fair sex, and are weak and delicate. Similarly, the organization of the Armenians, despite their weakness and small numbers when compared to other peoples, with its strong, self-sacrificing behavior, provides another proof of our observation.

and harmful consequence of this failure. By contrast, the people of misguidance and falsehood perceive the strength to be found in union, by virtue of their very weakness, and thus acquire union, that most important means for the attainment of all goals.

The cure and remedy for this disease of discord among the people of truth is to make one's rule of conduct the Divine prohibition contained in this verse, *Do not fall into dispute, lest you lose heart and your power de- part (Al-Anfal 8:46)* and the wise Divine command for social life contained in this verse, *Work together for the sake of virtue and piety (Al- Maedah 5:3)*

One must further realize how harmful to Islam dispute is, and how it helps the people of misguidance to triumph over the people of truth, and then, wholeheartedly and self-sacrificingly, join the caravan of the people of truth, with a sense of his own utter weakness and impotence. Finally, one must forget his own person, abandon hypocrisy and pretension, and lay hold of sincerity.

Sixth Cause

Discord among the people of truth does not arise from lack of manliness, aspiration and zeal; similarly, the wholehearted union among the misguided, neglectful and worldly with respect to their worldly affairs does not result from manliness, aspiration and zeal. It is rather that the people of truth are generally concerned with benefits to be had in the Hereafter and hence direct their zeal, aspiration and manliness to those important and numerous matters. Since they do not devote time-the true capital of man-to a single concern, their union with their fellows can never become firm. Their concerns are numerous and of a wide scope. As for the neglectful and worldly, they think only of the life of this world, and they firmly embrace the concerns of the life of this world with all their senses, their spirit and heart, and cling firmly to whoever aids them in those concerns. Like a mad diamond merchant who gives an exorbitant price for a piece of glass worth virtually nothing, they devote time, which is of the highest value, to matters which in reality and in the view of the people of truth are worth nothing. Paying such a high price and offering oneself with the devotion of all the senses will naturally result in a wholehearted sincerity that yields success in the matter at hand, so that the people of truth are defeated. As a result of this defeat, the people of truth decline into a state of abasement, humiliation, hypocrisy and ostentation, and sincerity is lost. Thus the people of truth are obliged to flatter and cringe before a handful of vile and lowly men of the world.

O people of truth! O people of the law, people of reality and people of the path, all worshipping God! Confronted by this awesome disease of discord, overlook each other's faults, close your eyes to each other's shortcomings! Behave according to the rule of courtesy established by the criterion that is the Qur'an in the verse, *When they pass by error, they pass by it with honorable avoidance (Al-Furqan 25:72).*

Regard it as your primary duty-one on which your state in the Hereafter depends-to abandon internal dissension when attacked by an enemy from the outside, and thereby to deliver the people of truth from their abasement and humiliation! Practice the brotherhood, love and co-operation insistently enjoined by hundreds of Qur'anic verses and traditions of the Prophet! Establish with all of your powers a union with your fellows and brothers in religion that is stronger than the union of the worldly! Do not fall into dispute! Do not say to yourself, "Instead of spending my valuable time on such petty matters, let me spend it on more valuable things such as the invocation of God and meditation;" then withdrawing and weakening unity. For precisely what you imagine to be a matter of slight importance in this moral *jihad* may in fact be very great. In just the same way that under certain special and unusual conditions the watch kept for one hour by a soldier may be equal to a whole year's worship, in this age when the people of truth have been defeated, the precious day that you spend on some apparently minor matter concerning the moral struggle may be worth a thousand days, just like the hour of that soldier. Whatever is undertaken for the sake of God cannot be divided into small and great, valuable and valueless. An atom expended in sincerity and for the sake of God's pleasure becomes like a star. What is important is not the nature of the means employed, but the result that it yields. As long as the result is God's pleasure and the substance employed is sincerity, any means to which recourse is had will be great, not small.

Seventh Cause

Dispute and rivalry among the people of truth do not arise from jealousy and greed for the world, and conversely union among the worldly and neglectful does not arise from generosity and magnanimity. It is rather that the people of truth are unable to preserve fully the magnanimity and high aspiration that proceed from the truth, or the laudable form of competition that exists on God's path. Infiltrated by the unworthy, they partially misuse that laudable form of competition and fall into rivalry and dispute, causing grave harm both to themselves and to the Islamic Community. As for the people of neglect and misguidance, in order not to lose the benefits with which they are infatuated and not to offend the leaders and companions they worship for the sake of benefit, in their utter humiliation, abasement and lack of manliness, they practice union at all costs with their companions, however abominable, treacherous and harmful they be, and wholeheartedly agree with their partners in whatever form may be dictated by their common interest. As a result of this wholeheartedness, they indeed attain the benefits desired.

So O people of truth given to dispute and afflicted with disaster! It is through your loss of sincerity and your failure to make God's pleasure your sole aim in this age of disaster that you have caused the people of truth to undergo this humiliation and defeat. In matters relating to religion and the Hereafter there should be no rivalry, envy or jealousy; indeed there can be none of these in truth. The reason for envy and jealousy is that when several hands reach out after a single object, when several eyes are fixed on a single position, when several stomachs hunger for a single loaf of bread, first envy arises as a result of conflict, dispute and rivalry, and then jealousy. Since many people desire the same thing in the world, and because the world, narrow and transitory as it is, cannot satisfy the limitless desires of man, people become rivals of each other. However, in the Hereafter a five-hundred-year para-dise will be given to a single individual; seventy thousand palaces and *houris*[99] will be granted to him; and every one of the people of Paradise will be perfectly satisfied with his share. It is thus clear that there is no cause for rivalry in the Hereafter, nor can there be rivalry. In that case, neither should there be any rivalry with respect to those good deeds that entail reward in the Hereafter; there is no room for jealousy here. The one jealous here is either a hypocrite, seeking worldly result through the performance of good deeds, or a sincere but ignorant devotee, not knowing the true purpose of good deeds and not comprehending that sincerity is the spirit and foundation of all good deeds. By cultivating a kind of rivalry and hostility toward God's saints, he is in fact placing in doubt the breadth of God's compassion.

An instance supporting this truth: One of my former compan-ions nurtured hostility to someone. His enemy's good deeds and sanctity were once favorably described in his presence. He was not jealous or upset. Then someone said, "That enemy of yours is cou-rageous and strong." We saw a strong vein of jealousy and rivalry suddenly appearing in that man. We said to him:

"Sanctity and righteousness bestow a strength and exaltation like a jewel of eternal life, yet you were not jealous of them. Now worldly strength is to be found in oxen, and courage in wild beasts; in comparison with sanctity and righteousness they are like a piece of glass compared to a diamond."

The man replied: "We have both fixed our eyes in this world on a single object. The steps that lead to it are provided by things such as courage and strength. It is for this reason that I was jealous of him. The objects and stations of the Hereafter are without number. Although he is my enemy here, there he can be my beloved and in-timate brother."

The Answer: In this world everyone has his private and tempo-rally limited world as broad as the world, the pillar of which is his life. He makes use of his world through his inner and outer senses. He says to himself, "The sun is my lamp, the stars are my candles." The

---

[99] Young women in Paradise.

existence of other creatures and animate beings in no way negates his ownership of these; on the contrary, they brighten and illumine his world. In the same way, although on an infinitely higher plane, in addition to the garden of each believer that contains thousands of palaces and *houris*, there is a private five-hundred-year paradise for everyone, apart from the general Paradise. He will benefit from this paradise and eternity through his senses and feelings, according to the degree of development they have reached. The fact that others share in the general Paradise in no way harms his ownership or benefit, but on the contrary strengthens these, and adorns that vast Paradise. Man in this world benefits from a garden lasting an hour, a spectacle lasting a day, a country lasting a month and a journey lasting a year, with his mouth, his ear, his eye, his taste and all his other senses. So too, in that realm of eternity, his sense of smell and touch, which in this transient world barely profit from a garden lasting an hour, will benefit as if from a garden lasting a year. The sense of sight and hearing which here barely profit from an excursion lasting a year, will there be able to benefit from a five-hundred-year excursion in a manner fitting that realm, adorned from end to end. Every believer will benefit there according to his spiritual rank, and gain delight and pleasure through his senses that will expand and develop in relation to the reward he has earned in this world and the good deeds he has performed.

O people of the truth and the path! The service of the truth is like carrying and preserving a great and weighty treasure. Those who carry that trust on their shoulders will be happy and grateful whenever powerful hands rush to their aid. Far from being jealous, one should proudly applaud the superior strength, effectiveness and capacity of those who in upright love come forward to offer their help. Why then look on true brothers and self-sacrificing helpers in a spirit of rivalry, thus losing sincerity? You will be exposed to fearsome accusations in the eyes of the people of misguidance, such as pursuing worldly interest through religion, even though it is something a hundred times lower than you and your belief, earning your livelihood through the knowledge of truth and rivaling others in greed and acquisitiveness.

The sole remedy for this disease is to accuse your own soul before others raise these charges, and always to take the side of your fellow, not your own soul. The rule of truth and equity established by the scholars of the art of debate is this: "Whoever desires, in debate on any subject, that his own word should turn out to be true, whoever is happy that he turns out to be right and his enemy to be wrong and mistaken-such a person has acted unjustly." Not only that, such a person loses, for when he emerges the victor in such a debate, he has not learned anything previously unknown to him, and his probable pride will cause him loss. But if his adversary turns out to be right, he will have learned something previously unknown to him and thereby gained something without any loss, as well as being saved from pride. In other words, one fair in his dealings and enamored of the truth will subject the desire of his own soul to the demands of the truth. If he sees his adversary to be right, he will accept it willingly and support it happily.

If then the people of religion, the people of truth, the people of the path, and the people of learning take this principle as their guide, they will attain sincerity, and be successful in those duties that prepare them for the Hereafter. Through God's mercy, they will be delivered from this appalling wretchedness and misfortune from which they presently suffer.

Glory be unto You! We have no knowledge save that which You have taught us; indeed You are All-Knowing, All Wise.

ON SINCERITY-2

This piece should be read at least once a fortnight.

In the Name of God, the All-Merciful, the All-Compassionate.

Do not dispute with one another, or else you may lose heart and your power and energy desert you; and remain steadfast. (Al-Anfal 8:46)

And stand before God in a devout [frame of mind].

(Al-Baqarah 2:238)

Truly he succeeds that purifies it,

And he fails that corrupts it. (Ash-Shams 91:9–10)

Nor sell my signs for a small price. (Al-Baqarah 2:41)

O my brothers of the Hereafter! And O my companions in the service of the Qur'an! You should know-and you do know-that in this world sincerity is the most important principle in works pertaining to the Hereafter in particular; it is the greatest strength, and the most acceptable intercessor, and the firmest point of support, and the shortest way to reality, and the most acceptable prayer, and the most wondrous means of achieving one's goal, and the highest quality, and the purest worship. Since in sincerity lies much strength and many lights like those mentioned above; and since at this dreadful time, despite our few number and weak, impoverished, and powerless state and our being confronted by terrible enemies and suffering severe oppression in the midst of aggressive innovations and misguidance, an extremely heavy, important, general, and sacred duty of serving belief and the Qur'an has been placed on our shoulders by Divine grace, we are certainly compelled more than anyone to work with all our strength to gain sincerity. We are in utter need of instilling sincerity in ourselves. Otherwise what we have achieved so far in our sacred service will in part be lost, and will not persist; and we shall be held responsible. We shall manifest the severe threat contained in the Divine prohibition, *nor sell my signs for a small price, (al-Baqarah 2:41)*and destroy sincerity, thus harming eternal happiness for the sake of meaningless, unnecessary, harmful, sad, self-centered, tedious, hypocritical base feelings and insignificant benefits. And in so doing we would violate all our brothers' rights, transgress against the duty of service to the Qur'an, and be disrespectful towards the sacredness of the truths of belief.

My brothers! There are many obstacles before great works of good. Satan puts up a powerful struggle against those who assist those works. One has to rely on the strength of sincerity in the face of these obstacles and satans. You should avoid things which harm sincerity the same as you avoid snakes and scorpions. In accordance with the words of Joseph, peace and blessings be upon him, *Nor do I absolve my own self [of blame]; the [human] soul is certainly prone to evil, unless my Sustainer do bestow His mercy (Yusuf 12:53)* the evil-commanding soul should not be relied on. Do not let egotism and the soul deceive you! You should take as your guide the following rules, in order to gain sincerity and preserve it:

Your First Rule

You should seek Divine pleasure in your actions. If Almighty God is pleased, it is of no importance even should the whole world be displeased. If He accepts an action and everyone else rejects it, it has no effect. Once His pleasure has been gained and He has accepted an action, even if you do not ask it of Him, should He wish it and His wisdom requires it, He will make others accept it. He will make them consent to it too. For this reason, the sole aim in this service should be the direct seeking of Divine pleasure.

Your Second Rule

This is not to criticize your brothers who are employed in this service of the Qur'an, and not to excite their envy by displaying superior virtues. For just as one of man's hands cannot compete with the other, neither can one of his eyes criticize the other, nor his tongue object to his ear, nor his heart see his spirit's faults. Each of his members completes the deficiencies of the others, veils their faults, assists their needs, and helps them out in their duties. Otherwise man's life would be extinguished, his spirit flee, and his body be dispersed.

Similarly, the components of machinery in a factory cannot compete with one another in rivalry, take precedence over each other, or dominate each other. They cannot spy out one another's faults and criticize each other, destroy the other's eagerness for work, and cause them to become idle. They rather assist each other's motions with all their capacity in order to achieve the common goal; they march towards the aim of their creation in true solidarity and unity. Should even the slightest aggression or desire to dominate interfere, it would throw the factory into confusion, causing it to be without product or result. Then the factory's owner would demolish the factory entirely.

And so, O *Risale-i Nur* students and servants of the Qur'an! You and I are members of a collective personality such as that, worthy of the title of 'perfect man.' We are like the components of a factory's machinery which produces eternal happiness within eternal life. We are hands working on a dominical boat which will disembark the Community of Muhammad, peace and blessings be upon him, at the Realm of Peace, the shore of salvation. So we are surely in need of solidarity and true union, obtained through gaining sincerity-for the mystery of sincerity secures through four individuals the moral strength of one thousand one hundred and eleven-indeed, we are compelled to obtain it.

Yes, if three Arabic first letter of *alifs* do not unite, they have the value of three. Whereas if they do unite, through the mystery of numbers they acquire the value of one hundred and eleven. If four times four remain apart, they have a value of sixteen. But if, through the mystery of brotherhood and having a common goal and joint duty, they unite coming together shoulder to shoulder on a line, they have the strength and value of four thousand four hundred and forty-four. Just as numerous historical events testify that the moral strength and value of sixteen self-sacrificing brothers have been greater than that of four thousand.

The underlying reason for this mystery is this: each member of a true and sincere union may see also with the eyes of the other brothers, and hear with their ears. As if each person of a true union of ten has the value and strength of seeing with twenty eyes, thinking with ten minds, hearing with twenty ears, and working with twenty hands.[100]

---

[100] 'Yes, heartfelt solidarity and union through the mystery of sincerity are the means to innumerable benefits, and so too are they an effective shield and point of support against fear, and even death. For, if death comes, it takes one spirit. But since through the mystery of true brotherhood on the way of Divine pleasure in works connected with the Hereafter there are spirits to the number of brothers, if one of them dies, he meets death happily, saying: "My other spirits remain alive, for they in effect make life contin- ue for me by constantly gaining reward for me, so I am not dying. By means of their spirits, I live in respect of merit; I am only dying in respect of sin." And he lays down in peace.

Your Third Rule

You should know that all your strength lies in sincerity and truth. Yes, strength lies in truth and sincerity. Even those who are wrong gain strength from their sincerity in their wrongdoing.

Evidence that strength lies in truth and sincerity is this service of ours. A small amount of sincerity in our work proves this claim and is evidence for itself. Because seven or eight years of service to learning and religion here has surpassed a hundredfold the twenty years of service I performed in my native region and in Istanbul. And in my own region and in Istanbul those assisting me were a hundred or even a thousand times more numerous than my brothers who work together with me here, where I am alone, with no one, a stranger, semi-literate, under the surveillance of unfair officials and persecuted by them. I have absolutely no doubt that the service I have carried out with you these seven or eight years and the moral strength which has resulted in success a hundred times greater than formerly, has resulted from the sincerity you have. I have also to confess that through your heartfelt sincerity, you have saved me to an extent from the hypocrisy which used to flatter my soul under the veil of fame and renown. God willing, you will be successful in gaining absolute sincerity, and you will cause me to gain it too.

You should be aware that Hadhrat Ali, may God be pleased with him, and *Ghawth al-A'zam,* may his mystery be sanctified, honor you with their miraculous wonder-working and wondrous vision of the Unseen because of this mystery of sincerity. They offer you consolation in protecting manner and applaud your service. Yes, you should have no doubt that this attention of theirs is because of sincerity. If you knowingly harm this sincerity, it is from them that you will receive punishment. You should bear in mind 'the blows of compassion' in the Tenth Flash in *The Flashes.*

If you want to have the support of spiritual heroes such as those behind you, and have them as masters at your head, gain complete sincerity in accordance with the verse, *But give them preference over themselves (Al-Hashr 59:9).* Choose your brothers' souls to your own soul in honor, rank, acclaim, in the things your soul enjoys like material benefits. Even in the most innocent, harmless benefits like informing a needy believer about one of the subtle, fine truths of belief. If possible, encourage one of your companions who does not want to, to inform him, so that your soul does not become conceited. If you have a desire like "Let me tell him this pleasant matter so I'll gain the reward," it surely is not a sin and there is no harm in it, but the meaning of sincerity between you could be damaged.

Your Fourth Rule

This is to imagine your brothers' virtues and merits in your own selves, and to thankfully take pride at their glory. The Sufis have terms they use among themselves, "annihilation in the sheikh," "annihilation in the Prophet;" I am not a Sufi, but these principles of theirs make a good rule in our way, in the form of "annihilation in the brothers." Among brothers this is called "*tafânî*;" that is, "annihilation in one another." That is to say, to forget the feelings of one's own carnal soul, and live in one's mind with one's brothers' virtues and feelings. In any event, the basis of our way is brotherhood. It is not the means which is between father and son, or sheikh and follower. It is the means of true brotherhood. At the very most a Master [*Ustad*] intervenes. Our way is the closest friendship. This friendship necessitates being the closest friend, the most sacrificing companion, the most appreciative comrade, the noblest brother. The essence of this friendship is true sincerity. One who spoils this true sincerity falls from the high pinnacle of this friendship. He may possibly fall to the bottom of a deep depression. There is nothing onto which he may cling in between.

Yes, the way is seen to be two. There is the possibility that those who part now from this way of ours, the great highway of the Qur'an, are unknowingly helping the forces of irreligion, who are hostile to us. God willing, those who enter the sacred bounds of the Qur'an of Miraculous Exposition by way of the *Risale-i Nur* will always add strength to light, sincerity, and belief, and will avoid such pitfalls.

O my companions in the service of the Qur'an! One of the

most effecetive means of attaining and preserving sincerity is "contemplation of death." Yes, like it is worldly ambition that damages sincerity and drives a person to hypocrisy and the world, so it is contemplation of death that causes disgust at hypocrisy and gains sincerity. That is, to think of death and realize that this world is transient, and so be saved from the tricks of the soul. Yes, through the instruction the Sufis and people of truth received from verses of the All-Wise Qur'an like, *Every soul shall taste death (Al-'Imran 3:185)* and *Truly you will die [one day], and truly they [too] will die [one day] (Az-Zumar 39:30)* they made the contemplation of death fundamental to their spiritual journeying, and dispelled the illusion of eternity, the source of worldly ambition. They imagined and conceived of themselves as dead and being placed in the grave. Through prolonged thought the evil-commanding soul becomes saddened and affected by such imagining and to an extent gives up its far-reaching ambitions and hopes. There are numerous advantages in this contemplation. The Hadith the meaning of which is, *"Frequently mention death which dispels pleasure and makes it bitter"*[101] teaches this contemplation.

However, since our way is not the Sufi path but the way of reality, we are not compelled to perform this contemplation in an imaginary and hypothetical form like the Sufis. To do so is anyway not in conformity with the way of reality. Our way is not to bring the future to the present by thinking of the end, but to go in the mind to the future from the present in respect of reality, and to gaze on it. Yes, having no need of imagination or conception, one may look on one's own corpse, the single fruit on the tree of this brief life. In this way, one may look on one's own death, and if one goes a bit further, one can see the death of this century, and going further still, observe the death of this world, opening up the way to complete sincerity.

The Second Means: Attaining a sense of the Divine presence through the strength of certain, verified belief and through the lights proceeding from reflective thought on creatures which leads to knowledge of the Maker; thinking that the Compassionate Creator is all-present

---

[101] *Tirmidhi, Zuhd 4; Qiyama 26; Nasa'i, Jana'iz 3; Ibn Majah, Zuhd 31; al-Hakim, Al-Mus- tadrak, iv, 321.*

and seeing; not seeking the attention of any other than He, and realizing that looking to others in His presence or seeking help from them is contrary to right con- duct in His presence; one may be saved from such hypocrisy and gain sincerity. However, there are many degrees and stages in this. However much a person may profit from his share, it is profit. Numerous truths are mentioned in the *Risale-i Nur* which will save a person from hypocrisy and gain him sincerity, so referring him to those, we cut short the discussion here.

Obstacles that destroy sincerity and drive one to hypocrisy

The first obstacle

Rivalry in regard to material advantages slowly destroys sincerity. It is also detrimental to the results of our service. So too it causes the material benefits to be lost. This nation has always nurtured respect for those who work for reality and the Hereafter, and assisted them. With the intention of actively sharing in their genuine sincerity and in the works they carry out devotedly, it has always showed respect by assisting them with material benefits like alms and gifts so that they should not become preoccupied with securing their material needs and wasting their time. But this assistance and benefit may not be sought; it is given. It may not even be sought through the tongue of disposition by desiring it with the heart or expecting it. It should rather be given when unexpected, otherwise sincerity will be harmed. It also approaches the prohibition of the verse, *Nor sell my signs for a small price (Al-Baqarah 2:41)* and in part destroys the action.

Thus, first desiring and expecting such a material benefit, then so as not to allow it to go to someone else, the evil-commanding soul selfishly excites a feeling of rivalry towards a true brother and companion in that particular service. Sincerity is damaged, and the sacredness of the service is lost, and the person becomes disagreeable in the eyes of the people of reality. He also loses the material benefit. This subject bears much discussion. However, I shall cut it short and only mention two examples which will strengthen sincerity and true union between my true brothers.

First Example: 'The worldly,' and even certain politicians and se-cret societies and manipulators of society, have taken as their guide the principle of shared property, in order to obtain great wealth and power. They acquire an extraordinary strength and advantage, despite all their exploitation and losses. However, the nature of common property does not change with sharing, despite its many harms. Although each partner is as though the owner and supervi-sor of the rest in one respect, he cannot profit from this.

Nevertheless, if this principle of shared property is applied to works pertaining to the Hereafter, it accumulates vast benefits which produce no loss. For it means that all the property passes to the hands of each partner. For example, there are four or five men. With the idea of sharing, one of them brings paraffin, another a wick, another the lamp, another the mantle, and the fifth match-es; they assemble the lamp and light it. Each of them becomes the owner of a complete lamp. If each of those partners has a full-length mirror on a wall, he will be reflected in it together with the lamp and room, without deficiency or being split up.

It is exactly the same with mutual participation in the goods of the Hereafter through the mystery of sincerity, and co-operation through the mystery of brotherhood, and joint enterprise through the mystery of unity-the total obtained through those joint acts, and all the light, enters the book of good deeds of each of those taking part. This is a fact and has been witnessed by the people of reality. It is also required by the breadth of Divine mercy and munificence.

And so, my brothers, God willing, material benefits will not pro-voke rivalry among you. It is possible that you might be deceived in regard to the benefits of the Hereafter like some of those who follow the Sufi path. But how can some personal, minor merit be compared with the merit and light manifested in respect of the shared actions mentioned in the above example?

Second Example: Craftsmen are obtaining significant wealth through co-operating in order to profit more from the products of their crafts. Formerly ten men who made sewing needles all worked on their own, and the fruit of their individual labor was three needles a day. Then in accordance with the rule of joint enterprise the ten men united. One brought the iron, one lit the furnace, one pierced the needles, one placed them in the furnace, and another sharpened the points, and so on... each was occupied with only part of the process of the craft of needle-making. Since the work in which he was employed was simple, time was not wasted, he gained skill, and performed the work with considerable speed. Then they divided up the work which had been in accordance with the rule of joint enterprise and the division of labor: they saw that instead of three needles a day, it worked out at three hundred for each man. This event was widely published among the craftsmen of 'the worldly' in order to encourage them to pool their labor.

And so, my brothers! Since union and accord in the matters of this world and in dense materials yield such results and huge total benefits, you can compare how vastly profitable it is for each to reflect in his own mirror through Divine grace the light of all, which is luminous and pertains to the Hereafter and does not need to be divided up and fragmented, and to gain the equivalent reward of all of them. This huge profit should not be lost through rivalry and insincerity.

The Second Obstacle that destroys sincerity

This is to flatter the ego and give high status to the evil-commanding soul through attracting attention to oneself and public acclaim, driven by the desire for fame, renown, and position. This is a serious spiritual sickness, so too it opens the door to the hypocrisy and self-centeredness called 'the hidden association of partners with God,' and damages sincerity.

My brothers! Our way in the service of the Qur'an is reality and brotherhood, and the true meaning of brotherhood is to annihilate one's personality among one's brothers[102] and to prefer their souls to one's own soul. Rivalry of this sort arising from desire for rank and position should not therefore be provoked. It is altogether

---

[102]   Yes, happy is he who, in order to gain access to a large pool of sweet water filtered from the spring of the Qur'an, casts his personality and egotism-which are like blocks of ice-into the pool and melts them.

opposed to our way. The brothers' honor may be all the individuals' generally; so I am hopeful that sacrificing that great collective honor for personal, selfish, competitive, minor fame and renown is far from being something the *Risale-i Nur* students would do. Yes, the heart, mind, and spirit of the *Risale-i Nur* students would not stoop to lowly, harmful, inferior things like that. But everyone has an evil-commanding soul, and sometimes the soul's emotions influence certain veins of character, and govern to an extent in spite of the heart, mind, and spirit; I am not accusing your hearts, minds, and spirits. I have confidence in you because of the effect of the *Risale-i Nur*. But the soul, desires, emotions, and imagination sometimes deceive. For this reason, you sometimes receive severe warnings. This severity looks to the soul, emotions, desires, and imagination; act cautiously.

Yes, if our way had been that of subjection to a sheikh, there would have been a single rank, or limited ranks, and numerous capacities would have been appointed to them. There could have been envy and selfishness. But our way is brotherhood. There can be no position of father among brothers, nor can they assume the position of spiritual guide. The rank in brotherhood is broad; it cannot be the cause of envious jostling. At the most brother helps and supports brother; he completes his service. Evidence that much harm and many mistakes have resulted from the envy, greed for spiritual reward, and high aspirations of the paths of spiritual guides are the conflict and rivalry among those who follow the Sufi path-their vast and significant attainments, perfections and benefits-which have had the disastrous consequence of that vast and sacred power of theirs being unable to withstand the gales of innovation.

The Third Obstacle

This is fear and greed. This obstacle has been expounded completely in the Six Attacks[103] together with certain other obstacles. We therefore refer you to that, and making all His Most Beautiful Names our intercessor, we beseech the Most Merciful of the Merciful that He will

---

[103] 'See Chapter 12. Deceits of the Devil.

grant us success in attaining complete sincerity.

O God! For the sake of *Surah al-Ikhlas*, place us among Your sincere servants who are saved. Amen. Amen.

Glory be unto You! We have no knowledge save that which You have taught us; indeed, You are All-Knowing, All-Wise. (Al-Baqarah 2:32)

A Confidential Letter to Some of my Brothers

I shall mention a point about two *hadiths* to my brothers who become bored of writing, and prefer other recitations during the Three Months,[104] the months of worship, to writing out the *Risale-i Nur*, although to do this is considered to be worship in five respects.[105] The two Hadiths are these:

The First: "At the Judgment Day, the ink spent by scholars of religion will weigh equally to the blood of the martyrs."[106]

The Second: "Whoever adheres to my *sunnah* when my community is corrupted shall earn the reward of a hundred martyrs."[107] That is, "Those who adhere to and serve the Practices of the Prophet and truths of the Qur'an when innovations and misguidance are rife may gain the reward of a hundred martyrs."

---

[104]   These are the 7th, 8th and 9th months of the Hijri Calendar, Rajab, Shaban and Ramadan.

[105]   'We asked for an explanation of the five sorts of worship which our Master indicates in this valuable letter. The explanation we received is below:

i. To strive against the people of misguidance, the most important struggle.

ii. To serve our Master in the form of helping him spread the truth.

iii. To serve Muslims in respect of belief.

iv. To obtain knowledge by means of the pen.

v. To perform worship in the form of reflective thought, one hour of which may sometimes be equal to a year's worship.

Signed: Rüştü, Hüsrev, Re'fet

[106]   hazzali, *Ihya 'Ulum ad-Din, i, 6; al-Munawi, Fayzu'l-Qadir, vi, 466; al-Ajluni, Kashf al-Khafa, ii, 561; Suyuti, Jami'u's-Saghir, 10026.*

[107]   3. Ibn Adiy, *Al-Kamil fi'd-Duafa ii, 739; al-Munziri, Al-Targhib wa't-Tarhib, i, 41; Tabarani, Al-Majma'u'l-Kabir, 1394; Ali ibn Husamuddin, Muntakhabat Kanzi'l-Ummal, i, 100; al-Haythami, Majma'u'z-Zawa'id, vii, 282.*

O my brothers who weary of writing due to laziness! And O my brothers who lean to Sufism! Together, these two Hadiths show that the black light flowing from the blessed, pure pens serving the truths of belief and mysteries of the Sharia and Practices of the Prophet peace and blessings be upon him, at a time such as this, even a drop of their water-of-life-like ink, may gain for you the advantage on the Day of Judgment equal to a hundred drops of the blood of martyrs. So you should try to gain it!

Question: It says "scholars" in the *hadith*, and some of us are only scribes. **Answer:** One who reads these treatises for a year, comprehending and accepting them, may become an important, correct scholar at this time. And even if he does not understand them, since the *Risale-i Nur* students have a collective personality, doubtless it is learned. As for your pens, they are the immaterial fingers of that collective personality. Although in my own view I am unworthy, due to your good opinion of me, you have afforded me the position of Master (*Ustad*) and religious scholar, and attached yourselves to me. Since I am unlettered and have difficulty in writing, your pens may be thought of as mine; you will receive the reward indicated in the Hadith.

Saïd Nursi

CHAPTER 10

REMEDIES TO THE SICK

Message for the Sick

This piece consists of twenty-five remedies.[108] It was written as a salve, a solace, and a prescription for the sick, and as a visit to the sick and a wish for their speedy recovery.

Warning and Apology

This immaterial prescription was written with a speed greater than all my other writings,[109] and since time could not be found in which to correct and study it, unlike all the others, it was read only once- and that at great speed like its composition. That is to say, it has remained in the disordered state of a first draft. I did not consider it necessary to go over carefully the things which had occurred to me in a natural manner, lest they be spoilt by arranging them and paying them undue attention. Readers and especially the sick should not feel upset and offended at any disagreeable expressions or harsh words and phrases; let them rather pray for me.

In the Name of God, the All-Merciful, the All-Compassionate.

---

[108] In fact, there are twenty-six remedies in this treatise as the sixth remedy appears twice. For Nursi's own explanation, see Footnote 110.

[109] This treatise was written in four and a half hours. Signed, Rüştü, Re'fet, Hüsrev, Saïd.

Those who, when a disaster befalls them, say, "Surely
we belong to God (as His creatures and servants), and
surely to Him we are bound to return. " (And they act
accordingly) (Al-Baqarah 2:156)
And He it is Who gives me food and drink; and Who,
when I fall ill, heals me. (Ash-Shu'ara 26:79)

In this Flash, we describe briefly Twenty-Five Remedies which may offer true consolation and a beneficial cure for the sick and those struck by disaster, who form one tenth of mankind.

First remedy

Unhappy sick person! Do not be anxious, have patience! Your illness is not a malady for you; it is a sort of cure. For life departs like capital. If it yields no fruits, it is wasted. And if it passes in ease and heedlessness, it passes most swiftly. Illness makes that capital of yours yield huge profits. Moreover, it does not allow your life to pass quickly; it restrains it and lengthens it, so that it will depart after yielding its fruits. An indication that your life is lengthened through illness is the following much repeated proverb: "The times of calamity are long, the times of happiness, most short."

Second remedy

O ill person who lacks patience! Be patient, indeed, offer thanks! Your illness may transform each of the minutes of your life into the equivalent of an hour's worship. For worship is of two kinds. One is positive like the well-known worship of supplication and the five Daily Prayers. The other are negative forms of worship like illness and calamities. By means of these, those afflicted realize their impotence and weakness; they beseech their All-Compassionate Creator and take refuge in Him; they manifest worship which is sincere and without hypocrisy. Yes, there is a sound narration stating that a life passed in illness is counted as worship for the believer-on condition he does not complain about God. It is even established by sound narrations and by those who uncover the realities of creation that one minute's illness of some who are completely patient and thankful becomes the equivalent of an hour's worship and a minute's illness of certain perfected men the equivalent of a day's worship. Thus, you should not complain about an illness which as though transforms one minute of your life into a thousand minutes and gains for you long life; you should rather offer thanks.

Third remedy

Impatient sick person! The fact that those who come to this world continuously depart, and the young grow old, and man perpetually revolves amid death and separation testifies that he did not come to this world to enjoy himself and receive pleasure.

Moreover, while man is the most perfect, the most elevated, of living beings and the best endowed in regard to members and faculties, through thinking of past pleasures and future pains, he passes only a grievous, troublesome life, lower than the animals. This means that man did not come to this world in order to live in fine manner and pass his life in ease and pleasure. Rather, possessing vast capital, he came here to work and do trade for an eternal, everlasting life.

The capital given to man is his lifetime. Had there been no illness, good health and well-being would have caused heedlessness, for they show the world to be pleasant and make the Hereafter forgotten. They do not want death and the grave to be thought of; they cause the capital of life to be wasted on trifles. Whereas illness suddenly opens the eyes, it says to the body: "You are not immortal. You have not been left to your own devices. You have a duty. Give up your pride, think of the One Who created you. Know that you will enter the grave, so prepare yourself for it!" Thus, from this point of view, illness is an admonishing guide and advisor that never deceives. It should not be complained about in this respect, indeed, should be thanked for. And if it is not too severe, patience should be sought to endure it.

Fourth remedy

Plaintive ill person! It is your right, not to complain, but to offer thanks and be patient. For your body and members and faculties are not your property. You did not make them, and you did not buy them from other workshops. That means they are the property of another. Their owner has disposal over his property as he wishes.

As is stated in the Twenty-Sixth Word,[110] an extremely wealthy and skillful craftsman, for example, employs a poor man as a model in order to show off his fine art and valuable wealth. In return for a wage, for a brief hour he clothes the poor man in a bejeweled and most skillfully wrought garment. He works it on him and gives it various states. In order to display the extraordinary varieties of his art, he cuts the garment, alters it, and lengthens and shortens it. Does the poor man working for a wage have the right to say to that person: "You are causing me trouble, you are causing me distress with the form you have given it, making me bow down and stand up;" has he the right to tell him that he is spoiling his fine appearance by cutting and shortening the garment which makes him beautiful? Can he tell him he is being unkind and unfair?

O sick person! Just like in this comparison, in order to display the garment of your body with which He has clothed you, bejeweled as it is with luminous faculties like the eye, the ear, the reason, and the heart, and the embroideries of His Most Beautiful Names, the All-Glorious Maker makes you revolve amid numerous states and changes you in many situations. Like you learn of His Name of Provider through hunger, come to know also His Name of Healer through your illness. Since suffering and calamities show the decrees of some of His Names, within those flashes of wisdom and rays of mercy are many instances of good to be found. If the veil of illness, which you fear and loathe, was to be lifted, behind it you would find many agreeable and beautiful meanings.

Fifth remedy

O you who is afflicted with illness! Through experience I have formed the opinion at this time that sickness is a Divine bounty for some people, a gift of the Most Merciful One.[111] Although I am not

---

[110]   See Chapter Three: Divine Determining (*Qadar*).

[111]   *Bukhari, Marda, 1; Muwatta', Ayn, 7; Musnad, ii, 237.*

worthy of it, for the past eight or nine years, a number of young people have come to me in connection with illness, seeking my prayers. I have noticed that each of those ill youths had begun to think of the Hereafter to a greater degree than other young people. He lacked the drunkenness of youth. He was saving himself to a degree from animal desires and heedlessness. So I would consider them and then warn them that their illnesses were a Divine bounty within the limits of their endurance. I would say: "I am not opposed to this illness of yours, my brother. I don't feel compassion and pity for you because of your illness, so that I should pray for you. Try to be patient until illness awakens you completely, and after it has performed its duty, God willing, the Compassionate Creator will restore you to health."

I would also say to them: "Through the calamity of good health, some of your fellows become neglectful, give up the five Daily Prayers, do not think of the grave, and forget God Almighty. Through the superficial pleasure of a brief hour's worldly life, they shake and damage an unending, eternal life, and even destroy it. Due to illness, you see the grave, which you will in any event enter, and the dwellings of the Hereafter beyond it, and you act in accordance with them. That means for you, illness is good health, while for some of your peers good health is a sickness..."

Sixth remedy

O sick person who complains about his suffering! I say to you: think of your past life and remember the pleasurable and happy days and the distressing and troublesome times. For sure, you will either say "Oh!" or "Ah!" That is, your heart and tongue will either say "All praise and thanks be to God!", or "Alas and alack!" Note carefully, what makes you exclaim "Praise and thanks be to God!" is thinking of the pains and calamities that have befallen you; it induces a sort of pleasure so that your heart offers thanks. For the passing of pain is a pleasure. With the passing of pains and calamities, a legacy of pleasure is left in the spirit, which on being aroused by thinking, pours forth from the spirit with thanks.

What makes you exclaim "Alas and alack!" are the pleasurable and happy times you have experienced in the former times, which, with their passing leave a legacy of constant pain in your spirit. Whenever you think of them, the pain is again stimulated, causing regret and sorrow to pour forth.

Since one day's illicit pleasure sometimes causes a year's suffering in the spirit, and with the pain of a fleeting day's illness are many days' pleasure and recompense in addition to the pleasure at being relieved at its passing and saved from it, think of the result of this temporary illness with which you are now afflicted, and of the merits of its inner face. Say: "All is from God! This too will pass!", and offer thanks instead of complaining.

Another remedy[112]

O brother who thinks of the pleasures of this world and suffers distress at illness! If this world was everlasting, and if on our way there was no death, and if the winds of separation and decease did not blow, and if there were no winters of the spirit in the calamitous and stormy future, I would have pitied you together with you. But since one day the world will bid us to leave it and will close its ears to our cries, we must forego our love of it now through the warnings of these illnesses, before it drives us out. We must try to abandon it in our hearts before it abandons us.

Yes, illness utters this warning to us: "Your body is not composed of stone and iron, but of various materials which are always disposed to parting. Leave off your pride, understand your impotence, recognize your Owner, know your duties, learn why you came to this world!" It declares this secretly in the heart's ear.

Moreover, since the pleasures and enjoyment of this world do not continue, and particularly if they are illicit, they are both fleeting, and full of pain, and sinful, do not weep on the pretext of illness because you have lost those pleasures. On the contrary, think of the aspects of worship and reward in the Hereafter to be found in illness, and try to receive pleasure from those.

---

[112] This Flash occurred to me in a natural manner, and two remedies have been included in the Sixth Remedy. We have left it thus in order not to spoil the naturalness; indeed, we did not change it thinking there may be some mystery contained in it.

Seventh remedy

O sick person who has lost the pleasures of health! Your illness does not spoil the pleasure of Divine bounties, on the contrary, it causes them to be experienced and increases them. For if something is continuous, it loses its effect. The people of reality even say, "Things are known through their opposites." For example, if there were no darkness, light would not be known and would contain no pleasure. If there was no cold, heat could not be comprehended. If there were no hunger, food would afford no pleasure. If there were no thirst of the stomach, there would be no pleasure in drinking water. If there were no sickness, no pleasure would be had from good health.

The All-Wise Creator's decking out man with truly numerous members and faculties, to the extent that he may experience and recognize the innumerable varieties of bounties in the universe, shows that He wants to make man aware of every sort of His bounty and to acquaint him with them and to impel man to offer constant thanks. Since this is so, He will give illness, sickness, and suffering, the same as He bestows good health and well-being. I ask you: "If there had not been this illness in your head or in your hand or stomach, would you have perceived the pleasurable and enjoyable Divine bounty of the good health of your head, hand or stomach, and offered thanks? For sure, it is not offering thanks for it, you would not have even thought of it! You would have unconsciously spent that good health on heedlessness, and perhaps even on dissipation.

Eight remedy

O sick person who thinks of the Hereafter! Sickness washes away the dirt of sins like soap, and cleanses. It is established in a sound Hadith that illnesses are atonement for sins. And in another Hadith, it says: "As ripe fruits fall on their tree being shaken, so the sins of a believer fall away on his shaking with illness."[113]

Sins are the lasting illnesses of eternal life, and in this worldly life they are sicknesses for the heart, conscience, and spirit. If you

---

[113]   *Bukhari, Marda, 1, 2, 13, 16; Muslim, Birr, 45; Darimi, Riqaq, 57; Musnad, i, 371, 441; ii, 303, 335; iii, 4, 18, 38, 48, 61, 81.*

are patient and do not complain, you will be saved through this temporary sickness from numerous perpetual sicknesses. If you do not think of your sins, or do not know the Hereafter, or do not recognize God, you suffer from an illness so fearsome it is a million times worse than your present minor illnesses. Cry out at that, for all the beings in the world are connected with your heart, spirit, and soul. Those connections are continuously severed by death and separation, opening up in you innumerable wounds. Particularly since you do not know the Hereafter and imagine death to be eternal non-existence, it is quite simply as though lacerated and bruised, your being suffers illness to the extent of the world.

Thus, the first thing you have to do is to search for the cure of belief, which is a certain healing remedy for the innumerable illnesses of that infinitely wounded and sick, extensive immaterial being of yours; you have to correct your beliefs, and the shortest way of finding such a cure is to recognize the power and mercy of the All-Powerful One of Glory by means of the window of your weakness and impotence shown you behind the curtain of heedlessness, rent by your physical illness.

Yes, one who does not recognize God is afflicted with a world-full of tribulations. While the world of one who does recognize Him is full of light and spiritual happiness; he perceives these in accordance with the strength of his belief. The suffering resulting from insignificant physical illnesses is dissolved by the immaterial joy, healing, and pleasure that arise from this belief; the suffering melts away.

Nineth remedy

O sick person who recognizes his Creator! The pain, fear, and anxiety in illness is because it is sometimes leads to death. Since superficially and to the heedless view death is frightening, illnesses which may lead to it cause fear and apprehension.

So know firstly and believe firmly that the appointed hour is determined and does not change. Those weeping beside the grievously sick and those in perfect health have died, while the grievously sick have been cured and lived.

Secondly death is not terrifying as it appears to be superficially. Through the light afforded by the All-Wise Qur'an, in many parts of the *Risale-i Nur* we have proved in completely certain and indubitable fashion that for believers death is to be discharged from the burdensome duties of life. And for them it is a rest from worship, which is the instruction and training in the arena of trial of this world. It is also a means of their re-joining friends and relations, ninety-nine out of a hundred of whom have already departed for the next world. And it is a means of entering their true homeland and eternal abodes of happiness. It is also an invitation to the gardens of Paradise from the dungeon of this world. And it is the time to receive their wage from the munificence of the Most Compassionate Creator in return for service rendered to Him. Since the reality of death is this, it should not be regarded as terrifying, but on the contrary, as the introduction to mercy and happiness.

Moreover, some of the people of God-fearing death have not been out of terror at it, but due to their hope of gaining more merit through performing more good works with the continuation of the duties of life.

Yes, for the people of belief, death is the door to Divine mercy, while for the people of misguidance; it is the pit of everlasting darkness.

Tenth remedy

O sick person who worries unnecessarily! You worry at the severity of your illness and that worry increases it. If you want your illness to be less severe, try not to worry. That is, think of the benefits of your illness, the recompense for it, and that it will pass quickly; it will remove the worry and cut the illness at the root.

Indeed, worry increases illness twice over. Worry causes an immaterial illness of the heart beneath the physical illness; the physical illness rests on that and persists. If the worry ceases through submission, contentment, and thinking of the wisdom in the illness, an important part of the illness is extirpated; it becomes lighter and in part disappears. Sometimes a minor physical illness increases tenfold just through anxiety. On the anxiety ceasing, nine tenths of the illness disappears.

Worry increases illness, so is it also like an accusation against Divine wisdom and a criticism of Divine mercy and complaint against the Compassionate Creator. For this reason, contrary to his intentions, the one who does so receives a rebuff and it increases his illness. Yes, just as thanks increases bounty, so also complaint increases illness and tribulations.

Furthermore, worry is itself an illness. The cure for it is to know the wisdom in illness and the purpose of it. Since you have learnt its purpose and benefit, apply that salve to your worry and find relief! Say "Ah!" instead of "Oh!", and "All praise be to God for every situation" instead of sighing and lamenting.

Eleventh remedy

O my impatient sick brother! Although illness causes you an immediate suffering, the passing of your illness in the past until today produces an immaterial pleasure and happiness for the spirit arising from the reward received for enduring it. From today forward, and even from this hour, there is no illness, and certainly no pain is to be had from non-being. And if there is no pain, there cannot be any grief. You become impatient because you imagine things wrongly. Because, with the physical aspect of your time of illness prior to today departing, its pain has departed with it; only its reward and the pleasure of its passing remains. While it should give you profit and happiness, to think of past days and feel grieved and become impatient is crazy. Future days have not yet come. To think of them now, and by imagining a day that does not exist and an illness that does not exist and grief that does not exist to be grieved and display impatience, is to give the color of existence to three degrees of non-existence-if that is not crazy, what is?

Since, if the hour previous to the present was one of illness, it produces joy; and since the time subsequent to the present hour is non-existent, and the illness is non-existent, and the grief is non-existent, do not scatter the power of patience given you by Almighty God to right and left, but muster it in the face of pain of the present hour; say: "O Most Patient One!" and withstand it.

Twelfth remedy

O sick person who due to illness cannot perform his worship and invocations and feels grief at the deprivation! Know that it is stated in a hadith that "A pious believer who due to illness cannot perform the invocations he normally regularly performs, receives an equal reward."[114] On an ill person carrying out his obligatory worship as far as it is possible with patience and relying on God, during that time of severe illness, the illness takes the place of *sunnah* worship-and in sincere form.

Moreover, illness makes a person understand his impotence and weakness. It causes him to offer supplication both verbally and through the tongue of his impotence and weakness. Almighty God bestowed on man a boundless impotence and infinite weakness so that he would perpetually seek refuge at the Divine Court and beseech and supplicate. According to the meaning of the verse, *Say: "My Lord would not care for you were it not for your prayer. (Al-Furqan 25:77)* that is, "what importance would you have if you did not offer prayer and supplication?", the wisdom in man's creation and reason for his value is sincere prayer and supplication. Since one cause of this is illness, from this point of view it should not be complained about, but God should be thanked for it, and the tap of supplication which illness opens should not be closed by regaining health.

Thirteenth remedy

O unhappy person who complains at illness! For some people illness is an important treasury, a most valuable Divine gift. Every sick person can think of his illness as being of that sort.

The appointed hour is not known: in order to deliver man from absolute despair and absolute heedlessness, and to hold him between hope and fear and so preserve both this world and the Hereafter, in His wisdom Almighty God has concealed the appointed hour. The appointed hour may come at any time; if it cap-

---

[114]   *Bukhari, Jihad, 134; Musnad, iv, 410, 418.*

tures man in heedlessness, it may cause grievous harm to eternal life. But illness dispels the heedlessness; it makes a person think of the Hereafter; it recalls death, and thus he may prepare himself. Some illnesses are so profitable that they gain for a person in twenty days a rank they could not otherwise have gained in twenty years.

For instance, from among my friends there were two youths, may God have mercy on them. One was Sabri from the village of Ilema, the other Vezirzâde Mustafa from Islamköy. I used to note with amazement that although these two could not write they were among the foremost in regard to sincerity and the service of belief. I did not know the reason for this. After their deaths I understood that both suffered from a serious illness. Through the guidance of the illness, unlike other neglectful youths who gave up obligatory worship, they had great fear of God, performed most valuable service, and attained a state beneficial to the Hereafter. God willing, the distress of two years' illness was the means to the happiness of millions of years of eternal life. I now understand that the prayers I sometimes offered for their health were maledictions in respect to this world. God willing, my prayers were accepted for their well-being in the Hereafter.

Thus, according to my belief, these two gained profit equivalent to that which may be gained through ten years' fear of God [taqwa].[115] If like some young people, they had relied on their youth and good health and thrown themselves into heedlessness and vice, and watching them, death had grabbed them right in the midst of the filth of their sins, they would have made their graves into lairs of scorpions and snakes, instead of that treasury of lights.

Since illnesses contain such benefits, they should be not complained about, but borne with patience and relying on God, indeed, thanking God and having confidence in His mercy.

---

[115] The Hadith's meaning is this: "If a person has standing in God's sight and he cannot reach that station through good works and taqwa, God afflicts him with such tribulations as illness until he does attain it." Al-Hakim, Al-Mustadrak, i, 344.

Fourteenth remedy

O sick person whose eyes have developed cataracts! If you knew what a light and spiritual eye is to be found beneath the cataract that may cover a believer's eyes, you would exclaim: "A hundred thousand thanks to my Compassionate Sustainer." I shall recount an incident to you to explain this salve. It is as follows:

One time, the aunt of Süleyman from Barla, who served me for eight years with total loyalty and willingness, became blind. Thinking well of me a hundred times more than was my due, the righteous woman caught me by the door of the mosque and asked me to pray for her sight to be restored. So I made the blessed woman's righteousness the intercessor for my supplication, and beseeching Almighty God, I prayed: "O Lord! Restore her sight out of respect for her righteousness." Two days later, an oculist from Burdur came and removed the cataract. Forty days later she again lost her sight. I was most upset and prayed fervently for her. God willing, the prayer was accepted for her life in the Hereafter, otherwise that prayer of mine would have been a most mistaken malediction for her. For forty days had remained till her death; forty days later she had died-May God have mercy on her.

Thus, in place of the woman looking sorrowfully at the gardens of Barla with the eye of old age, she profited by in her grave being able to gaze for forty thousand days on the gardens of Paradise. For her belief was strong and she was completely righteous.

Yes, if a believer loses his sight and enters the grave blind, in accordance with his degree he may gaze on the world of light to a much greater extent than others in their graves. Just as we see many things in this world that blind believers do not see, if they depart with belief, those blind people see to a greater extent than other dead in their graves. As though looking through the most powerful telescopes, they can see and gaze on the gardens of Paradise like the cinema, in accordance with their degree.

Thus, with thanks and patience you can find beneath the veil on your present eye an eye which is thus light-filled, and with which while beneath the earth you can see and observe Paradise above the skies. That which will raise the veil from your eye, the eye doctor that will allow you to look with that eye, is the All-Wise Qur'an.

Fifteenth remedy

O sick person who sighs and laments! Do not look at the outward aspect of illness and sigh, look at its meaning and be pleased. If the meaning of illness had not been good, the All-Compassionate Creator would not have given illness to the servants He loves most. Whereas, there is a Hadith the meaning of which is, "Those afflicted with the severest trials are the

Prophets, then the saints and those like them."[116] That is, "Those most afflicted with tribulations and difficulties are the best of men, the most perfect." Foremost the Prophet Job, peace be upon him, and the other Prophets, then the saints, then the righteous, have regarded the illnesses they have suffered as sincere worship, as gifts of the Most Merciful; they have offered thanks in patience. They have seen them as surgical operations performed by the All-Compassionate Creator's mercy.

O you who cries out and laments! If you want to join this luminous caravan, offer thanks in patience. For if you complain, they will not accept you. You will fall into the pits of the people of misguidance, and travel a dark road.

Yes, there are some illnesses which if they lead to death, are like a sort of martyrdom; they result in a degree of sainthood like martyrdom. For example, those who die from the illnesses accompanying childbirth[117] and pains of the abdomen, and by drowning, burning, and plague, become martyrs. So also there are many blessed illnesses which gain the degree of sainthood for those who die from them. Moreover, since illness lessens love of the world and attachment to it, it lightens parting from the world through death, which for the worldly is extremely grievous and painful, and it sometimes even makes it desirable.

---

[116] Al-Munawi, *Fayzu'l-Qadir*, i, 519 no:1056; al-Hakim, *Al-Mustadrak*, iii, 343; Bukhari, Marda, 3; Tirmidhi, Zuhd, 57; Ibn Majah, Fitan, 23; Darimi, Riqaq, 67; Musnad, i, 172, 174, 180, 185; vi, 369.

[117] The period this martyrdom may be gained through illness is around the forty days of 'lying-in.'

Sixteenth remedy

O sick person who complains of his distress! Illness prompts respect and compassion, which are most important and good in human social life for it saves man from self-sufficiency, which drives him to unsociableness and unkindness. For according to the meaning of, *No indeed, but (despite all His favors to him), human is unruly and rebels. In that he sees himself as self-sufficient, independent (of his Lord) (Al-'Alaq 96:6)* an evil-commanding soul which feels self-sufficient due to good health and well-being, does not feel respect towards his brothers in many instances, who are deserving of it. And he does not feel compassion towards the sick and those smitten by disaster, although they deserve kindness and pity. Whenever he is ill, he understands his own impotence and want, and he has respect towards his brothers who are worthy of it. He feels respect towards his believing brothers who visit him or assist him. And he feels human kindness, which arises from fellow-feeling, and compassion for those struck by disaster-a most important Islamic characteristic. And comparing them to himself, he pities them in the true meaning of the word and feels compassion for them. He does what he can to help them, and at the very least prays for them and goes to visit them to ask them how they are, which is *Sunnah* according to the Sharia, and thus earns reward.

Seventeenth remedy

O sick person who complains at not being able to perform good works due to illness! Offer thanks! It is illness that opens to you the door of the most sincere of good works. In addition to continuously gaining reward for the sick person and for those who look after him for God's sake, illness is a most important means for supplications being accepted.

Indeed, there is significant reward for believers for looking after the sick. Enquiring after their health and visiting the sick-on condition it does not tax them-is *sunna*[118] and also atonement for sins. There is a Hadith which says, "Receive the prayers of the sick, for their prayers are acceptable."[119]

---

[118] Al-Munawi, *Fayzu'l-Qadir, ii, 45 no: 1285.*

[119] *Ibn Majah, Jana'iz, 1; Daylami, Musnadu'l-Firdaws, i, 280.*

Especially if the sick are relations, and parents in particular, to look after them is important worship, yielding significant reward. To please a sick person's heart and console him, is like significant alms-giving. Fortunate is the person who pleases the easily touched hearts of father and mother at the time of illness, and receives their prayer. Indeed, even the angels applaud saying: *"Ma'shallah! Barakallah!"* before loyal scenes of those good offspring who respond at the time of their illness to the compassion of their parents-those most worthy of respect in the life of society-with perfect respect and filial kindness, showing the exaltedness of humanity.

Yes, there are pleasures at the time of illness which arise from the kindness, pity, and compassion of those around them, and are most pleasant and agreeable and reduce the pains of illness to nothing. The acceptability of the prayers of the sick is an important matter. For the past thirty or forty years, I myself have prayed to be cured from the illness of lumbago from which I suffer. However, I understood that the illness had been given for prayer. Since through prayer, prayer cannot be removed, that is, since prayer cannot remove itself, I understood that the results of prayer pertain to the Hereafter,[120] and that it is itself a sort of worship, for through illness one understands one's impotence and seeks refuge at the Divine Court. Therefore, although for thirty years I have offered supplications to be healed and apparently my prayer has not been accepted, it has not occurred to me to give it up. For illness is the time for supplication. To be cured is not the result of the supplication. If the All-Wise and Compassionate One bestows healing, He bestows it out of His abundant grace.

Furthermore, if supplications are not accepted in the form we wish, it may not be said that they have not been accepted. The All-Wise Creator knows better than us; He gives whatever is in our interests. Sometimes for our interests, he directs our prayers for this world towards the Hereafter, and accepts them in that way. In any event, a supplication that acquires sincerity due to illness and arises

---

[120] Certain illnesses encourage and are the reason for prayer. Therefore, if a prayer causes the termination of the illness, then prayer would annul the reason for it. This cannot be admitted.

from weakness, impotence, humility and need in particular, is very close to being acceptable. Illness is the means to supplication that is thus sincere. Both the sick who are religious, and believers who look after the sick, should take advantage of this supplication.

Eighteenth remedy

O sick person who gives up offering thanks and takes up complaining! Complaint arises from a right. None of your rights have been lost that you should complain. Indeed, there are numerous thanks which are an obligation for you, a right over you, and these you have not performed. Without Almighty God giving you the right, you are complaining as though demanding rights in a manner which is not rightful. You cannot look at others superior to you in degree who are healthy, and complain. You are rather charged with looking at the sick who from the point of view of health are at a lower degree than yourself, and offering thanks. If your hand is broken, look at theirs, which is severed. If you have only one eye, look at the blind, who lack both eyes. And offer thanks to God!

For sure, no one has the right to look to those superior to him in regard to bounties and to complain. And in tribulations it is everyone's right to look to those above themselves in regard to tribulation, so that they should offer thanks. This mystery has been explained in a number of places in the *Risale-i Nur* with a comparison; a summary of it is as follows:

A person takes a wretched man to the top of a minaret. On every step he gives him a different gift, a different bounty. Right at the top of the minaret he gives him the largest present. Although he wants thanks and gratitude in return for all those various gifts, the peevish man forgets the presents he has received on each of the stairs, or considers them to be of no importance, and offering no thanks, looks above him and starts to complain, saying, "If only this minaret had been higher I could have climbed even further. Why isn't it as tall as that mountain over there or that other minaret?" If he begins to complain like this, what great ingratitude it would be, what a wrong!

In just the same way, man comes into existence from nothing, not as a rock or a tree or an animal, but becomes a man and a Muslim, and most of the time sees good health and acquires a high level of bounties. Despite all this, to complain and display impatience because he is not worthy of some bounties, or because he loses them through wrong choice or abuse, or because he could not obtain them, and to criticize Divine lordship saying "What have I done that this has happened to me?", is a condition and immaterial sickness more calamitous than the physical one. Like fighting with a broken hand, complaint makes his illness worse. Sensible is the one who in accordance with the meaning of the verse,

Those who, when a disaster befalls them, say, "Surely we belong to God (as His creatures and servants), and surely to Him we are bound to return." (And they act accordingly.) (Al-Baqarah 2:156) submits and is patient, so that the illness may complete its duty, then depart.

Nineteenth remedy

As the term of the Eternally Besought One, 'the Most Beautiful Names' shows, all the Names of the All-Beauteous One of Glory are beautiful. Among beings, the most subtle, the most beautiful, the most comprehensive mirror of Eternal Besoughtedness is life. The mirror to the beautiful is beautiful. The mirror that shows the virtues of beauty becomes beautiful. Just as whatever is done to the mirror by such beauty is good and beautiful, whatever befalls life too, in respect of reality, is good. Because it displays the beautiful impresses of the Most Beautiful Names, which are good and beautiful.

If life passes monotonously with permanent health and well-being, it becomes a deficient mirror. Indeed, in one respect, it tells of non-existence, non-being, and nothingness, and causes weariness. It reduces the life's value, and transforms the pleasure of life into distress. Because thinking he will pass his time quickly, out of boredom, a person throws himself either into vice or into amusements. Like a prison sentence, he becomes hostile to his valuable life and wants to kill it and make it pass quickly. Whereas a life that revolves in change and action and different states makes its value felt, and makes known the importance and pleasure of life. Even if it is in hardship and tribulation, such a person does not want his life to pass quickly. He does not complain out of boredom, saying, "Alas! The sun hasn't set yet," or, "it is still night-time."

Yes, ask a fine gentleman who is rich and idle and living in the lap of luxury, "How are you?" You are bound to hear a pathetic reply like: "The time never passes. Let's have a game of backgammon. Or let's find some amusement to pass the time." Or else you will hear complaints arising from worldly ambition, like: "I haven't got that; if only I had done such-and-such."

Then ask someone struck by disaster or a worker or poor man living in hardship: "How are you?" If he is sensible, he will reply: "All thanks be to God, I am working. If only the evening did not come so quickly, I could have finished this work! Time passes so quickly, and so does life, they pass so quickly. For sure things are hard for me, but that will pass too. Everything passes quickly." He in effect says how valuable life is and how regretful he is at its passing. That means he understands the pleasure and value of life through hardship and labor. As for ease and health, they make life bitter and make it wanted to be passed.

My sick brother! Know that the origin and leaven of calamities and evils, and even of sins, is non-existence, as is proved decisively and in detail in other parts of the *Risale-i Nur*. As for non-existence, it is evil. It is because monotonous states like ease, silence, tranquility, and arrest are close to non-existence and nothingness that they make felt the darkness of non-existence and cause distress. As for action and change, they are existence and make existence felt. And existence is pure good, it is light.

Since the reality is thus, your illness has been sent to your being as a guest to perform many duties like purifying your valuable life, and strengthening it and making it progress, and to make the other human faculties in your being turn in assistance towards your sick member, and to display various Names of the All-Wise Maker. God willing, it will carry out its duties quickly and depart. And it will say to good health: "Come, and stay permanently in my place, and carry out your duties. This house is yours. Remain here in good health."

Twentieth remedy

O sick person who is searching for a remedy for his ills! Illness is of two sorts. One sort is real, the other, imaginary. As for the real sort, the All-Wise and Glorious Healer has stored up in His mighty pharmacy of the earth a cure for every illness. It is licit to obtain medicines and use them as treatment, but one should know that their effect and the cure are from Almighty God. He gives the cure just as He provides the medicine.

Following the recommendations of skillful and God-fearing doctors is an important medicine. For most illnesses arise from abuses, lack of abstinence, wastefulness, mistakes, dissipation, and lack of care. A religious doctor will certainly give advice and orders within the bounds of the lawful. He will forbid abuses and excesses, and give consolation. The sick person has confidence in his orders and consolation, and his illness lessens; it produces as easiness for him in place of distress.

But when it comes to imaginary illness, the most effective medicine for it is to give it no importance. The more importance is given it, the more it grows and swells. If no importance is given it, it lessens and disperses. The more bees are upset the more they swarm around a person's head and if no attention is paid to them they disperse. So too, the more importance one pays to a piece of string waving in front of one's eyes in the darkness and to the apprehension it causes one, the more it grows and makes one flee from it like a madman. While if one pays it no importance, one sees that it is an ordinary bit of string and not a snake, and laughs at one's fright and anxiety.

If hypochondria continue a long time, it is transformed into reality. It is a bad illness for the nervous and those given to imaginings; such people make a mountain out of a molehill and their morale is destroyed. Especially if they encounter unkind 'half' doctors or unfair doctors, it further provokes their hypochondria. For the rich, they lose their wealth, or they lose their wits, or their health.

Twenty-first remedy

My sick brother! There is physical pain with your illness, but a significant immaterial pleasure encompasses you that will remove the effect of your physical pain. For if you have father, mother, and relations, their most pleasurable compassion towards which you have forgotten since childhood will be reawakened and you will see again their kind looks which you received in childhood. In addition, the friendships around you which had remained secret and hidden again look towards you with love through the attraction of illness, and so, in the face of these your physical pain becomes very cheap. Also, since those whom you have served proudly through the decree of illness now serve you kindly, you have become a master to the masters. Moreover, since you have attracted towards yourself the fellow-feeling and human kindness in people, you have found numerous helpful friends and kind companions. And again, you have received the order from your illness to rest from many taxing duties, and you are taking a rest. For sure, in the face of these immaterial pleasures, your minor pain should drive you to thanks, not complaint.

Twenty-second remedy

My brother who suffers from a severe illness like apoplexy! Firstly I give you the good news that apoplexy is considered blessed for believers. A long time ago I used to hear this from holy men and I did not know the reason. Now, one reason for it occurs to me as follows:

In order to attain union with Almighty God, be saved from the great spiritual dangers of this world, and to obtain eternal happiness, the people of God have chosen to follow two principles:

The first is contemplation of death. Thinking that like the world is transitory, they too are transient guests charged with duties, they worked for eternal life in that way.

The second; through fasting, religious exercises and asceticism, they tried to kill the evil-commanding soul and so be saved from its dangers and from the blind emotions.

And you, my brother who has lost the health of half his body! Without choosing it, you have been given these two principles, which are short and easy and the cause of happiness. Thus, the state of your being perpetually warns you of the fleeting nature of the world and that man is transient. The world can no longer drown you, nor heedlessness closes your eyes. And for sure, the evil-commanding soul cannot deceive with base lusts and animal appetites someone in the state of half a man; he is quickly saved from the trials of the soul.

Thus, through the mystery of belief in God and submission to Him and reliance on Him, a believer can benefit in a brief time from a severe illness like apoplexy, like the severe trials of the saints. Then a severe illness such as that becomes exceedingly cheap.

Twenty-third remedy

Unhappy ill person who is alone and a stranger! Even if your aloneness and exile together with your illness were to arouse sympathy towards you in the hardest hearts and attract kindness and compassion, could that be a substitute for your All-Compassionate Creator? For He presents Himself to us at the start of all the Qur'an's Surahs with the Attributes of "the Merciful and the Compassionate," and with one flash of His compassion makes all mothers nurture their young with that wonderful tenderness, and with one manifestation of His mercy every spring fills the face of the earth with bounties, and a single manifestation of His mercy is eternal life in Paradise together with all its wonders. Then surely your relation to Him through belief, your recognizing Him and beseeching Him through the tongue of impotence of your illness, and your illness of loneliness in exile, will attract the glance of His mercy towards you, which takes the place of everything. Since He exists and He looks to you, everything exists for you. Those who are truly alone and in exile are those who are not connected with Him through belief and submission, or attach no importance to that relation.

Twenty-fourth remedy

O you who look after innocent sick children or after the elderly, who are like innocent children! Before you is important trade for the Hereafter. Gain that trade through enthusiasm and endeavor! It is established by the people of reality that the illnesses of innocent children are like exercises and training for their delicate bodies, and injections and dominical training to allow them to withstand in the future the upheavals of the world; that in addition to many instances of wisdom pertaining to the child's

worldly life, instead of the atonement for sins in adults which looks to spiritual life and is the means to purifying life, illnesses are like injections ensuring the child's spiritual progress in the future or in the Hereafter; and that the merits accruing from such illnesses pass to the book of good works of the parents, and particularly of the mother who through the mystery of compassion prefers the health of her child to her own health. As for looking after the elderly, it is established in sound narrations and many historical events that together with receiving huge reward, to receive the prayers of the elderly and especially of parents, and to make their hearts happy and serve them loyally, is the means to happiness both in this world and in the Hereafter. And it is established by many events that a fortunate child who obeys to the letter his elderly parents will be treated in the same way by his children, and that if a wretched child wounds his parents he will be punished by means of many disasters in this world as well as in the Hereafter. Yes, to look after not only relatives who are elderly or innocents, but also those of the believers if one encounters them-since through the mystery of belief there is true brotherhood-and to serve the venerable sick elderly if they are in need of it to one's utmost ability, is required by Islam.

Twenty-fifth remedy

My sick brothers! If you want a most beneficial and truly pleasurable sacred cure, develop your belief! That is, through repentance and seeking forgiveness, and the five Daily Prayers and worship, make use of belief, that sacred cure-and of the medicine which arises from belief.

Indeed, due to love of this world and attachment to it, it is as if you possess a sick immaterial being as large as the world, like the heedless. We have proved in many parts of the *Risale-i Nur* that belief at once heals that immaterial being of yours as large as the world, which is bruised and battered by the blows of death and separation, and saves it from the wounds and truly heals it. I cut short the discussion here so as not to weary you.

As for the medicine of belief, it shows its effect through your carrying out your religious obligations as far as is possible. Heedlessness, vice, the lusts of the soul, and illicit amusements prevent the effectiveness of that remedy. Since illness removes heedlessness, cuts the appetites, is an obstacle to illicit pleasures, take advantage of it. Make use of the sacred medicines and lights of belief through repentance and seeking forgiveness, and prayer and supplication.

May Almighty God restore you to health and make your illnesses expiation for your sins. Amen. Amen. Amen.

They say: "All praise and gratitude are for God, Who has guided us to this. If God had not guided us, we would certainly not have found the right way. The Messengers of our Lord did indeed come with the truth." (Al-A'raf 7: 43)

All-Glorified You are. We have no knowledge save what You have taught us. Surely You are the All-Knowing, the All-Wise. (Al-Baqarah 2:32)

O God! Grant blessings to our master Muhammad, the medicine for our hearts and their remedy, the good health of our bodies and their healing, the light of our eyes and their radiance, and to his Family and Companions, and grant them peace.

A LETTER OF CONDOLENCE ON THE DEATH OF A CHILD

And in His Name, be He glorified!
And there is nothing but it glorifies Him with praise.
In the Name of God, the All-Merciful, the All-Compassionate.
And give good news to the patient,
Those who when afflicted with calamity say: To God do we belong and to Him is our return. (Al-Baqarah 2:155)

My Dear Brother of the Hereafter, Hafiz Halid Efendi!

Your child's death saddened me. But, "the command is God's," contentment with the Divine decree and submission to Divine Determining is a mark of Islam. May Almighty God grant you all patience. And may He make the deceased a supporter and intercessor for you in the Hereafter. I shall explain Five Points which are truly good news and offer real consolation for you, and pious believers like you:

First Point

The meaning of the phrase, *immortal youths (Al-Waqi'ah 56:17)* in the All- Wise Qur'an is this: with this phrase, the verse indicates and gives the good news that the children of believers who die before reaching maturity will remain perpetually as eternal, lovable children in a form worthy of Paradise; that they will be an everlasting means of happiness in the embrace of their fathers and mothers who go to Paradise; that they will be the means for ensuring for their parents the sweetest of pleasures like loving and caressing children; that all pleasurable things will be found in Paradise; that the statements of those who say that since Paradise is not the place for reproduction, there will be no loving and caressing of children are not correct; and that gaining millions of years of pure, pain free loving and caressing of eternal children in place of a short time like ten years of loving children mixed with sorrows in this world is a great source of happiness for believers.

Second Point

One time, a man was in prison. They sent one of his lovable children to him. The unhappy prisoner suffered both his own sorrows, and since he could not make the child comfortable, he was grieved also at his hardship. Then the compassionate judge sent a man to him with a message which said: "For sure this child is yours, but he is my subject and of my people. I shall take him and look after him in a fine palace." The man wept in anguish. He said: "I won't give you my child who is my solace!" His friends said to him: "Your grief is meaningless. If it is the child you pity, he will go to a spacious and happy palace in place of this dirty, stinking, distressing dungeon. If you are grieved for yourself and are seeking your own benefits, if your child remains here, you will suffer much distress and pain at the child's difficulties in addition to your single dubious, temporary benefit. If he goes there, it will be of manifold advantage for you, for it will be the cause of attracting the king's mercy and will be an intercessor for you. The king will want to make you meet with him. He surely will not send him to the prison so that you can see him; he will release you from the prison, summon you to the palace, and allow you to meet with the child there. On condition that you have confidence in the king and you obey him..."

My dear brother, like this comparison, you must think as follows, like other believers when their children die: the child was innocent, and his Creator is All-Compassionate and All-Generous. He has taken him to His most perfect grace and mercy in place of my deficient upbringing and compassion. He has released him from the grievous, calamitous, difficult prison of this world and sent him to the gardens of Paradise. How happy for the child! If he had stayed in this world, who knows what form he would have taken. Therefore, I do not pity him, I know him to be fortunate. There remain the benefits for myself, and I don't pity myself for those, and I do not grieve and be sorrowful. For if he had remained in the world, he would have secured ten years of a child's temporary love mixed with pains. If he had been righteous and if he had been capable in the matters of the world, perhaps he would have helped me. But with his death, he has become like an intercessor who is the means to ten million years of a child's love in eternal Paradise and to everlasting happiness. Most certainly, one who loses some dubious, immediate benefit and gains a thousand certain, postponed benefits does not display grief and sorrow, he does not cry out in despair.

Third Point

The child who died was the creature, possession, servant, and together with all his members, the artifact of a Most Compassionate Creator, and belonging to Him, was a friend of his parents, put temporarily under their supervision. The Creator made the father and mother servants of the child. In return for their services, He gave them pleasurable compassion as an immediate wage. Now, if as the requirement of mercy and wisdom, that All-Compassionate Creator, Who owns nine hundred and ninety-nine shares out of a thousand of the child, takes the child from you and puts an end to your service, to cry out in grief and despair due to that ap- parent single share in the face of the true owner of the thousand shares in a manner that recalls complaint, does not befit a believer; it befits rath- er the people of neglect and misguidance.

Fourth Point

If the world had been eternal, and man was to have remained in it eternally, and separation had been eternal; grievous sorrow and despairing woe would have had some meaning. But since this world is a guesthouse, wherever the dead child has gone, you, and we too, shall go there. Moreover, this death is not particular to him, it is a general highway. And, since separation is not forever, in the future, both in the Intermediate Realm and in the Hereafter, he will be met with. One must say, the command is God's. He gave him and He took him away. One must say, "All praise be to God for every situation," and offer thanks in patience.

Fifth Point

Compassion, one of the most subtle, beautiful, agreeable, and sweet manifestations of Divine mercy, is a luminous elixir. It is much more direct than passionate love; it swiftly becomes a means to union with Almighty God. Metaphorical love and worldly love are transformed into true love with the greatest difficulty, and find Almighty God, but compassion binds the heart to Him in a shorter, purer fashion-and without difficulty. Both father and mother love their child more than the entire world. When their child is taken from them, if they are fortunate and if they are true believers, its turns their faces from this world and finds the True Bestower of Bounties. It says: "Since the world is transitory, it is not worthy of the heart's attachment." Wherever the child has gone, a person forms an attachment with that place, and this gains for him high spiritual rank.

The people of neglect and misguidance are deprived of the happiness and good news of these Five Points. You can see from the following how grievous their situation is: they see their only child in the throes of death and due to their imagining the world to be eternal and as a result of their heedlessness and misguidance, they think death is non-existence and eternal separation. They think of him in the earth of his grave in place of his soft bed, and due to their heedlessness or misguidance, they do not think of the Paradise of mercy and heaven of bounty of the Most Compassionate of the Compassionate; you can see by comparison what despairing sorrow and grief they suffer. Whereas belief and Islam say to the believer: his All-Compassionate Creator will take this child of yours who is in the throes of death from this base world and take him to Paradise. He will make him both an intercessor for you, and an eternal child. Separation is temporary, do not worry.

The command is God's.
To God do we belong and to Him is our return.
(Al-Baqarah 2:155)

Saïd Nursi

CHAPTER 11

FASTING OF RAMADAN

This piece explains nine of the many examples of wisdom in the month of Ramadan.

In the Name of God, the All-Merciful, the All-Compas-sionate.

It was the month of Ramadan in which the Qur'an was bestowed from on high as a guidance unto man and a self-evident proof of that guidance, and as the standard to discern true from false. (Al-Baqarah 2:185)

First Wisdom

The fasting during the month of Ramadan is one of the five pillars of Islam, and it is one of the greatest of the marks and obser-vances of Islam. There are many purposes and instances of wisdom in the fast of Ramadan which look to both God Almighty's lordship, and to man's social life, his personal life and the training of his in-stinctual soul (*nafs*), and to his gratitude for Divine bounties. One of the many instances of wisdom in fasting from the point of view of God Almighty's lordship is as follows:

God Almighty created the face of the earth in the form of a table laden with bounties, and arranged on the table every sort of bounty in a form of *From whence he does not expect, (At-Talaaq 65:3)* in this way stating the perfection of His Lordship and His mercifulness and compassionateness. Human beings are unable to discern clearly the reality of this situation while in the sphere of causes, under the veil of heedlessness, and they sometimes forget it. However, during the month of Ramadan, the people of belief suddenly become like a well drawn-up army. As sunset approaches, they display a worshipful attitude as though, having been invited to the Pre-Eternal Monarch's banquet, they are awaiting the command of "Fall to and help yourselves!" They are responding to that compassionate, illustrious, and universal mercy with comprehensive, exalted, and orderly worship. Do you think those who do not participate in such elevated worship and noble bounties are worthy to be called human beings?

Second Wisdom

One of the many instances of wisdom in the fast of the blessed month of Ramadan with respect to thankfulness for God Almighty's bounties is as follows:

As is stated in the First Word, a price is required for the foods a tray-bearer brings from a royal kitchen. But, to give a tip to the tray-bearer, and to suppose those priceless bounties to be valueless and not to recognize the one who bestowed them would be the greatest foolishness.

God Almighty has spread innumerable sorts of bounties over the face of the earth for mankind, in return for which He wishes thanks, as the price of those bounties. The apparent causes and possessors of the bounties are like tray-bearers. We pay a certain price to them and are indebted to them, and even though they do not merit it, are over-respectful and grateful to them. Whereas the True Bestower of Bounties is infinitely more deserving of thanks than those causes which are merely the means for the bounty. To thank Him, then, is to recognize that the bounties come directly from Him; it is to appreciate their worth and to perceive one's own need for them.

Fasting in Ramadan, then, is the key to a true, sincere, extensive, and universal thankfulness. For at other times of the year, most of those who are not in difficult circumstances do not realize the value of many bounties since they do not experience real hunger. Those whose stomachs are full and especially if they are rich, do not understand the degree of bounty there is in a piece of dry bread. But when it is time to break the fast, the sense of taste testifies that the dry bread is a most valuable Divine bounty in the eyes of a believer. During Ramadan, everyone from the monarch to the destitute, manifests a sort of gratitude through understanding the value of those bounties.

Furthermore, since eating is prohibited during the day, they will say: "Those bounties do not belong to me. I am not free to eat them, for they are another's property and gift. I await his command." They will recognize the bounty to be bounty and so will be giving thanks. Thus, fasting in this way is in many respects like a key to gratitude; gratitude being man's fundamental duty.

Third Wisdom

One of the many instances of wisdom in fasting from the point of view of man's social life is as follows:

Human beings have been created differently with regard to their livelihoods. As a consequence of the difference, God Almighty invites the rich to assist the poor, so that through the hunger experienced in fasting, the rich can truly understand the pains and hunger which the poor suffer. If there was no fasting, there would be many self-indulgent rich unable to perceive just how grievous is hunger and poverty and how needy of compassion are those who suffer them.

Compassion for one's fellow men is an essential of true thankfulness. Whoever a person is, there will always be someone poorer than himself in some respect. He is enjoined to be compassionate towards that person. If he was not himself compelled to suffer hunger, he would be unable give the person-by means of compassion-the help and assistance which he is obliged to offer. And even if he was able, it would be deficient, for he would not have truly experienced the state of hunger himself.

Fourth Wisdom

One instance of wisdom in fasting in Ramadan with respect to training the instinctual soul is as follows:

The instinctual soul wants to be free and independent, and considers itself to be thus. According to the dictates of its nature, it even desires an imaginary lordship and to act as it pleases. It does not want to admit that it is being sustained and trained through innumerable bounties. Especially if it possesses wealth and power in this world, and if heedlessness also encourages it, it will devour God's bounties like a usurping, thieving animal. Thus, in the month of Ramadan, the instinctual soul of everyone, from the richest to the poorest, may understand that it does not own itself, but is totally owned; that it is not free, but is a slave. It understands that if it receives no command, it is unable to do the simplest and easiest thing, it cannot even stretch out its hand towards water. Its imaginary lordship is therefore shattered; it performs its worship and begins to offer thanks, its true duty.

Fifth Wisdom

One of the many instances of wisdom in fasting in Ramadan from the point of view of improving the conduct of the instinctual soul and giving up its rebellious habits is as follows:

The human soul forgets itself through heedlessness. It cannot see the utter powerlessness, want, and deficiency within itself and it does not wish to see them. And it does not think of just how weak it is, and how subject to transience and to disasters, nor of the fact that it consists merely of flesh and bones, which quickly decline and are dispersed.

Simply, it assaults the world as though it possessed a body made of steel and imagined itself to be undying and eternal. It hurls itself onto the world with intense greed and voracity and passionate attachment and love. It is captivated by anything that gives its pleasure or that benefits it. Moreover, it forgets its Creator Who sustains it with perfect compassion, and it does not think of the results of its life and its life in the Hereafter. Indeed, it wallows in dissipation and misconduct.

However, fasting in the month of Ramadan awakens even the most heedless and obstinate to their weakness, impotence, and want. By means of hunger, they think of their stomachs; they understand the need therein. They realize how unsound are their weak bodies, and perceive how needy they are for kindness and compassion. So they abandon the soul's pharaoh-like despotism, and through recognizing their utter impotence and want, perceive a desire to take refuge at the Divine Court. And they prepare themselves to knock at the door of mercy with the hands of thankfulness. So long as heedlessness has not destroyed their hearts, that is.

Sixth Wisdom

One of the many instances of wisdom in fasting in Ramadan from the point of view of the revelation of the All-Wise Qur'an, and with respect to the fact that the month of Ramadan was the most important time in its revelation, is as follows:

Since the All-Wise Qur'an was revealed in the month of Ramadan, to shun the lower demands of the soul and trivialities and to resemble the angelic state by abstaining from food and drink in order to greet that heavenly address in the best manner, is to attain to a holy state. And to read and listen to the Qur'an as though it was just revealed, to listen to the Divine address in it as if it was being revealed that very instant, to listen to that address as though hearing it from God's Noble Messenger (Upon whom be blessings and peace), indeed, from the Angel Gabriel, or from the Pre-Eternal Speaker Himself, is to attain to that same holy state. To act in this way is to act as an interpreter and to cause others to listen to it and in some degree to demonstrate the wisdom in the Qur'an's revelation.

Indeed, it is as if the world of Islam becomes a mosque during the month of Ramadan. In every corner of that mighty mosque millions of those who know the whole Qur'an by heart cause the dwellers on the earth to hear the heavenly address. Each Ramadan displays the verse *It was the month of Ramadan in which the Qur'an was bestowed from on high (Al-Baqarah 2:185)* in luminous shining manner. It proves that Ramadan is the month of the Qur'an. Some of the members of the vast congregation listen to the reciters with reverence, while others read it themselves.

Following the appetites of the base instinctual soul while in a sacred mosque that is such, and quitting that luminous condition through eating and drinking, is truly loathsome and makes such a person the target of the aversion and disgust of the congregation in the mosque. In the same way, people who oppose those who fast during Ramadan are to the same extent the target of the aversion and disgust of the whole world of Islam.

Seventh Wisdom

One of the many instances of wisdom in the fast of Ramadan with re-spect to mankind's gain and profit, who comes to this world in order to cultivate and trade for the Hereafter, is as follows:

The reward for actions in the month of Ramadan is a thousand fold. According to Hadith, each word of the All-Wise Qur'an has ten merits; each is counted as ten merits and will yield ten fruits in Par-adise. While during Ramadan, each word bears not ten fruits but a thousand, and verses like *Ayat al-Kursi*[121] thousands for each word, and on Fridays in Ramadan it is even more. And on the Night of Pow-er, each word is count- ed as thirty thousand merits.

Indeed, the All-Wise Qur'an, each of whose words yield thirty thousand eternal fruits, is like a luminous Tree of Tuba that gains for believers in Ramadan millions of those eternal fruits. So, come and look at this sacred, eternal profitable trade, then consider it and un-derstand the infinite loss of those who do not appreciate the value of those words.

To put it simply, the month of Ramadan is an extremely profita-ble display and market for the trade of the Hereafter. It is an extreme-ly fertile piece of land for the crops of the Hereafter. For the growth and flourishing of actions it is like April showers in the spring. It is like a brilliant holy festival for the parade of mankind's worship in the face of the sovereignty of Divine lordship. Since it is thus, man-kind has been charged with fasting in order not to heedlessly in-

---

[121]   Al-Baqarah 2:255.

dulge the animal needs of the instinctual soul like eating and drinking, nor to indulge the appetites lustfully and in trivialities. For, by
temporarily rising above the state of being an animal and quitting
the calls of this world, man approaches the angelic state and enters
upon the trade of the Hereafter. And by fasting, he approaches the
state of the Hereafter and that of a spirit appearing in bodily form.
It is as if man then becomes a sort of mirror reflecting the Eternally
Besought One. Indeed, the month of Ramadan comprises and gains
a permanent and eternal life in this fleeting world and brief transient life.

Certainly, a single Ramadan can produce fruits equal to that of
a lifetime of eighty years. The fact that, according to the Qur'an, the
Night of Power is more auspicious than a thousand months is a decisive proof of this.

For example, a monarch may declare certain days to be festivals
during his reign, or perhaps once a year. Either on his accession to
the throne or on some other days which reflect a glittering manifestation of his sovereignty. On those days, he favors his subjects, not
within the general sphere of the law, but with his special bounties
and favors, with his presence without veil and his wondrous activities. And he favors with his especial regard and attention those of his
nation who are completely loyal and worthy.

In the same way, the All-Glorious Monarch of eighteen thousand worlds, Who is the Sovereign of Pre-Eternity and Post-Eternity,
revealed in Ramadan the illustrious decree of the All-Wise Qur'an,
which looks to the eighteen thousand worlds. It is a requirement of
wisdom, then, that Ramadan should be like special Divine festival, a
dominical display, and a spiritual gathering. Since Ramadan is such
festival, God has commanded man to fast, in order to disengage him
to a degree from base and animal activities.

The most excellent fasting is to make the human senses and
organs, like the eyes, ears, heart, and thoughts, fast together with
the stomach. That is, to withdraw them from all unlawful things and
from trivia, and to urge each of them to their particular worship.

For example, to ban the tongue from lying, back-biting, and obscene
language and to make it fast. And to busy it with activities like reciting

the Qur'an, praying, glorifying God's Names, asking for God's blessings on the Prophet Muhammad, peace and blessings be upon him, and seeking forgiveness for sins. And for example, to prevent the eyes looking at members of the opposite sex outside the stipulated degrees of kinship, and the ears from hearing harmful things, and to use the eyes to take lessons and the ears to listen to the truth and to the Qur'an, is to make other organs fast too. As a matter of fact, since the stomach is the largest factory, if it has an enforced holiday from work through fasting, the other small work- shops will be made to follow it easily.

Eighth Wisdom

One of the many instances of wisdom in Ramadan from the point of view of man's personal life is as follows:

It is a healing physical and spiritual diet of the most important kind. When man's instinctual soul eats and drinks just as it pleases, it is both harmful for man's physical life from the medical point of view, and when it hurls itself on everything it encounters without considering whether it is licit or illicit, it quite simply poisons his spiritual life. Further, it is difficult for such a soul to obey the heart and the spirit. It willfully takes the reins into its own hands, and then man cannot ride it, it rather rides man. But by means of fasting in Ramadan, it becomes accustomed to a sort of diet. It tries to discipline itself and learns to listen to commands.

Furthermore, it will not be attracting illness to that miserable, weak stomach by cramming it with food before the previous consignment has been digested. And by abandoning even licit actions as it is commanded, it will acquire the ability to listen to the commands of the Sharia and the reason, and so to avoid illicit actions. It will try not to destroy his spiritual life.

Moreover, the great majority of mankind frequently suffer from hunger. Man, therefore, needs hunger and discipline, which are training for patience and endurance. Fasting in Ramadan is patient endurance of a period of hunger that continues for fifteen hours, or for twenty-four if the pre-dawn meal is not eaten, and it is a discipline and training. That is to say, fasting is also a cure for impatience and lack of endurance, which double man's afflictions.

Furthermore, the factory of the stomach has many workers. And many of the human organs are connected to it. If the instinctual soul does not have a rest from activity during the day for a month, it makes the factory's workers and those organs forget their particular duties. It makes them busy with itself so that they remain under its tyranny. Also, it confuses the rest of the organs in the human body with the clangor and steam of the factory's machinery. It continuously attracts their attention to itself, making them temporarily forget their exalted duties. It is because of this that for centuries those closest to God have accustomed themselves to discipline and to eating and drinking little in order to be perfected.

However, through fasting in Ramadan the factory's workers understand that they were not created for the factory only. While the rest of the organs, instead of delighting in the lowly amusements of the factory, take pleasure in angelic and spiritual amusements, and fix their gazes on them. It is for this reason that in Ramadan the believers experience enlightenment, fruitfulness, and spiritual joys which differ according to their degrees. Their subtle faculties, such as the heart, spirit, and intellect, make great progress and advancement in that blessed month by means of fasting. They laugh with innocent joy in spite of the stomach's weeping.

Ninth Wisdom

One of the instances of wisdom in fasting in Ramadan with regard to shattering the instinctual soul's imaginary lordship and making known its worship through pointing out its impotence is as follows:

The instinctual soul does not want to recognize its Sustainer; it wants its own lordship, like Pharaoh. However much torment it suffers, that character remains in it. It is however destroyed through hunger. And so, fasting in Ramadan strikes direct blows at the soul's pharaoh-like front, shattering it. It demonstrates its impotence, weakness, and want. It makes it realize that it is a slave.

Among the narrations of Hadith is the following: "God Almighty said to the instinctual soul: 'What am I and what are you?' The soul replied: 'I am myself and You are Yourself.' So He punished it and cast it into Hell, then asked it again. Again it replied: 'I am myself and You are Yourself.' However He punished it, it did not give up its egoism. Finally He punished it with hunger. That is, He left it hungry. Then again He asked it: 'Who am I and who are you?' And the soul replied: 'You are my Compassionate Sustainer and I am your impotent slave.'"

O God! Grant blessings and peace to our master Muhammad, that will be pleasing to You and fulfillment of his truth to the number of the merits of the words of the Qur'an in the month of Ramadan, and to his Family and Companions, and grant them peace.

ON THANKING GOD

> *In the Name of God, the All-Merciful, the All-Compassionate. And there is nothing but it glorifies Him with praise. Will they not then give thanks? (Ya-Sin 36:35)*

> *And we shall surely reward those who give thanks. (Al-'Imran 3:145) If you give thanks, I shall increase [my favors] to you. (Ibrahim 14:7) Worship God and be of those who give thanks (Az-Zumar 39:66)*

Through repeating verses like these, the Qur'an of Miraculous Exposition shows that the most important thing the Most Merciful Creator wants from His servants is thanks. The Qur'an, the All-Wise Distinguisher between Truth and Falsehood, calls men to offer thanks, giving it the greatest importance. It shows ingratitude to be a denial of bounties, and in *Surah ar-Rahman*, utters a severe and fearsome threat thirty-three times with the decree, *So which of the favors of your Lord do you deny? (Ar- Rahman 55:13)*. It shows that ingratitude is denial and negation. Indeed, both the All-Wise Qur'an shows thanks to be the result of creation, and the mighty Qur'an of the universe shows that the most important result of the creation of the world is thanks. For if the universe is observed carefully, it is apparent that all things result in thanks in the way each is arranged within it; to a degree each looks to thanks and is turned towards it. It is as if the most important fruit of the tree of creation is thanks, and the most elevated product of the factory of the universe is thanks. The reason for this is as follows:

We see in the creation of the world that its beings are arranged as though in a circle with life as its central point. All beings look to life, and serve life, and produce the necessities of life. That is to say, the One Who created the universe chose life from it.

Then we see that He created the animal kingdom in the form of a circle and placed man at its center. Simply, He centered the aims intended from animate beings on man, gathering all living creatures around him, and subjugating them to him. He made them serve him and him dominant over them. That is to say, the Glorious Creator chose man from among living beings, and willed and decreed this position for him in the world.

Then we see that the world of man, and the animal world too, are formed like circles, with sustenance placed at their center. He has made mankind and the animals enamored of sustenance, has subjugated them to it, and made them serve it. What rules them is sustenance. And He has made sustenance such a vast and rich treasury that it encompasses His innumerable bounties. Even, with a faculty called the sense of taste, He has placed on the tongue fine and sensitive scales to the number of foods, so that they can recognize the tastes of the many varieties of sustenance. That is to say, the strangest, richest, most wonderful, most agreeable, most comprehensive, and most marvelous truth in the universe lies in sustenance.

Now we see that just as everything has been gathered around sustenance and looks to it, so does sustenance in all its varieties subsist through thanks, both material and immaterial and that offered by word and by state; it exists through thanks, it produces thanks, its shows thanks. For appetite and desire for sustenance are sorts of innate or instinctive thanks. Enjoyment and pleasure also are a sort of unconscious thanks, offered by all animals. It is only man who changes the nature of that innate thanks through misguidance and unbelief; he deviates from thanks to associating partners with God.

Furthermore, the exquisitely adorned forms, the fragrant smells, the wonderfully delicious tastes in the bounties which are sustenance invite thanks; they awake an eagerness in animate beings, and through eagerness urge a sort of appreciation and respect, and prompt thanks of a sort. They attract the attention of conscious beings and engender admiration. They encourage them to respect the bounties; through this, they lead them to offer thanks verbally and by act, and to be grateful; they cause them to experience the highest and sweetest pleasure and enjoyment within thanks. That is, they show that, as well as a brief and temporary superficial pleasure, through thanks, these delicious foods and bounties gain the favors of the Most Merciful One, which provide a permanent, true, boundless pleasure. They cause conscious beings to ponder over the infinite, pleasurable favors of the All-Generous Owner of the treasuries of mercy, and in effect to taste the everlasting delights of Paradise while still in this world. Thus, although by means of thanks sustenance becomes such a valuable, rich, all-embracing treasury, through ingratitude it becomes utterly valueless.

As is explained in the Sixth Word,[122] when the sense of taste in the tongue is turned towards sustenance for the sake of Almighty God, that is, when it performs its duty of thanks, it becomes like a grateful inspector of the numberless kitchens of Divine mercy and a highly-esteemed super- visor full of praise. If it is turned towards it for the sake of the soul, that is, without thinking of giving thanks to the One Who has bestowed the sustenance, the sense of taste falls from the rank of being a highly-esteemed supervisor to the level of a watchman of the factory of the stom- ach and a doorkeeper of the stable of the belly. Just as through ingratitude these servants of sustenance descend to such a level, so does the nature of sustenance and its other servants fall; they descend from the highest rank to the lowest; they sink to a state opposed to the Creator of the universe's wisdom.

The measure of thanks is contentment, frugality, and being satisfied and grateful. While the measure of ingratitude is greed, wastefulness and extravagance; it is disrespect; it is eating whatever one comes across, whether lawful or unlawful.

Like ingratitude, greed causes both loss and degradation. For example, it is as though because of greed the blessed ant even, which has a social life, is crushed underfoot. For, although a few grains of

---

[122] See Chapter 5: Logic behind worship and supplication.

wheat would be sufficient for a year, it is not contented with this, and collects thousands if it can. While the blessed honeybee flies overhead due to its contentment, and through a Divine command bestows honey on human beings for them to eat.

The Name of All-Merciful—the Greatest Name after the Name of Allah, which signifies the Divine Essence and is the Greatest Name of the Most

Pure and Holy One—looks to sustenance, and is attained to through the thanks provoked by sustenance. Also, the most apparent meaning of All- Merciful is Provider.

Moreover, there are different varieties of thanks. The most compre- hensive of these and their universal index are the Prescribed Prayers.

Furthermore, within thanks is a pure belief, a sincere affirmation of God's Unity. For a person who eats an apple and utters, "Praise be to God!" is proclaiming through his thanks: "This apple is a souvenir bestowed directly by the hand of power, a gift directly from the treasury of mercy." With saying this and believing it, he is surrendering everything, particular and universal, to the hand of power. He recognizes the manifestation of mercy in everything. He announces through thanks a true belief and sincere affirmation of Divine Unity.

Of the many aspects of the great loss which heedless man incurs through ingratitude for bounties, we shall describe only one. It is as follows:

If someone eats a delicious bounty and gives thanks, the bounty be- comes a light through his thanks and a fruit of Paradise in the Hereafter. Through thinking of it being a work of Almighty God's favor and mercy due to the pleasure it affords, it gives a true, lasting delight and enjoyment. He sends kernels and essences pertaining to its meaning, and immaterial substances like these, to the abodes above, while the material husk-like residue, that is, the matter that has completed its duty and now is unnecessary, becomes excreta and goes to be transformed into its original substances, that is, into the elements. If he does not give thanks, the temporary pleasure leaves a pain and sorrow at its passing, and itself becomes waste.

Bounty which is of the nature of diamonds is transformed into coal. Through thanks, transient sustenance produces enduring pleasures, everlasting fruits. But bounty which is met with ingratitude is turned from the very best of forms into the most distasteful. For according to a heedless person such as that, after a temporary pleasure, the end of sustenance is waste-matter.

For sure, sustenance is in a form worthy of love, and that form becomes apparent through thanks. While the passion of the misguided and heedless for sustenance is animality. You can make further comparisons in this way and see what a loss the heedless and misguided suffer.

Among animate species the most needy for the varieties of sustenance is man. Almighty God created man as a comprehensive mirror to all His Names; as a miracle of power with the capacity to weigh up and recognize the contents of all His treasuries of mercy; and as His vicegerent on earth possessing the faculties to draw to the scales all the subtleties of the different manifestations of His Names. He therefore gave him a boundless need, making him needy for the endless different varieties of sustenance, material and immaterial. The means of raising man to 'the best of forms,' which is the highest position in accordance with this comprehensiveness, is thanks. If he does not give thanks, he falls to 'the lowest of the low,' and perpetrates a great wrong.

In short, the most essential of the four fundamental principles of the way of worship and winning God's love, the highest and most elevated way, is thanks. These four principles have been defined as follows:

"Four things are necessary on the way of the impotent, my friend: "Absolute impotence, absolute poverty, absolute fervor, and absolute thanks, my friend...."

O God, through Your mercy, appoint us among those who give thanks, O Most Merciful of the Merciful!

All-Glorified You are. We have no knowledge save what You have taught us. Surely You are the All-Knowing, the All-Wise. (Al-Baqarah 2:32)

O God, grant blessings and peace to our master Muhammad, master of those who offer thanks and praise, and to all his Family and Companions. Amen.

And the close of their cry will be, "All praise be to God, Sustainer of All the Worlds." (Yunus 10:10)

CHAPTER 12

DECEITS OF THE DEVIL

This piece was written to warn students and servants of the All-Wise Qur'an, so that they should not be deceived by Satan.

In the Name of God, the All-Merciful, the All-Compassionate.

And do not incline towards those who do wrong, or the Fire will seize you. (Hud 11:113)

God willing, this piece will baffle six tricks and tactics of satans, and block up six of their ways of attack.

First Satanic Tactic: Desire For Rank And Position

As a consequence of the instruction they have received from satans among the jinn, human satans want to deceive, by means of the desire for rank and position, the self-sacrificing servants of the party of the Qur'an, and to make them give up their sacred service and elevated 'jihad of the word.' It is as follows:

Present in most people is the hypocritical desire to be seen by people and hold a position in the public view, which is the ambition for fame and acclaim, and self-advertisement; this desire for rank and position is present to a lesser or greater extent in all those who seek this world. To accomplish this ambition, the desire for fame will drive a person to sacrifice his life even. This ambition is exceedingly dangerous for those who seek the Hereafter. And for those who seek this world it is a rough road, is also the source of many bad morals and is man's weakest vein of character. In order to get possession of someone and draw him to himself, a person only has to gratify this ambition; this ties the man to him, and he is defeated by him. My greatest fear for my brothers is the possibility that the atheists will take advantage of this weak vein of theirs. It has caused me much thought. For in that way they attracted some unfortunates who were not truly friends, drawing them into a dangerous situation.[123]

My brothers and friends in the service of the Qur'an! Say the following to the secret agents of the cunning 'worldly,' or the propagandists of the people of misguidance, or the students of Satan, who try to deceive you through the desire for rank: "Firstly, Divine pleasure, the favors of the Merciful One, and dominical acceptance are such a position that the regard and admiration of men is worth virtually nothing beside them. If one receives Divine mercy, that is sufficient. The regard of men is acceptable in respect of its being the reflection and shadow of the regard of mercy; otherwise it is not something to be desired. For it is extinguished at the door of the grave, so worth nothing!"

If the desire for rank and position is not silenced and eliminated, it has to be directed towards something else, like this: in accordance with the following comparison, perhaps the emotion may have a licit side; if it is for reward in the Hereafter, or with the intention of being prayed for, or from the point of view of the effectiveness of service.

For example, at a time Hagia Sophia Mosque in Istanbul is filled with eminent and blessed people, the virtuous and excellent, there are one or two idle youths and immoral loafers around the entrance and porch, while by the windows and in front of them are a few Europeans watching for amusement. A man enters the mosque and joins the congregation, then recites a passage from the Qur'an beautifully in a fine voice; the gazes of thousands of the people of truth are turned on him, and they gain reward for him through their regard and prayers. Only,

---

[123] *Those unfortunates suppose themselves to be in no danger through thinking: "Our hearts are together with Ustad." But someone who strengthens the atheists' current*

this does not please the idle youths and heretic loafers and the one or two Europeans. If when the man had entered the blessed mosque and joined the huge congregation, he had shouted out disgraceful, rude, indecent songs, and danced and jumped around, then it would have made the idle youths laugh, have pleased the dissolute loafers since it encouraged immorality, and made the Europeans smile mockingly, who receive pleasure at seeing any faults in Islam. But it would have attracted looks of disgust and contempt from the vast and blessed congregation; he would have appeared in their view to have fallen to the very lowest of the low. and is carried away by their propaganda, offering the possibility of perhaps unknowingly being used in spying activities, saying: "My heart is pure, and loyal to Ustad's way" resembles the following example: While performing the obligatory prayers, someone cannot hold his wind and expels it; and his Prayer is invalidated. When he is told that his prayers are invalid, he replies: "Why should they be? My heart is pure."

Exactly like this example, the World of Islam and Asia is a huge mosque, and the people of belief and truth within it are the respected congregation in the mosque. The idle youths are the sycophants with the minds of children. The dissolute loafers are those villains who follow Europe and have no nation or religion. While the European spectators are the journalists who spread the ideas of the Europeans. All Muslims, and especially the virtuous and perfected ones, have a place in the mosque according to their degree; they are seen and attention is turned towards them. If they perform actions and works proceeding from the injunctions and sacred truths the All-Wise Qur'an teaches, in regard to the sincerity and Divine pleasure which are a fundamental of Islam, and if their tongues of disposition recite Qur'anic verses, they will then be included in the prayer: *O God, grant forgiveness to all believing men and to all believing women*, which is constantly uttered by all individuals in the World of Islam, and will have a share of it, and they will become connected to them all in brotherly fashion. Only, its value will not be apparent to some of the people of misguidance who are like harmful beasts and to some idiots who are like bearded children. If the man disowns all his forefathers, the source of honor, and all the past, the cause of pride, and abandons in the spirit the luminous highway of his righteous predecessors, which they considered to be their point of support, and performs actions following his own whims and passions, hypocritically, seeking fame, and following innovations, he will fall to the very lowest position in the view of all the people of truth and belief. In accordance with: "Beware the insight of the believer, for he sees with the light of God,"[124] however common and ignorant a believer is, even if his mind does not realize it, his heart looks coldly and in disgust on such boastful, selfish men.

And so, the man carried away by love of position and rank and obsessed by the desire for fame-the second man, descends to the very lowest of the low in the view of that numberless congregation. And he gains a temporary and inauspicious position in the view of a number of insignificant, mocking, raving loafers. In accordance with the verse, *Friends on that Day will be foes, one to another-except the righteous. (Az-Zukhruf (43:67)* he will find a few false friends who will be harmful in this world, torment in the Intermediate Realm, and enemies in the Hereafter.

As for the first man, even if he does not expunge from his heart the desire for position, on condition he takes sincerity and Divine pleasure as basic and does not make rank and position his goal, he will attain a sort of spiritual rank, and a glorious one at that, which will perfectly satisfy his desire for rank. This man will lose something insignificant, very insignificant, and find in place of it many, very many, valuable and harmless things. Indeed, he will chase away a few snakes, and find numerous blessed creatures in their place; he will become familiar with them. Or he will ward off stinging wild hornets, and draw to himself blessed bees, the sherbert-sellers of mercy. He will eat honey at their hand, and find such friends that from all parts of the Islamic world his spirit will be given effulgence like the water of *al-Kawthar*[125] to imbibe through their prayers,

---

[124] *Tirmidhi, Tafsiru Sura, 156; Abu Na'im, Hilyat al-Awliya', iv, 94; al-Haythami, Majma' al-Zawa'id, x, 268; al-'Ajluni, Kashf al-Khafa, i, 42.*

[125] *Al-Kawthar* is a great cistern, a tank for holding water, which will be set up in the place of gathering on the Day of Resurrection, to which the *ummah* of Prophet Muhammad, peace and blessings be upon him, will come. The water of this cistern will come from the river of *al-Kawthar* which is in Paradise, hence it is called the Cistern of *al-Kawthar*.

which will pass to his book of good deeds.

At one time, when through perpetrating a great wrong due to the desire for fame, a little man who was occupying a high worldly position became a laughing-stock in the eyes of the World of Islam, I spoke to him teaching him the meaning of the above comparison; I hit him over the head with it. He was well shaken, but because I had not been able to save myself from the desire for rank and position, my warning did not arouse him.

Second Satanic Tactic: Fear

One of the most important and fundamental emotions in man is the sense of fear. Scheming oppressors profit greatly from the vein of fear. They restrain the pusillanimous with it. The agents of the worldly and propagandists of the people of misguidance take advantage of this vein of the common people and of the religious scholars in particular. They frighten them and excite their groundless fears. For example, in order to throw someone on a roof into danger, a scheming man shows the fearful one something which he supposes is harmful; he excites his fear and draws him gradually towards the edge of the roof; then he makes him fall and break his neck. In exactly the same way, they make people sacrifice most important things through most unimportant fears. Thinking, Don't let this mosquito bite me, they flee into the dragon's mouth.

One time, an eminent person—May God have mercy on him—was frightened of climbing into a rowing boat. One evening, we walked together in Istanbul to the Bridge. We had to board a boat; there was no carriage, and we had to go to Eyüp Sultan. I insisted. He said: "I'm frightened. Perhaps it will sink!" I said to him: "How many boats do you reckon there are, here on the Golden Horn?" He replied: "Perhaps a thousand." So I asked him: "How many boats sink in a year?" He said: "One or two. Perhaps none at all." I asked him: "How many days are there in a year?" "Three hundred and sixty," he replied. Then I said to him: "The possibility of sinking, which arouses groundless fears in you and makes you anxious, is one in three hundred and sixty thousand. Someone who is frightened at such a possibility is not a human being, he could not even be an animal!"

Then I asked him: "How long do you reckon you will live?" He replied: "I am old; perhaps I shall live another ten years." So I said to him: "Because the appointed hour of death is secret, every day there is the possibility of dying. In which case, you might die on any day of the three thousand six hundred. You see, it is not a possibility of one in three hundred thousand like the boat; rather one in three thousand, that you might die today; so tremble and weep, and write your will!" He came to his senses, and I got him trembling to board the boat. When on board, I said to him: "Almighty God gave the sense of fear to preserve life, not to destroy it! He did not give life to make it burdensome, difficult, painful, and torment. If fear is due to a possibility of one in two, three, or four, or even one in five or six, it is a precautionary fear and may be accepted. But to have fear at a possibility of one in twenty, thirty, or forty, is a groundless fear, and makes life torture!"

And so, my brothers, if those who toady to the atheists attack you by frightening you into giving up your sacred 'jihad of the word,' say to them: "We are the party of the Qur'an. According to the verse, *We have, without doubt, sent down the Message; and We will assuredly guard it (Al-Hijr 15:9)* we are in the citadel of the Qur'an. The verse, *For us God suffices, and He is the Best Disposer of Affairs (Al-'Imran 3:173)* is a firm bastion surrounding us. Through fear at the possibility of one in thousands of some minor harm coming to our fleeting transient lives here, you cannot drive us through our own wills down a way which with a hundred per cent possibility will cause thousand fold harm to our eternal lives!" And say too: "Is there anyone who has suffered harm due to Saïd Nursi, our friend in the service of the Qur'an and Master and foreman in running this sacred service, or from the people of truth like us who are his companions on the way of truth? Is there anyone who has suffered any trouble due to his close students, so that we might suffer it too? So should we be anxious at the possibility of suffering it? This brother of ours has thousands of friends and brothers of the Hereafter. Although for twenty to thirty years he played an effective role in the social life of this world, we have not heard of a single of his brothers suffering harm due to him. Especially at that time, he was carrying the club of politics. Now in place of that club, he has the light of reality. For sure, long ago they mixed him up in the Thirty-First of March Incident and they crushed some of his friends, but it later became evident that the affair had erupted due to others. His friends suffered misfortune, not because of him, but because of his enemies. Moreover, at that time, he saved very many of his friends. So satans like you shouldn't get it into their minds to make us throw away an eternal treasury through fear of a danger the possibility of which is one in not a thousand but thousands." You should say that, hit those toadies of the people of misguidance in the mouth, and drive them away! And tell them this:

"And if the possibility of death is not one in hundreds of thousands but a hundred per cent probability, if we have a jot of sense, we will not be frightened and leave him and flee!" Because it has been seen through repeated experiences, and it is seen, that the calamity which is visited on those who betray their elder brother or their Master in times of danger, strikes them first. And they are punished mercilessly and they are looked down upon contemptuously. Both physically dead, and their spirits abased, they are dead in meaning. Those who torment them feel no pity for them, for they say: "Since they betrayed their Master who was loyal and kind to them, they must be completely despicable, and worthy not of pity but contempt."

Yes, the reality is this. Also, if a tyrannical, unscrupulous man throws someone to the ground and stands over him certain to crush his head with his foot, and the man on the ground kisses that savage oppressor's foot, through his abasement, his heart will be crushed before his head, and his spirit will die before his body. He will lose his head, and his self-respect and pride will be destroyed. By displaying weakness before that savage tyrant without conscience, he emboldens him to crush him. But if the oppressed man under his foot spits in the tyrant's face, he will save his heart and his spirit, and his body will be a wronged martyr. Yes, spit in the shameless faces of the oppressors!

One time when the British had destroyed the guns on the Bosporus and occupied Istanbul, the head clergyman of the Anglican Church, the main religious establishment of that country, asked six questions of the Sheikh al-Islam's Office. I was a member of the

Daru'l-Hikmeti'l-Islamiye[126] at the time. They asked me to answer them, saying that they wanted a six-hundred-word reply to their six questions. But I said to them: "I shall answer them not with six hundred words, and not even with six words, or even a single word, but with a mouthful of spit! For you can see that government; the moment it set foot on our Bosporus, its clergyman arrogantly asked us six questions. In the face of this, we should spit in his face. So spit in the pitiless faces of those tyrants!" And now I say: My brothers! Since at a time a tyrannical government like the British had occupied us the protection of the Qur'an was enough for me, despite the danger of confronting them in this way through the tongue of the press being a hundred per cent, it is certainly a hundred times more sufficient for you in the face of the harm that comes to you at the hand of insignificant bullies, the possibility of which is only one in a hundred.

Furthermore, my brothers! Most of you have done your military service. Those that have not, have certainly heard this. And those who have not heard it, let them hear it from me: "Those who receive most wounds are those who abandon their trenches and run away. While those who receive fewest wounds are those who persevere in their trenches!"

The allusive meaning of the verse, *Say: "The death from which you flee will truly overtake you" (Al-Jumu'ah 62:8)* shows that those who run away are more likely to meet death through their flight!

Third Satanic Tactic: Greed

We have proved in many treatises with certain proofs that have issued forth from the clear verses of the All-Wise Qur'an that "Licit sustenance comes not in accordance with power and will, but in relation to powerlessness and want." There are numerous signs, indications, and evidences demonstrating this truth. For instance:

Trees, which are animate beings of a sort and in need of sustenance, remain in their places and their sustenance comes hastening

---

[126]   *Daru'l-Hikmeti'l-Islamiye* was the committee of consultants at the office of the Sheikh al-Islam *(Islam's foremost authority)* in The Ottoman Empire.

to them. While since animals chase after their sustenance greedily, they are not nurtured as perfectly as trees.

Also, although fishes are the most stupid and powerless of the animals, and are found in sand, their being the best nourished and generally appearing fat, while intelligent and capable animals like the monkey and fox are weak and thin from their scanty sustenance, shows that "the means of sustenance is not power, but want."

Also, the fine sustenance of all young, whether human or animal, and a most delicate gift of the treasury of mercy like milk being bestowed on them in an unexpected way out of compassion for their weakness and impotence, and the difficult circumstances of wild animals, show that the means of licit sustenance is impotence and want, it is not intelligence and power.

Also, among the nations of the world there is none which pursues sustenance more than the Jewish nation, which is notorious for its intense greed. Whereas they have suffered more than any from poor livelihoods amid degradation and poverty. Even the rich among them live in lowly fashion. In any event, the possessions they have acquired by illicit means like usury are not licit sustenance so that it might refute our discussion here.

Also, the poverty of many literary figures and scholars, and the wealth and riches of many stupid people shows that the means of attracting sustenance is not intelligence and power, but impotence and want; it is submitting to God while relying on Him, and supplication by word, state, and deed.

The verse, *For God is He Who gives [all] sustenance, Lord of Power, and Steadfast [for ever] (adh-Dhariyat 51:58)* proclaims this truth, and is a powerful and firm proof of this assertion of ours which all plants and animals and young recite. Every group of creature which seeks sustenance recites the verse through the tongue of disposition.

Since sustenance is appointed and bestowed and the one who gives it is Almighty God, and since He is both All-Compassionate and Munificent, let those who degrade themselves through illicit gain in a way that accuses His mercy and insults

His munificence, giving their consciences and even certain sacred matters as bribes and accepting things which are unlawful and inauspicious-let them ponder over just what a compounded lunacy this is.

Yes, 'the worldly' and especially the people of misguidance do not give away their money cheaply; they sell it at a high price. Sometimes some- thing which may help a little towards a year of worldly life is the means to destroying infinite eternal life. And through that vile greed, the person draws Divine wrath on himself and tries to attract the pleasure of the people of misguidance.

Yes, my brothers! If those who toady to 'the worldly' and the dissemblers among the misguided lay hold of you due to this weak vein in human nature, think of the above truth and take this poor brother of yours as an example. I assure you with all my strength that contentment and frugality ensure your life and sustenance more than does a salary. Especially any unlawful money that is given you, they will want a price a thousand times higher in return. It may also be an obstacle to service of the Qur'an, which may open for you an everlasting treasury, or it may make you slack in that service. And that would be such a loss and emptiness that even if they gave you a thousand salaries every month, they could not fill its place.

Warning

The people of misguidance are not able to defend themselves and reply to the truths of belief and the Qur'an which we take from the All-Wise Qur'an and disseminate, therefore, through intrigue and dissembling they employ snares of deception and wile. They want to deceive my friends through the desire for position, greed, and fear, and to refute me by ascribing certain things to me. In our sacred service, we always act positively. But unfortunately, sometimes the duty of removing the obstacles in the way of some good matter impels us to act negatively.

It is because of this that I am warning my brothers concerning the above-mentioned three points, in the face of the cunning propaganda of the dissemblers. I am trying to rebuff the attacks which are leveled at them.

The most significant attack now is at my person. They say: "Saïd is a Kurd. Why do you show him so much respect, and follow him?" So I am forced to mention the Fourth Satanic Stratagem in the language of the Old Saïd, although I do not want to, in order to silence such villains.

Fourth Satanic Tactic: Nationalist Feelings

In order to deceive my brothers and excite their nationalist feelings, certain irreligious people who occupy high positions and attack me by means of propaganda, through the promptings of Satan and suggestions of the people of misguidance, say: "You are Turks. Thanks be to God, among the Turks are religious scholars and people of perfection of every sort. Saïd is a Kurd. To work along with someone who does not share your nationality is unpatriotic."

The answer: You miserable person without religion! All praise be to God, I am a Muslim. At all times there are three hundred and fifty million members of my sacred nation. I seek refuge with God a hundred thousand times from sacrificing three hundred and fifty million brothers who establish an eternal brotherhood, and who help me with their prayers, and among whom are the vast majority of Kurds, for the idea of racialism and negative nationalism, and from gaining in place of those innumerable blessed brothers a few who have embarked on a way which is without religion or belongs to no school of law, who bear the name of Kurd and are reckoned to belong to the Kurdish people. O you without religion! There would have to have been some idiots like you who would abandon the everlasting brotherhood of a luminous beneficial community of three hundred and fifty million true brothers in order to gain the brotherhood— which even in this world is without benefit—of a handful of Hungarian infidels or Europeanized Turks who have lost their religion. Since, in the Third Matter of the Twenty-Sixth Letter, we have shown together with the evidences the nature of negative nationalism and its harms, we refer you to that, and here only explain a truth which was mentioned briefly at the end of the Third Matter. It is as follows:

I say to those pseudo-patriotic irreligious deviants who hide under the veil of Turkism and in reality are enemies of the Turks: "I am closely and most truly connected by means of an eternal and true brotherhood with the nation of Islam, with the believers of this country who are called Turks. On account of Islam, I have a proud and partial love for the sons of this land who for close on a thousand years victoriously carried the banner of the Qur'an to every corner of the world. As for you, you pseudo-patriotic imposters! You possess in a way that will make you forget the true national pride of the Turks, a metaphorical, racial, temporary, and hateful brotherhood. I ask you: does the Turkish nation consist only of heedless and lustful youths between the ages of twenty and forty? And is what is beneficial for them and will serve them—as demanded by nationalist patriotism—an European education which will only increase their heedlessness, accustom them to immorality, and encourage them in what is forbidden? Is it to amuse them temporarily, which will make them weep in old age? If nationalist patriotism consists of this, and this is progress and the happiness of life, yes, if you are a Turkist and nationalist like that, I flee from such Turkism, and you can flee from me, too! If you have even a jot of patriotism, intelligence, and fairness, consider the following divisions of society and give me an answer. It is like this:

The sons of this land known as the Turkish nation consist of six parts. The first part is the righteous and the pious. The second are the sick and those stricken by disaster. The third are the elderly. The fourth are the children. The fifth are the poor and the weak. And the sixth are the young. Are the first five groups not Turks? Do they have no share of nationalist patriotism? Is it nationalist patriotism to vex those five groups, destroy their pleasure in life, and destroy those things which console them on the way of giving drunken enjoyment to the sixth group? Or is that enmity towards the nation? According to the rule "The word is with the majority," that which harms the majority is inimical, not friendly!

I ask you, is the greatest benefit of the believers and the pious, the first group, to be found in a European-type civilization? Or is it to be found in thinking of eternal happiness by means of the truths of belief, in travelling the way of truth, for which they are most de-sirous, and in finding a true solace? The way that the misguided and bogus patriots like you have taken extinguishes the spiritual lights of the pious people of belief, destroys their true consolation, and shows death to be eternal nothingness and the grave to be the door to everlasting separation.

Are the benefits of the disaster-stricken, the sick, and those who have despaired of life, who form the second group, to be found in the way of a European-type, irreligious civilization? For those un-fortunates want a light, a solace. They want a reward in return for the calamities they have suffered. They want to take their revenge on those who have oppressed them. They want to repulse the ter-rors at the door of the grave, which they are approaching. Through their false patriotism, those like you plunge a needle into the hearts of those unhappy victims of disaster who are much in need of com-passion, soothing, and healing, and worthy of them. You hit them over the head! You mercilessly destroy all their hopes! You cast them into absolute despair! Is this nationalist patriotism? Is that how you provide benefits for the nation?

The elderly, the third group, forms a third. They are approaching the grave, drawing close to death, growing distant from the world, coming close to the Hereafter. Are their benefits, lights, and conso-lation to be found in listening to the cruel adventures of tyrants like Hulagu[127] and Genghis[128]? Do they have a place in your modern-type movements which make the Hereafter forgotten, bind a person to the world, are without result, and have the meaning of decline while being superficially progress? Is the light of the Hereafter to be found in the cinema? Is true solace to be found in the theatre? If nationalist patriotism is in effect to slaughter them with an immaterial knife,

---

[127] Hulagu Khan (1217–1265) was one of the Mongol Rulers. He was the grandson of Genghis Khan. Hulagu Khan received the western provinces of the Mongol Empire. Hulagu Khan conquered Persia, eliminated the Abbasid caliphate, de-stroyed Baghdad (a city of a million inhabitants) and established the Mongol empire of the Il-Khans in Persia.

[128] Genghis Khan (1165–1227) was the Khan of the Mongols. Genghis Khan be-came the creator of the Mongol nation and founder of one of the vastest em-pires in world history which stretched from Northern China to the Black Sea.

and give them the idea that "you are being impelled towards ever-lasting nothingness," and to transform the grave, which they consider to be the gate of mercy, into the dragon's mouth, and to breathe in their ears: "You too will enter there!"-if, while these unhappy elderly people want respect from patriotism, that is what it is, "I seek refuge with God" a hundred thousand times from such patriotism!

The fourth group is the children. These want kindness from nationalist patriotism; they await compassion. Also, in respect of their weakness, impotence, and powerlessness, their spirits may expand through knowing a compassionate and powerful Creator; their abilities may unfold in happy manner. Through being instilled with reliance on God springing from belief and with the submission of Islam which may withstand the awesome fears and situations of the world in the future, these innocents may look eagerly to life. Could this be achieved by teaching them things concerning the progress of civilization, with which they have little connection, and the principles of lightless, purely materialist philosophy, which destroys their morale and extinguishes their spirits? If man consisted only of an animal body and he had no mind in his head, perhaps these European principles which you fancifully call civilized education and national education could have afforded these innocent children some worldly benefit in the form of some temporary childish amusement. Since those innocents are going to be cast onto the upheavals of life, and since they are human beings, they will certainly have far-reaching desires in their small hearts and large goals will be born in their little heads. Since the reality is thus, what compassion requires for them is to place in their hearts in the form of belief in God and belief in the Hereafter, an extremely powerful support and inexhaustible place of recourse in the face of their infinite want and impotence. Kindness and compassion to them is in this way. Otherwise, through the drunkenness of nationalist patriotism, it has the meaning of slaughtering those wretched innocents, like a crazy mother slaughtering her child with a knife. It is a savage cruelty and wrong, like pulling out their brains and hearts and making them eat them to nourish their bodies.

The fifth group are the poor and the weak. The poor, who, because of their poverty, suffer greatly from the heavy burdens of

life, and the weak, who are grieved at life's awesome upheavals—
do they not receive a share from nationalist patriotism? Is it to be
found in the movements which you have instituted under the name
of European-style, unveiled, Pharaoh-like civilization, which only
increase the despair and suffering of these unfortunates? The salve
for the wound of indigence of these poor may be found, not in the
idea of racialism, but in the sacred pharmacy of Islam. The weak
cannot receive strength and resistance from the philosophy of Naturalism, which is dark, lacks consciousness, and is bound to chance;
they may rather obtain strength from Islamic zeal and the sacred
nationhood of Islam!

The sixth group is the youth. If the youth of these young people
had been perpetual, the wine you have given them to drink through
negative nationalism would have had some temporary benefit and
use. But on their painfully coming to their senses when they advance in years, on awakening from that sweet sleep in the morning
of old age, distress and sorrow at the pleasurable drunkenness of
youth will make them weep, and the sorrow at the passing of their
pleasant dream will cause them much grief. It will make them exclaim: "Alas! Both my youth has gone, and my life has departed, and I
am approaching the grave bankrupt; if only I had used my head!" Is
the share of nationalist patriotism for this group to enjoy themselves
briefly and temporarily, and to be made to weep with sorrow for a
very long time? Or is their worldly happiness and pleasure in life to
be found in making permanent through worship that fleeting youth
by spending the bounty of fine, sweet youth, not on the way of dissipation, but on the straight path, in the form of offering thanks for the
bounty, and in that way gaining eternal youth in the Realm of Bliss?
You say, if you possess even a grain of intelligence!

In short, if the Turkish nation consisted only of young people, and if their youth was perpetual, and they had no place other than this world, your European-style movement under the
screen of Turkism might have been counted as nationalist patriotism. Then you might have been able to say to me, someone
who attaches little importance to the life of this world, considers racialism to be a sickness like 'the European disease,' tries

to prevent young people pursuing illicit amusements and vices, and came into the world in another country: "He is a Kurd. Don't follow him!", and you might have been right to say it. But since, as explained above, the sons of this land, who go under the name of Turks, consist of six groups, to cause harm to five of the groups and spoil their pleasure in life, and to afford a temporary, worldly pleasure the consequences of which are bad, to only one group, rather, to intoxicate them, is scarcely friendship to the Turkish nation; it is enmity.

Yes, according to race, I am not counted as a Turk, but I have worked with all my strength, with complete eagerness, in compassionate and brotherly fashion, for the group of the God-fearing, and the disaster-stricken, and the elderly, and the children, and the weak and the poor among the Turks. I have worked for the young people as well, who are the sixth group; I want them to forego illicit actions which will poison their worldly life, destroy their lives in the Hereafter, and for one hour's laughter, produce a year of weeping. The works I have taken from the Qur'an and published in the Turkish language—not only these six or seven years, but for twenty years—are there for everyone to see. Yes, Praise be to God, through these works derived from the All-Wise Qur'an's mine of lights, are shown the light which the group of the elderly wants more than anything. The most efficacious remedies for the disaster-stricken and the sick are shown in the sacred pharmacy of the Qur'an. Through those lights of the Qur'an, the door of the grave, which causes more thought to the elderly than anything else, is shown to be the door of mercy, and not the door leading to execution. A most powerful point of support in the face of the calamities and harmful things confronting the sensitive hearts of children, and a place of recourse to meet all their hopes and desires, have been extracted from the mine of the All-Wise Qur'an, and they have been demonstrated and profited from in fact. And the heavy obligations of life which crush most the poor and weak have been lightened by the truths of belief of the All-Wise Qur'an.

Thus, these five groups are five out of the six parts of the Turkish nation, and we are working for their benefit. The sixth group are the young people. We feel powerful brotherhood towards the good ones from among them. But between those like you who have deviated from the straight path, and us, there is no friendship at all! Because we do not recognize as Turks those who embrace misguidance and want to abandon Islamic nationhood, which holds all the true causes of pride of the Turks. We consider them to be Europeans hiding behind the screen of Turkishness! Because even if they claim to be Turkists a hundred thousand times over, they could not deceive the people of truth. For their actions and works would give the lie to what they claim.

O you who follow European ways, and you deviants who try to make my true brothers look coldly on me through your propaganda! How do you benefit this nation? You extinguish the lights of the first group, the pious and the righteous. You scatter poison on the wounds of the second group, who deserve kindness and care. You destroy the solace of the third group, who are most worthy of respect, and you cast them into despair. You destroy completely the morale of the fourth group, who are truly in need of compassion, and you extinguish their true humanity. You make fruitless the hopes and calls for help of the fifth group, who are most needy for assistance, help, and solace, and in their eyes, you turn life into something more ghastly than death. And to the sixth group, who need to be warned and to come to their senses, you give such a heady wine to drink in the sleep of youth that its hangover is truly grievous and terrible. Is this your nationalist patriotism for the sake of which you sacrifice numerous sacred things? Is this what Turkism has to offer the Turks? I seek refuge with God from it a hundred thousand times!

Sirs! I know that when you are defeated in the face of truth, you have recourse to force. In accordance with the fact that power lies in the truth, not in force, you can set fire to the world around my head, but this head, which has been sacrificed for the truth of the Qur'an, will not bow before you. And I tell you this, that not a limited number of people like you who are in effect despised by the nation, but if thousands like you were physically hostile to me, I would pay them no attention, attaching no more value to them than to injurious animals. Because what can you do to me? All you can do is to either bring my life to an end, or spoil my work and service. I am attached to nothing else in the world apart from these. As for the appointed hour which befalls life, I believe as certainly as witnessing it that it does not change, it is determined. Since this is so, if I die as a martyr on the way of truth, I do not hang back from it, I await it longingly. Especially since I am old; I find it hard to believe that I shall live for more than another year. To transform one year's apparent life into everlasting eternal life by means of martyrdom is an exalted aim for those like me. As for my work and service, through His mercy, Almighty God has given such brothers in the service of belief and the Qur'an that through my death it will be carried out in numerous centers instead of one. If my tongue is silenced by death, powerful tongues will speak in its place, continuing my work. I can even say that just as with entering the earth and dying, a single seed produces the life of a shoot, then a hundred seeds perform their duties in place of one, so I nourish the hope that my death will be the means to service greater than was my life!

Fifth Satanic Tactic: Egotism

Profiting from egotism, the supporters of the people of misguidance want to draw away my brothers from me. Truly, man's most dangerous vein is egotism. It is his weakest vein, too. They can make people do terrible things by encouraging it. My brothers! Beware, do not let them strike you with egotism, do not let them hunt you with it! You should know that this century the people of misguidance have mounted the ego and are galloping through the valleys of misguidance. The people of truth have to give up the ego if they are to serve the truth. Even if a person is justified in making use of the ego, since he will resemble the others and they too will suppose he is self-seeking like them, it is an injustice to the service of the truth. In any event, the service of the Qur'an around which we are gathered does not accept the 'I', it requires the 'we.' It says: "Don't say 'I', say 'we.'"

Of course, you have realized that this poor brother of yours did not set out with the 'I.' And he did not make you serve it. Indeed, he showed himself to you as an ego-free servant of the Qur'an. He does not care for himself and has taken as his way not taking the part of his ego. In any event, he has proved to you with decisive evidence that the works that have been presented for general benefit are common property; that is, they have issued from the All-Wise Qur'an. Nobody can claim ownership of them through his ego. Even if, to suppose the impossible, I did claim them as my own through my ego, as one of my brothers said: since this door of Qur'anic truth has been opened, the scholars and those seeking perfection should not consider my defects and insignificance, and hold back from following me; they should not consider themselves self-sufficient. For sure, the works of the former righteous and exacting religious scholars are a huge treasury sufficient for every ill, but it sometimes happens that a key has more importance than the treasury. For the treasury is closed, while the key may open lots of treasuries.

I reckon that those whose egotism in regard to their learning is excessive have understood that the Words that have been published are each keys to the truths of the Qur'an and diamonds swords smiting those who try to deny those truths. The people of virtue and perfection and those who are strongly egotistical in regard to their learning should know that the students are students not of me, but of the All-Wise Qur'an, and I study along with them.

And so, if, to suppose the impossible, I claimed to be the master, since we have a way of saving all the classes of the people of belief—from the common people to the upper classes—from the doubts and skepticism to which they are exposed, then let those scholars either find an easier solution, or let them take the part of our solution, and teach it and support it. There is a grave threat towards the 'bad religious scholars.' Religious scholars have to be especially careful at this time. So suppose, like my enemies, that I perform a service like this for the sake of egotism. Since a large number of people give up their egotism and gather around a Pharaoh-like man with complete loyalty for some worldly and national aim and carry out their work in complete solidarity, does this brother of yours not have the right to ask of you solidarity around the truths of be- lief and the Qur'an by giving up egotism, like those corporals of that worldly society, so long as he concealed his egotism? If even the greatest

of the scholars among you were not to agree, would they not be in the wrong?

My brothers! The most dangerous aspect of egotism in our work is jealousy. If it is not purely for God's sake, jealousy interferes and spoils it. Just as one of a person's hands cannot be jealous of the other, and his eye cannot envy his ear, and his heart cannot compete with his reason, so each of you is like one sense, one member, of the collective personality of the totality we make up. It is not being rivals to one another, on the contrary, to take pride and pleasure in one another's good qualities is a basic obligation springing from the conscience.

One other thing remains and it is the most dangerous: among yourselves and among your friends to feel jealous of this poor brother of yours is most dangerous. There are scholars of standing among you, and some scholars are egotistical in regard to their learning. Even if they themselves are modest, they are egotistical in that respect. They cannot easily give it up. Whatever their hearts and minds may do, their evil-commanding souls want eminence, to sell themselves, and even to dispute the treatises that have been written. Although their hearts love the treatises and their minds appreciate them and recognize their worth, due to jealousy arising from the egotism of learning, their souls want to reduce the value of the Words, as though nurturing an implicit enmity towards them, so that the products of their own thought can compete with them and be sold like them. But I have to tell them this:

Even if those in this circle of Qur'anic teaching are leading scholars and authorities on the Law, their duties in respect of the sciences of belief are only explanations and elucidations of *Risale-i Nur* that have been written, or the ordering of them. For I have understood through many signs that we have been charged with the duty of issuing fatwas concerning these sciences of belief. If someone within our circle writes some things outside an explanation or elucidation due to a feeling in his soul arising from the egotism of learning, it will be like a cold dispute or a deficient plagiarism. Because it has become established through numerous evidences and signs that the parts of the *Risale-i Nur* have issued from the Qur'an. In accordance with the rule of the division of labor, each of us has undertaken a duty, and we make those distillations of the water of life reach those who are in need of them!

Sixth Satanic Tactic: Laziness

It is this: they take advantage of the human characteristics of laziness, the desire for physical comfort, and attachment to other duties. Yes, the satans among jinn and men attack from every angle. When they see those from among our friends whose hearts are stout, intentions pure, loyalty strong, and enterprise, elevated, they attack from other points. As follows:

In order to put a stop to our work and discourage from our service, they profit from their laziness, desire for physical comfort, and attachment to other duties. They keep people from the service of the Qur'an with every kind of trick, so that without their being aware of it, they find more work for some of them. Then they cannot find the time to serve the Qur'an. And to some, they show them the enticing things of this world, so that arousing their desires, they become slack in their service; and so on. These ways of attack are lengthy, so, cutting them short, we refer them to your perspicacious understanding.

And so, my brothers, take great care: your duty is sacred, your service, elevated. Every hour of your time may acquire the value of a day's worship. Be aware of this and do not waste any of them!

> *O you who believe! Persevere in patience and constancy; vie in such perseverance, strengthen each other; and fear God, that you may prosper. (Al-'Im- ran 3:200)*

> *And sell not My signs for a miserable price. (Al-Maedah 5:44)*

Glory to your Sustainer, the Lord of Honor and Power! [He is free] from what they ascribe [to Him]!

And peace be on the Prophets!

And praise be to God, the Sustainer of All the Worlds. (As-Saf-faat 37:180)

All-Glorified You are. We have no knowledge save what You have taught us. Surely You are the All-Knowing, the All-Wise. (Al-Baqarah 2:32)

O God! Grant blessings and peace to our master Muhammad, the Beloved Unlettered Prophet, of Mighty Stature and Exalted Rank, and to his Family and Companions. Amen.

Appendix 1: Chronology and Diagram of the

Risale-i Nur Collection

A.   Chronology of the Risale-i Nur Collection

1877	Saïd Nursi is born.
1892	Nicknamed *'Bediüzzaman'* (wonder of the ages).
1911	*Muhakemat* (The Reasonings) published.
1913	*Münazarat* (Discussions) published.
1916	He began writing *Al-Isharat al-I'jaz* (Signs of Miraculousness).
1919–1921	Small treaties *Tuluat, Sünuhat, Lemaat,* İşarat and *Hutuvat-ı Sitte* written.
1920–1921	Collapse of the Ottoman Empire, emergence of Republic of Turkey. Beginning of the New Saïd Era.
1923	*Al-Mathnawi al-'Arabi al-Nuri* translated into Turkish.
1926	Writing of *Risale-i Nur* begun in exile in Barla.
1926–1929	*The Words.*
1929–1932	*The Letters.*
1932–1934	*The Flashes.*
1936–1940	Majority of *The Rays* written.
1948	Writing of the *Risale-i Nur* completed.
1950	First democratically elected government came to power. Beginning of the Third Saïd Era.
1956	*The Risale-i Nur* is printed in Latin alphabet.
1960	Saïd Nursi dies.

B. Diagram of the Risale-i Nur Collection

The Words *(Sözler)*			
1st Word			
.			
.			
.			
33rd Word >>>becomes	**The Letters** *(Mektūbat)*		
	1st Letter		
	.		
	.		
	.		
	27th Letter >>>>	**(Barla-Kastamonu and Emirdağ Lâhikası)**	
	.		
	.		
	30th Letter >>>>	**(Al-Isharat al-I'jaz)**	
	31st Letter >>>>becomes	**The Flashes** *(Lem'alar)*	
	.	1st Flash	
	33rd Letter	.	
		.	
		.	
		31st Flash >>>>becomes	**The Rays** *(Şualar)*
		.	1st Ray
		33rd Flash **(Al- Mathnawi al-Nuri)**	.
			.
			.
			15th Ray

Appendix 2: Names and Attributes of God in Islam (Al-Asma al-Husna)

Names in Transliterations	Meaning	Names in Transliterations	Meaning
Allāh	*The God.* The only one Almighty. He alone is worthy of worship.	Al-Mubdī	*The Originator.* He who creates all creatures initially without matter or model.
Al-'Adl	*The Just.* He who is Equitable.	Al-Mughnī	*The Enricher.* The Sufficer.
Al-Ākhir	*The Last.*	Al-Muhaymin	*The Guardian.* He who watches over and protects all things. (Helper in Peril)
al-'Afuw	*The Pardoner.* He who pardons all who sincerely repents.	Al-Muḥsī	*The Appraiser.* He who knows the number of every single thing in existence, even to infinity.
al-'Alīm	*The Knower of All.* He who has full knowledge of all things.	al-Mu'īd	*The Restorer.* He who recreates His creatures after He has annihilated them.
al-Aḥad	*The One.* The only one.	al-Mu'izz	*The Bestower of Honours.* He who confers honor and dignity.
al-Awwal	*The First.*	al-Mujīb	*The Responder to Prayer.* He who grants the wishes who appeals to him.
al-'Azīz	*The Mighty and Strong.*	al-Mun'īm	*The Nourisher.* He who gives every creature its sustenance.
al-'Azīm	*The Magnificent. The Most High.* He who is Most Splendid.	al-Muqaddim	*The Expediter.* He who brings forward whatever He wills (Forewarner).
al-Badī'	*The Incomparable.* He who is without model or match, and who brings into being worlds of amazing wonder.	al-Muqsīt	*The Equitable One.* He who does everything with proper balance and harmony.

al-Bā'ith	*The Resurrector.* He who brings the dead to life, and raises them from their tombs.	al-Muqtadir	*The Creator of All Power.* He who disposes at His will even of the strongest and mightiest of His creatures.
al-Bāqī	*The Everlasting One.* Eternal (in the future).	al-Mumīt	*The Taker of Life.* He who creates the death of a living creature.
al-Bāri'	*The Maker of Order* (Skilled Worker). O Evolver who created all things so that each whole and its parts are in perfect conformity and harmony.	al-Muntaqīm	*The Avenger.* He who justly inflicts upon wrongdoers the punishment they deserve.
al-Barr	Source of all Goodness. He who treats His servants tolerantly, and whose goodness and kindness are very great indeed.	al-Muṣawwir	*The Shaper of Beauty.* He who designs all things, giving each its particular form and character (Sculptor).
al-Baṣīr	*The All-Seeing.* To those who invoke this Name one hundred times between the obligatory and customary Prayers in Friday congregation, Allah grants esteem in the eyes of others.	al-Muta'āli	*The Supreme One.* He is exalted in every respect, far beyond anything the mind could possibly attribute to His creatures.
al-Bāsiṭ	*The Reliever (Uncloser).* He who releases, letting things expand.	al-Mutakabbir	*The Majestic.* He who demonstrates His greatness in all things and in all ways.
al-Bāṭin	*The Hidden One.* He who is hidden, concealed.	al-Mudhill	*The Humiliator.* He who degrades and abases.
al-Dhārr	*The Distresser.* The Creator of the Harmful. He who creates things that cause pain and injury.	An-Nāfi'	*The Creator of Good.* He who creates things that yields advantages and benefit.
al-Fattāh	*The Opener.* He who opens the solution to all problems and makes things easy.	al-Nūr	*The Light.* He who gives light to all the worlds, who illuminates the faces, minds and hearts of His servants.

al-Ghaffār	*The Forgiving.* He who is always ready to forgive.	al-Qābiḍ	*The Constrictor.* He who constricts and restricts.
al-Ghafūr	*The Forgiver* and Hider of Faults.	al-Qādir	*The All-Powerful.* He who is Able to do what He wills as He wills (Providence).
al-Ghanī	*The Rich One.* He who is infinitely rich and completely Independent.	al-Qahhār	*The Subduer.* He who dominates all things, and prevails upon them to do whatever He wills (Dominant).
al-Hādī	*The Guide.* He who provides guidance.	al-Qawī	*The Most Strong.* The Possessor of All Strength.
al-Ḥāfiẓ	*The Preserver.* He who guards all creatures in every detail.	al-Qayyūm	*The Self-Existing One.* He who maintains the heavens, the earth, and everything that exists.
al-Ḥayy	*The Ever Living One.* The living who knows all things and whose strength is sufficient for everything.	al-Quddūs	*The Pure One.* He who is free from all errors.
al-Ḥakīm	*The Perfectly Wise.* He whose every command and action is pure wisdom.	al-Rāfi'	*The Exalter.* He who raises up.
al-Ḥakam	*The Judge.* He who judges and makes right prevails.	al-Raḥīm	*The All Compassionate.* He who acts with extreme kindness.
al-'Ali-yyu	*The Highest.* The Exalted.	al-Raḥmān	*The All Merciful.* He who wills goodness and mercy for all His creatures.
al-Ḥalīm	*The Forbearing.* He who is Most Clement.	al-Raqīb	*The Watchful One.*
al-Ḥamīd	*The Praiseworthy.* All praise belongs to Him, and who alone do the tongues of all creation laud.	al-Rashīd	*The Righteous Teacher.* He who moves all things in accordance with His eternal plan, bringing them without error and with order and wisdom to their ultimate destiny (Unerring).

al-Ḥaqq	*The Truth.* He who's being endures unchangingly.	al-Ra'ūf	*The Kind.* He who is very compassionate (Indulgent).
al-Ḥasīb	*The Accounter.* He who knows every detail.	al-Razzāq	*The Sustainer.* He who provides all things useful to His creatures.

al-Jabbār	*The Compelling.* He who repairs all broken thing, and completes that which is incomplete.	as-Ṣabūr	*The Patient One.* He who is characterized by infinite patience.
al-Jalīl	*The Glorious.* He who is Lord of Majesty and Grandeur.	al-Salām	*The Source of Peace.* He who frees His servants from all danger.
al-Jāmi'	*The Gatherer.* He who brings together what He wills, when He wills, where He wills.	al-Ṣamad	*The Eternal.* He who is the only recourse for the ending of need and the removal of affliction.
al-Kabīr	*The Greatest.* He who supremely great.	al-Samī'u	*The Hearer of All.* Allah takes care of all the needs of those who invoke this glorious Name one hundred times.
al-Karīm	*The Generous.* He whose generosity is most abundant.	al-Shāhid	*The Witness.* He who is present everywhere and observes all things.
al-Khabīr	*The All Aware.* He who has the knowledge of inner and most secret aspects of all things.	al-Shakūr	*The Rewarder of Thankfulness.* He who gratefully rewards good deeds (Appreciator).
al-Khāfiḍ	*The Abaser.* He who brings down, diminishes.	al-Tawwāb	*The Acceptor to Repentance.* He who is ever ready to accept repentance and to forgive sins (Relenting).
al-Khāliq	*The Creator.* He who brings from non- being into being, creating all things in such a way that He determines their existence and the conditions and events they are to experience.	al-Wakīl	*The Trustee/ Guardian.* He who manages the affairs of those who duly commit them to His charge, and who looks after them better than they could themselves.
al-Laṭīf	*The Subtle One.* He who knows the minutest subtleties of all things.	al-Wālī	*The Protecting Friend.* He who is a nearest friend to His good servants.
al-Majīd	*The Majestic One.* He whose glory is most great and most high.	al-Wahhāb	*The Giver of All.* He who constantly bestows blessings of every kind.

al-Majīd	*The Glorious.* He, whose dignity and glory are most great, and whose generosity and munificence are bountiful.	al-Wāḥid	*The Unique.* He who is Single, absolutely without partner or equal in His Essence, Attributes, Actions, Names and Decrees.
al-Mālik	*The Absolute Ruler.* The Ruler of the entire universe (King of Kings).	al-Wājid	*The Finder.* He who finds what He wishes when He wishes (Perceiving).
Mālik-ul-Mulk	*The Owner of All.* The King of the Kingdom.	al-Wadūd	*The Loving One.* He who loves His good servants, and bestows his compassion upon them.
al-Māni'	*The Preventer of Harm.* The Withholder.	Al-Wālī	*The Governor.* The Protecting Friend. He who administers this vast universe and all its passing phenomena.
al-Mu'min	*The Inspirer of Faith.* He who awakes the light of faith in our hearts.	al-Wās'i	*The All Comprehending.* He who has limitless capacity and abundance.
al-Matīn	*The Firm.* He who is very steadfast.	al-Wārith	*The Inheritor of All.* He who is the Real Owner of all riches.
Al-Muhyi	*The Giver of Life.* He who confers life, gives vitality, revives.	Az-Zāhir	*The Manifest One.* He who is Evident.
al-Mu'akh-khir	*The Delayer.* He who sets back or delays whatever He wills.	Zul-Jalāli-Wal-Ikrām	*The Lord of Majesty and Bounty.* He who possesses both greatness and gracious magnanimity.

Appendix 3: Images

Nursi before
The First World War

Nursi during
The First World War

Nursi in Barla
in 1926

Nursi is in Court defend-
ing the *Risale-i Nur*.

Nursi's Barla home where he wrote most of his
Risale-i Nur Collection

Nursi in the courtyard of
Fatih Mosque in Istanbul
in 1952

Nursi in his last days

The Turpentine Tree near
Barla. Nursi spent long
nights on it to pray and
supplicate.

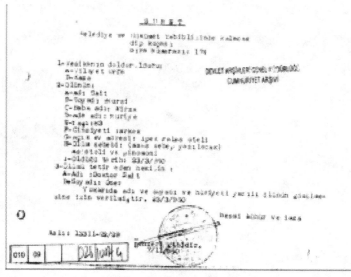

Death certificate of Nursi

Appendix 4: Schools of Thoughts

(*Madhhabs*) in Islam

There are five very distinct schools of theology in the Islamic philosophical tradition, which are: [1] Sunni, within which are [1.a] Ash'ari, [1.b] Athari (Salafi), and [1.c] Maturidi; [2] Shia, with the sub-schools of [2.a] Imami and [2.b] Ismaili; [3] Khariji; [4] Mu'tazili; and finally [5] Murjiah.

[1]. Sunni schools: The Sunni school is one of the largest branches of the Islamic faith. The word *Sunni* originates from *sunnah*, which means the tradition of Islām's Prophet Muḥammad. There are four Sunni schools of law (*madhhab*), which are Hanafi, Shafi'i, Hambali and Maliki. All four schools of law take their creed (*aqīdah*) from the three schools of theology, Ash'ari, Athari and Māturidī.

[2]. Shi'a school: It is the second largest Islamic school after the *Sunni* school. In 'aqi☐dah they are based on the Imami and Ismaili. Among other differences, the main one we are concerned with is the interpretation of Islām's Holy book the Qur'an, hence the faith itself. Shias believe that the true interpreters of Islām are the direct descendants of the Prophet Muḥammad's daughter Fatima and son-in-law Ali, who was also the fourth righteous caliph. These descendants are called *imāms* and they are the only ones to follow.

Whereas the Sunni school believes that *sunnah* is narrated by the Companions and that there is no need to have a direct blood link with Fatima and Ali in order to interpret Islām.

[3]. Khariji: Khariji literally means *those who went out. Kharijites* believed that the act of sinning is analogous to *kufr* (disbelief) and that every grave sinner was regarded as *kafir* (a disbeliever) unless he repented. They considered the Qur'an to be the source of Islamic Jurisprudence (*fiqh*), but regarding the other two sources (*hadīth* and *ijmā*) their concepts were different from ordinary Muslims.'

[4]. Mu'tazili: This school of Islamic theology came into being through controversies involving the interpretation (*ta'wil*) of the Qur'an in its anthropomorphic description of God and the denial of free will. The *Mu'tazilites* denied literal interpretation of the Qur'anic passages and affirmed man's free will, while the orthodox traditionalists adhered to literalism and determinism.

[5]. Murji'ah: As opposed to the Kharijites, Murjites advocated the idea of deferred judgement of people's beliefs. The Murjite doctrine held that only God has the authority to judge who is a true Muslim and who is not, and that Muslims should consider all other Muslims as part of the community. In another contrast to the Kharijites, who believed that committing a grave sin would render a person non-Muslim, Murjites considered genuine belief in and submission to God to be more important than acts of piety and good deeds. They believed that Muslims committing grave sins would remain Muslim and be eligible for Paradise if they remained faithful.

FURTHER READING

Books

Translations of Bediüzzaman Said Nursi's Books by Şükran Vahide

1. Nursi, Said. (Translated by Şükran Vahide). (1992). *The Words*.
Cağaloğlu, Istanbul, Turkey: Sözler Neşriyat.
2. --- *The Letters*
3. --- *The Flashes*
4. --- *The Rays*
5. --- *The Staff of Moses*
6. --- *Signs of Miraculousness*
7. --- *The Author of Risale-i Nur Collection: Bediuzzaman Said Nursi*

Translations of Bediüzzaman Said Nursi's Books by Hüseyin Akarsu

8. Nursi, Said. (Translated by Hüseyin Akarsu). (2007). *The Words:*
Epistles on Islamic thought, belief, and life. Somerset, N.J.: The Light.

9. --- *The Letters*

10.---*The Gleams*

11.---*The Rays*

12.--- *Al-Mathnawi al-Nuri*

Other recommended books on Bediüzzaman Said Nursi

13.Vahide, Şükran and Abu-Rabi, Ibrahim M. (2005). *Islam in modern Turkey: an intellectual biography of Bediuzzaman Said Nursi*. State Üniversity of New York Press.

14.Turner, Colin and Horkuc, Hasan. (2009). *Said Nursi.* I.B. Tauris.

London, New York

15.Turner, Colin. (2013). *The Qur'an Revealed: A Critical Analysis of*

Said Nursi's Epistles of Light. Gerlach Press. Berlin

16.Abu-Rabi', Ibrahim M. (2003). *Islam at the crossroads: on the life and thought of Bediuzzaman Said Nursi.* Albany: State University of New York Press.

Online resources

http://www.erisale.com/en

http://www.saidnur.com/en/

http://www.nur.gen.tr/en.html

BIBLIOGRAPHY

Abu-Rabi, Ibrahim M. (2003), *Islam at the crossroads: on the life and thought of Bediuzzaman Said Nursi* (Albany: State Üniversity of New York Press).

Faroqhi, Suraiya 'Approaching Ottoman history an introduction to the sources.'

Hanioğlu, M. Şükrü *Bir Siyasi Düşünür Olarak Dr Abdullah Cevded ve Dönemi* (Istanbul).

Mürsel, Safa (1976), *Bediüzzaman Said Nursi ve Devlet Felsefesi* (Istanbul: Yeni Asya Yayınları).

Nursi, Said (1994), *Hutbe-i Şamiye* (The Damascus Sermon) (Istanbul: Nesil).

--- (2004a), *The Flashes* (Istanbul: Nesil).

--- (2004b), *The Rays* (Istanbul: Nesil).

--- (2004c), *Muhakemat (The Reasonings)* (Istanbul: Nesil).

--- (2005), *The Words* (Istanbul: Nesil).

Nursi, Said (2004d), *Signs of miraculousness* (Istanbul: Nesil).

--- (2004e), *Divan-ı Harbi Örfi* (Istanbul: Nesil).

--- (2004f), *The Letters* (Istanbul: Nesil).

Olson, Robert W. (1989), *The emergence of Kurdish nationalism and the Sheikh Said rebellion, 1880-1925* (Austin: Üniversity of Texas Press).

Şahiner, Necmeddin (1997), *Bilinmeyen taraflarıyla Bediüzzaman Said Nursi: kronolojik hayatı* (Istanbul: Nesil).

Sarıtoprak, Zeki (2008), 'Said Nursi on Muslim-Christian Relations Leading to World Peace', *ISLAM AND CHRISTIAN MUSLIM RELATIONS,* 19 (1), 25–37.

Sarıtoprak, Zeki (2014), 'Islam's Jesus.'

Turner, Colin and Horkuc, Hasan (2009), *Said Nursi* (London, New York: I.B. Tauris).

Vahide, Şükran and Abu-Rabi, Ibrahim M. 'Islam in modern Turkey an intellectual biography of Bediuzzaman Said Nursi.'

Webster, Donald Everett (1939), *The Turkey of Ataturk: social process in the Turkish reformation.*